Frontières

The Food of France's Borderlands

ALEX JACKSON

PAVILION

Contents

The Alps

Alsace

Borderlands

The word 'border' has a negative connotation to it: a hard stop, a looming wall – metaphorical, linguistic, cultural or otherwise – that prompts anyone approaching it to slow down and take stock of what lies ahead. A border can be a barrier in a physical sense, sure, but also a limitation on the intellectual. Sadly, in the past few years, we have seen a closing of borders and a shift away from the cooperative spirit that once fuelled great international projects.

Thankfully for all involved this book is not about politics but about cooking, so let us think of its title as meaning borderlands, or in the more literal sense, frontiers. A borderland is, of course, the stretch of land on either side of a border, but also, and more interestingly for our purposes, a zone of indeterminate overlap: the grey area between fantasy and reality, between sleep and waking, between *pesto* and *pistou*. I do realize that a Genoese and a Provençal may disagree on this point, but from where I stand, as an Englishman, I see no conflict of interest. Much as I enjoy watching a good argument from afar, the appeal of a tasty green paste to stir into my soup or put on my spaghetti is undiminished. What I lack in heritage I hopefully make up for in idiotic enthusiasm, and an observer from a distance has in one sense an advantage: to see the similarities in recipes from rival villages, techniques from across the sea and the cooking from one side of a mountain range to another.

But what has always existed in France, and hopefully always will, is the staple fare of the farmhouse and the home kitchen.

When I look at the food of France I see numerous things. Myriad dishes, from the simplest country fare to the inventions of the multi-starred kitchens, as many recipes as there are cooks. France has undoubtedly produced one of the world's great cuisines. Indeed, no other country has codified its cooking so successfully, even to such an extreme that it might be perceived as a detriment. The recipes and systems of Taillevent, La Varenne, Carême and Escoffier paved the way for a consistency in fine French food that made it world famous: a kitchen organized like a military unit, canons of standardized recipes, a tall paper hat and a deserved, uniquely Gallic arrogance – a recipe for success.

French food, for all the pomp associated with it, has recently been maligned by some as pretentious, over-complicated and passé. They might well be right about some of it. But what has always existed in France, and hopefully always will, is the staple fare of the farmhouse and the home kitchen. *This* is the French food that we are interested in – *rustique*, simple, humble and delicious. Why have these attributes become so far removed from our perception of French food? It is said that the French invented the restaurant (or at least our modern idea of it, and certainly the word itself) but the characteristics we seek are nowadays more readily associated with two other great European cuisines, those of Italy and Spain.

Of course, regional cuisine in France is still very much alive and kicking. The cooking traditions of the Loire and the Languedoc, for example, are equally delicious yet wildly different. Zoom in, and inter-village rivalry over the 'correct' recipe exists just as we imagine it does in Italy. Such local variation, a depth and breadth of good cooking right across the country, laid the foundations for the greatness of French cuisine.

What we may now identify as French food came from a patchwork of recipes from across Europe, the Mediterranean and North Africa.

I want to explore the idea that good cooking is not unique to either the Loire or Languedoc, no more than it is to Provence or Liguria, to Roussillon or Catalonia, nor from one side of the Basque Country to the other. France's borderlands contain some of the most exciting food that I know – the Franco-German traditions of Alsace, the entire coastal sweep of the Riviera, from Toulon all the way to Italy's Cinque Terre; the Pyrenées, French Catalonia and the long mountain border with Spain; the maritime Alps where Piedmont meets Provence; and the port of Marseille, France's ancient connection with the rest of the Mediterranean, a city with the sound of the music of North Africa in its markets and the smell of its spices in the air.

The history of French cuisine spans many centuries, maybe millennia. It is a cuisine that has been shaped by an amalgam of different cultures: Gallic, Norman, Saxon, Anglo-Saxon, Celtic, Frankish, Jewish, Roman, Moorish and Catalan, to omit a few. What we may now identify as French food came from a patchwork of recipes from across Europe, the Mediterranean and North Africa. Some of these dishes are simple variations, using the same locally sourced ingredients from the land and the sea: a bit like visiting cousins from along the coast. Others hold connections somehow more secret, a rumour of a civilization long departed, or an ancient murmur in the soil, whispers from traders and travellers past. These are well-trodden culinary paths, and I hope that this book can follow in their footsteps.

Chapter One

South West

The Southwest

I am perpetually entertained by the broad definition of southwest France, which seems to mean anything west of Avignon. This city sits where Provence ends and the newly named region of Occitanie begins not to be confused with the historical Occitania, which covered the entire sweep of southern France from the Atlantic coast to the current Italian border.

Whatever the modern definition of the Southwest, I think it fits the idea that Waverley Root sets out in *The Food of France*: that France is a country of three cooking fats. There is butter in the North, Provence has its famous olive oil, while the Southwest is the land of duck fat. Simply put, the cooking and culture of each region are identified by the fat the people have chosen to put in the bottom of their cooking pot. Their choice, of course, is tied to many factors, geographical, anthropological and historical, but our interest is perhaps less in the history of the Southwest and more in the character of its cooking.

Duck is a ubiquitous feature on restaurant menus all the way from Montpellier to Biarritz. To anyone familiar with this region the vocabulary for duck – *canard* – is well known: *magret, confit, gésiers, foie gras*. There are slices of sweet smoked duck breast to tumble through a mustardy salad of green beans; jars of *confit* sitting preserved in white fat, yielding salty soft meat to enrich a *cassoulet* or a *garbure*; whole *magrets* with the skin scored so it crisps up over a charcoal grill, blistered golden black, with the meat a rare purple. Or a slab of *foie gras*, well crusted in the pan but silken pink within, with grapes, *verjus* and butter in the sauce, part of a meal that had me retiring in the afternoon to lie down in a darkened room.

But the cooking of the Southwest is rich and varied, due in part to the large area that it covers. On its Mediterranean flank is the Roussillon, the French Catalonia, with Catalan, Spanish, Arab and even Italian flourishes in its cooking – salt cod fried with saffron, pine kernels and raisins, salads of salted anchovies, grilled peppers, black olives and basil, or lamb cooked with beans and many cloves of garlic. And on its western, Atlantic margin lies the Pays Basque (the French Basque Country), where the *jambon de Bayonne* or *noir de Bigorre* is (almost) as delicious as the air-dried hams made over the border, and where the famous local chilli, *piment d'espelette*, is dried, powdered and sprinkled on everything from fish stew to chocolate ice cream; the region's cuisine a clear product of its proud people.

Between French Catalonia and the Basque Country the land rises steeply to form the Pyrénées. The inaccessibility of the mountains has long made travel and trade difficult, the tiny country of Andorra perhaps illustrating the point, for, were it more accessible, it would surely have been swallowed up by either of its larger neighbours, but there are similar cooking techniques on either side of the border. At its most rustic, the image I associate with the region is of a pot simmering slowly over a fire, to be filled with pulses, vegetables and perhaps some salted *confit*.

It was over (or perhaps, more wisely, around) these mountain ranges that invading Arabs came, bringing with them techniques and ingredients that have helped to form the cuisine of the region, including the dried beans and perhaps an earthenware pot that set the scene for the invention of the Southwest's signature dish: *cassoulet*. It has long been touted as the king of peasant dishes: rustic, bold-flavoured, but with some well-established rules (part of the fun, I think, is debating them in detail). What draws my attention is how it came to be, for a thing like *cassoulet* does not simply magic into being, despite the whimsical tales about its origin (see page 30). Perhaps nothing is more romantic than the real story: that a dish such as this is the product of thousands of years of *human* stories. These tell of techniques learned out of necessity and hardship, but also the movement of people, a sharing of old traditions, and a sprinkling of innovation.

There is a sense that somewhere over the high peaks, bubbling away in a pot, is a meal that has much in common with one's own.

I will not pretend to provide a comprehensive account of the entire region of the Southwest. Volumes could be written individually on the Basque Country, the whole sweep of the Pyrénées, or on French Catalonia; on their histories, geographies and all the delicious foods to be found within. These are regions with complicated histories and thousands of idiosyncratic dishes. I merely offer a selection of recipes that I find most appealing, and hope to illustrate a point: that along the length and breadth of the mountain ranges there is a sense that somewhere over the high peaks, bubbling away in a pot, is a meal that has much in common with one's own.

Raw Salt Cod & Tomato Salad

A few years back Rachel Roddy and I cooked a Sicilian-inspired lunch at my (now closed) restaurant Sardine. One of our antipasti was a salt cod *crudo* with lemon: just thin slices of lightly cured cod, Amalfi lemon, lemon zest and good olive oil. Most delicious! This salt cod salad, only a little more complicated, takes its inspiration from the classic Catalan *esqueixada*, a salad of hand-torn raw salt cod, tomatoes, olives and onion.

I have found that a brief salting for a salad of raw cod works very well. The cod has not much of the funk associated with real salt cod (not that this is a bad thing), but its flavour will be concentrated and the texture transformed.

SERVES 2

Quantity	Ingredient
200G/ 7OZ	COD FILLET, FROM THE THICK LOIN RATHER THAN THE TAIL
	SEA SALT
2	VERY RIPE BULL'S HEART OR BEEF TOMATOES
I	SMALL SWEET SALAD ONION — AN ITALIAN TROPEA OR SIMILAR IS BEST — FINELY SLICED INTO HALF-MOONS
I	CELERY HEART (PALE YELLOW STALKS AND LEAVES ONLY), FINELY SLICED
	BLACK OLIVES, PITTED
	RED WINE VINEGAR
	BEST OLIVE OIL
	SALT AND FRESHLY GROUND BLACK PEPPER

Skin the cod and bury in sea salt for 4 hours. Remove from the salt, rinse and dry well on kitchen paper.

Slice the tomatoes, season with salt (not too much) and pepper, then lay on a big plate.

Cut the salt cod into long, thin slices and lay on top of the tomatoes. Scatter the onion, celery and olives over the top. Drizzle with good red wine vinegar and a lot of your best olive oil. Eat with crusty bread.

Trout Carpaccio with Basil

SERVES 2

I ate this high up in a mountain pass in the Ariège, at a charming little restaurant overlooking the valley, with an Occitan flag fluttering in the wind. It was the start of August and it was hot. The food in simple restaurants like that one is often the same the whole year round – duck *confit*, *salade de gésiers* (giblets), stews, grilled meat with chips – all lovely, but not quite what you want to eat in the heat of the afternoon, even with the mountain breeze and a bottle of wine to cool you down.

The fishing in these parts is for trout or *omble chevalier* (char), and we had a lovely little char dusted in flour and fried up a treat with some excellent fried potatoes and a (random, inexplicable) carrot purée, but the real star of the meal was a plate of fresh raw trout, dressed simply with oil, lemon, salt and basil.

Writing down a recipe as simple as this always makes me feel a bit of a cheat, but to me this is one of those rare dishes that actually represents summer cooking in the mountains. Anyway, this is an excellent idea.

Raw trout with basil is fresh and delicious. I would go heavy on the seasoning – plenty of salt, lemon juice and black pepper, but don't drown it in olive oil as you might with a less oily fish: let the fresh trout speak for itself.

I	FILLET OF RIVER TROUT, NICE AND FRESH
	A FEW BASIL LEAVES
I	LEMON
	OLIVE OIL
	SALT AND FRESHLY GROUND BLACK PEPPER

Lay the fish skin side down on a board. Slice the trout thinly, leaving the skin on the board, and lay it on a plate. Tear the basil over the top. Zest a little of the lemon and squeeze over some juice. Season with salt and lots of black pepper. Drizzle with olive oil. There you go!

Morue à la Rouergate

A salt cod *brandade* with an earthy twist. Before the age of the railways, the River Lot was the main thoroughfare for produce travelling up country, and barges transported coal, wood and cheeses down to Bordeaux, and took fish and other goods back. Salted cod was perfect for the long journeys upriver.

À la Rouergate refers to the area of Rouergue, now Aveyron, and this dish is also known in the Lot as *estofinado*. This is walnut country, and here we encounter a little fresh chopped walnut as well as their flavoursome oil. Mashed potato with walnut oil is delicious in itself, particularly with a little cream as used here. A traditional addition is pieces of hard-boiled egg – shades of an English fish pie! I think it looks prettiest when grated on top.

300G/ 10½OZ	PIECE OF SALTED COD FILLET, SOAKED OVERNIGHT
I TSP	BLACK PEPPERCORNS
2	BAY LEAVES
	MILK, TO COVER
200G/ 7OZ	FLOURY POTATOES, PEELED
2	GARLIC CLOVES, CRUSHED TO A PASTE USING A PESTLE AND MORTAR
2 TBSP	OLIVE OIL
2 TBSP	DOUBLE CREAM
2 TBSP	WALNUT OIL, PLUS EXTRA TO SERVE
2 TBSP	FINELY CHOPPED PARSLEY
	A HANDFUL OF SHELLED WALNUTS, LIGHTLY TOASTED AND ROUGHLY CHOPPED
I	EGG, HARD-BOILED AND PEELED

Place the salt cod, peppercorns and bay leaves in a saucepan and cover with milk. Bring very slowly to a simmer, then turn off the heat. Leave the cod to poach for 5 minutes in the hot milk, then remove carefully. Skin the fillet and check for bones. Remove and discard the peppercorns and bay leaves, but reserve the milk. Cut the potatoes into chunks and boil in the fishy milk until soft. Taste the milk to see whether any salt is required – usually the answer is no. Drain and mash or rice the potatoes into a bowl.

Put the cooked salt cod in a blender and blitz to a rough purée with the crushed garlic, the olive oil and the cream. Transfer to the bowl with the potatoes and mix well. Add a little more cream if you think it needs it. Just before serving, mix in the walnut oil. Transfer to a serving dish, make a well in the centre, sprinkle in the chopped parsley and walnuts, and drizzle over a little more walnut oil. Finely grate the boiled egg on top. Serve the *brandade* with toast.

Wood-grilled Mussels (Brasucade)

SERVES 4
or 2 hungry people

I am a total sucker for anything cooked over a wood fire, and when on the Languedoc coast near Sète and Marseillan, *brasucade* is the dish to seek out: mussels, cooked over a smoky wood fire and doused in an aromatic, oily marinade. The word comes from Occitan: *braso* is a glowing ember, and a *brasucado* is a mountain practice of roasting chestnuts in a perforated pan over a fire so that they take up the smoky flavour.

It's the same idea here with mussels. The shellfish are cooked on a thick-bottomed *plancha* (grill) that sits above the flames. The mussels absorb a little of the wood smoke,

and the *plancha* catches the juices that emerge as the shells open. Recipes for the sauce vary from family to family. The version I first had was a gently spiced oil spiked with onion, garlic, thin pieces of lemon, chilli and a tiny bit of ginger. Mine is a little different; feel free to omit, add or improvise on the theme.

The best way to cook this on a barbeque is in a large, flat pan with sides that will hold the cooking liquid – a paella pan would be perfect. Ideally you will be able to shut the barbeque lid over the pan as the mussels cook, so that more of the smoky flavour is absorbed.

2KG/ 4LB 8OZ	MUSSELS, SHELLS SCRUBBED AND DE-BEARDED

FOR THE SAUCE:

100ML/ 3½FL OZ/ SCANT ½ CUP	OLIVE OIL
2	GARLIC CLOVES, ROUGHLY SMASHED
½	SHALLOT, DICED
I	SPRIG OF THYME
2	BAY LEAVES
I	SPRIG OF ROSEMARY
½ TSP	FENNEL SEEDS
½ TSP	CORIANDER SEEDS
I	WHOLE DRIED CHILLI
I	STRIP OF ORANGE PEEL
2½FL OZ/ ⅓ CUP	*PASTIS*

First, and preferably the day before, make the sauce by combining all the ingredients together.

Clean the mussels – debeard, wash well and discard any that are broken or that refuse to close when tapped hard on the edge of the sink.

Build a nice smoky fire of oak or birch wood on your barbeque. When hot, introduce your cooking pan, heat well then add the mussels. Cook, stirring, until all the shells are open – this might take a while, so have a cold drink to sip while you do it. Cover the barbeque (but not the pan) with a lid whenever possible as this will keep the smoke in.

As the mussels cook, pour off excess juices into a waiting vessel (we'll use some of it to finish the dish, and keep any excess for fish soups/stews etc). When all the shells are open, pour over the oily sauce and stir until all smells wonderful. Reintroduce a little of the mussel juices if you think the pan looks a bit dry or anything starts to fry too hard.

Pour the cooked mussels and their sauce into a big bowl and attack immediately, armed with crusty bread and copious amounts of chilled wine.

Fried Salt Cod, Chard, Pine Kernels, Raisins & Saffron

SERVES 2

Chard with pine kernels and raisins is a classical Catalan preparation, but one that crops up all over the Mediterranean: in Provence, Languedoc, Lazio, Liguria and Venice (with spinach instead of chard), Sicily, Sardinia and Corsica. Clifford A. Wright, in his magnum opus *A Mediterranean Feast*, writes of a 'medieval culinary connection between Catalonia and Italy' that might help to explain the prevalence of this tasty combination. In Andalucía this is sometimes made with almonds instead of pine kernels, and spiced subtly with saffron, showing that its Moorish roots run deep.

I'm not sure that this recipe really belongs to any of the aforementioned regions, but it certainly fits in as a product of the Mediterranean as a whole. When fried, the salt cod takes on extra savoury dimensions; sticky, salty and golden. The chard is quickly boiled, then heated through in warm oil with garlic, pine kernels, raisins and a little saffron, before being tossed with the cod in an oily, vinegary jumble.

I like to eat this on toast, with a boiled egg to take the edge off the salty-sharpness of it all.

You can buy salt cod in Spanish or Portugeuse delis, but I often make my own with fresh cod fillet: salt the fish well for 3 hours, rinse, pat dry and leave in the fridge overnight.

200G/ 7OZ	SALT COD, SOAKED OVERNIGHT IF APPROPRIATE, CUT INTO 2 PIECES
	PLAIN FLOUR, TO DUST THE FISH
	OLIVE OIL
200G/ 7OZ	RAINBOW CHARD
I	FAT GARLIC CLOVE, FINELY SLICED
I TBSP	PINE KERNELS
	A SMALL PINCH OF SAFFRON STRANDS
I TBSP	RAISINS, SOAKED IN WARM WATER BRIEFLY
	RED WINE VINEGAR, TO TASTE

TO SERVE:

	TOASTED BREAD
	OIL FOR DRIZZLING
I	HARD-BOILED EGG, HALVED

Pat the fish dry on kitchen paper and dredge in flour; tap to remove any excess. Heat some olive oil in a large pan and fry the pieces of cod until sticky, golden and cooked through – about 3–4 minutes, turning once, as a rough guide, but this will depend on the thickness of your cod. Transfer the fish to a plate, remove any excess oil and wipe out the pan.

If the chard is thick-stemmed, separate the stalks from the leaves and cut the stalks into 1-cm/½-in pieces. If the chard is young and the stalks tender, leave it whole. Boil the chard in a saucepan of lightly salted water until just cooked. Squeeze lightly and set aside.

Add 2 tbsp of fresh olive oil to the cleaned frying pan. Fry the garlic and pine kernels until lightly golden, then add the saffron and raisins. Cook slowly for a minute, then add the chard and heat gently in the flavoursome oil. Pull apart the cooked salt cod and jumble the flakes through the chard. Season to taste with red wine vinegar – it will take a fair whack. Arrange the tasty jumble on pieces of oily toast and serve with the boiled egg.

Salt Cod & Potato Omelette

SERVES 1

I first ate an omelette like this in a cider house in the Spanish Basque Country, where the excellent cider – sharp, dry and lightly sparkling – is poured in a violent thin stream from a 15,000-litre/4,000-gallon wooden barrel. Catch the stream in your glass and you're away! We ate plates of chorizo cooked in cider, sheep's milk cheese with walnuts, vast dishes of fried salt cod with onions and peppers, huge rare steaks grilled over wood and served with chips, and a deeply savoury salt cod omelette. The food was very good and all quite salty: just the ticket!

This is no *tortilla Española*, rather a quick, lightly browned and folded omelette as you might encounter in France. The one I had in Spain was a wondrous beige; just salt cod and egg, but in mine thin slices of potato and onion, fried slowly in oil until golden, add to the umami, and a bit of parsley freshens things up. *Piment d'espelette* is another very good addition. This omelette should definitely be served on the runny side, and with dry cider for extra Basque points.

	OLIVE OIL
I	SMALL WAXY POTATO, FINELY SLICED
¼	YELLOW ONION, FINELY SLICED
50G/ I ¾OZ	SALT COD, SOAKED, SKIN REMOVED, TORN INTO PIECES
I TSP	CHOPPED PARSLEY
	A GOOD OF PINCH OF *PIMENT D'ESPELETTE* (OR TURKISH PEPPER FLAKES, *PUL BIBER*)
	A KNOB OF UNSALTED BUTTER
2	EGGS, BEATEN, VERY LIGHTLY SALTED

Heat few tablespoons of olive oil in an omelette pan over a medium heat. Add the potato and onion and cook for 10–15 minutes. The onion will soften and the potatoes crisp up a bit – all will be golden and stick together. Chuck in the torn salt cod and cook for a further minute until the fish turns opaque. Add the parsley and *piment d'espelette*, then tip the lot out of the pan and set aside. Wipe the pan clean and return to the heat.

Add the knob of butter to the pan and swirl it around until it just starts to froth, then add the beaten eggs. Cook as you would a normal omelette; when still very runny add the potato, onion and cod and fold in half. Take the pan off the heat and wait for 30 seconds or so, then tip out, folding it over in half as you do so, onto a plate. Eat the omelette and drink some dry cider.

Sardines en Escabèche

SERVES 6–12
depending on appetites

Colman Andrews, who wrote magnificently on catalan cuisine, theorizes that *escabèche* (*escabetx* in Catalan) was a technique that the Catalans taught to Europe, although the word might well have its roots in the Perso-Arabic word *sikbaj*, meaning 'vinegary stew'. Either way, this quick preparation has long been popular in French Catalonia as well as south of the border.

This is a well-travelled recipe: I have seen this style of escabèche crop up in collections of Pieds-Noirs (Algerian-born people of European descent) recipes issuing from the North African coast, and this type of recipe also travelled with Spanish colonizers to South America.

Sardines are the best fish for this by far, but by all means try it with trout or mackerel fillets too. I have seen many iterations of *escabèche* – including Escoffier's, no less – that mess around with bits of onion and crunchy carrots, but I am more interested in the earthy Catalan original, with just quick-fried fish, olive oil, vinegar, paprika, bay and garlic. This recipe is adapted from Irving Davis's *A Catalan Cookery Book*, which is a grumpy, terse, illuminating delight.

Escabèche is a tasty method of preservation, and your sardines will keep for more than a few days in their vinegary marinade, but are equally good eaten straight away if you simply can't wait.

12	BUTTERFLIED SARDINES
	FLOUR, FOR DUSTING
	OLIVE OIL
6	GARLIC CLOVES, UNPEELED
2	BAY LEAVES
1	SPRIG OF THYME
2 TSP	SWEET PAPRIKA
½ TSP	HOT PAPRIKA
5 TBSP	SHERRY VINEGAR OR RED WINE VINEGAR
	SALT

Season the sardines with salt and leave for 1 hour. Pat dry with kitchen paper and lightly flour the skin side only. Heat some olive oil in a large frying pan and briefly fry the sardines on the skin side only until coloured gold but not cooked through – the fish should keep its raw appearance on the flesh side. Transfer the sardines to a shallow dish – arrange them in one layer.

Wipe out the pan and pour in a fresh slick of olive oil, around 5mm/¼in deep. Slowly fry the garlic cloves until they have softened and turned golden brown. Remove the pan from the heat, pop in the bay leaves and thyme, and stir around until you are happy that the oil has been infused with their flavour. With the pan still off the heat but the oil hot, add both paprikas and stir thoroughly for 30 seconds to cook the paprika without burning it. Finally, pour in the vinegar, give the pan a shake, and allow to cool slightly before pouring the lot over the fish.

Cool to room temperature, then refrigerate for a good couple of days before eating. Eat slightly cooler than room temperature, with a selection of other snacks: olives, crisps, bread, beer etc, or on top of toast rubbed with tomato and garlic.

Ttoro

This one is a Basque fish stew from the fishing town of St-Jean-de-Luz, seasoned with the local chilli, *piment d'espelette*. This pepper is only mildly spicy, but most flavourful, and is used with abandon in the French Basque Country. I have seen it for sale in good French delis – pick some up if you find it and make this delicious stew. For this I like a mixture of hake, monkfish and – if you can get it – gurnard, plus a few mussels and a langoustine or two to crown the bowl.

The combination of duck fat, Armagnac, tomato and shellfish makes for a rich, satisfying bowlful. The nicest bit when making this is the initial stage, which is when you are layering up all the flavour: smash up a langoustine and sacrifice it in the hot duck fat, throw in the *piment d'espelette* and fry it gently, which will infuse the soup with a deep-red colour, then stew your vegetables until soft and flambé with the Armagnac. I find this stew particularly fun to make.

5	LANGOUSTINES, UNPEELED
4 TBSP	DUCK FAT
I TBSP	*PIMENT D'ESPELETTE*, PLUS I TSP TO SERVE
2	ONIONS, DICED
I	CARROT, SLICED INTO ROUNDS
2	CELERY STICKS (WITH LEAVES IF POSSIBLE), CHOPPED
I	SMALL LEEK, SLICED INTO ROUNDS
8	GARLIC CLOVES, SQUISHED
	A SPRIG OF THYME
I	BAY LEAF
	A FEW PARSLEY STALKS, IF AVAILABLE
200G/ 7OZ	HAKE FILLET, PLUS A SMALL HEAD OR NICE PIECE OF BACKBONE
200G/ 7OZ	MONKFISH FILLET, PLUS THE BACKBONE IF YOU HAVE IT
200G/ 7OZ	GURNARD FILLET, PLUS THE HEAD AND BONES FOR THE SOUP
6	JUICY RIPE TOMATOES, CHOPPED, OR 400G/14OZ CAN CHOPPED PLUM TOMATOES
50ML/ 2FL OZ/ SCANT ¼ CUP	ARMAGNAC
I	SMALL GLASS OF WHITE WINE
500G/ ILB 2OZ	MUSSELS, SCRUBBED AND DEBEARDED (DISCARD ANY WITH BROKEN SHELLS OR THAT DO NOT CLOSE)
	LEMON JUICE (OPTIONAL)
	SALT

Roughly chop one of the langoustines with a heavy knife, or simply smash it with a rolling pin. A noble death! Heat the duck fat in a roomy, deep-sided pan. Fry the langoustine in the duck fat, then add the *piment d'espelette*. Stir, then throw in the vegetables, garlic, herbs and a good pinch of salt. Cook slowly until everything is soft and sweet, stirring occasionally. Add more duck fat or a drizzle of olive oil if you think it looks a little dry.

Chop the fish bones into manageable pieces, and pull the gills out of the heads, washing them of any red/black gunk. Add the bones and heads to the soup and try to fry them in the fat a little before adding the chopped tomatoes. Turn the heat up and fry the tomatoes a bit. When the tomatoes have started to break down into a sauce, add the Armagnac, which the heat might well set alight, so take half a step back! Add the white wine, bring to the boil, then top up with water to cover the ingredients by about 5cm/2in. Simmer for about 30–40 minutes; top up with water if it reduces too fast. Towards the end of the cooking, before you strain the broth, chuck in a big handful of the mussels, which will deepen the flavour.

Strain the broth through a sieve, mushing the softened solids with the back of a spoon to squish all the precious liquid out of them. Return the broth to the heat and set at a fast simmer. Reduce the broth slightly until it has thickened a bit and tastes delicious.

Cut all the fish fillets into four pieces (one piece of each fish per person), season with salt, and drop into the simmering broth along with the langoustines and remaining mussels. Cover with a lid and simmer for a few minutes until all the fish is cooked through and the mussel shells have opened. Taste again for salt; it might need a little squeeze of lemon juice.

Serve the fish and the hot broth in bowls. Sprinkle with parsley and the extra *piment d'espelette*. Drizzle with olive oil, and eat with bread or slices of oily toast rubbed with garlic.

TO SERVE:

4 TBSP	CHOPPED PARSLEY
	OLIVE OIL

Salmon & Sorrel Sauce

SERVES 4
as a starter, or a light lunch with bread and salad

The *nouvelle cuisine* movement of the 1970s was a great leap forward in French cuisine: a philosophy that embraced innovation, new techniques and technologies, shortened menus, that utilized the freshest ingredients, championed regional cooking, and dropped the heavier, flour-thickened traditional sauces in favour of herbs, lemon juice and good butter. It was a slow shift away from *haute cuisine* towards a lighter style of cooking.

The Troisgros brothers, based west of Lyon in the small town of Roanne, were at the vanguard of *nouvelle cuisine*. Their *saumon à l'oseille* (salmon with sorrel) was emblematic of the movement, and was at the time revolutionary and deeply controversial. It is said to have been inspired by a trip to San Sebastian, where they ate a salmon cooked pink as is to the Basque taste.

Back in Roanne their dish initially received a hostile reception; angry customers sent it back, appalled, until the veteran restaurant critic of *Le Monde*, Robert Courtine, tasted it and pronounced 'Finally, an intelligent salmon'. From that point the Troisgros brothers made their name, and the dish became not only famous around the world but one of the most famous French restaurant dishes ever; in Roanne the railway station opposite the family's restaurant was painted pink and green in its honour.

The cooking of the fish, the making of the sauce and even the plating of the dish were revolutions in themselves. The salmon, a thin piece of skinned fillet, is cooked for the briefest time, to a more-than-blushing pink inside, in a non-stick pan (itself an innovation that made this dish possible). The sauce, light, bright and sharp, is thickened not with flour but through the reduction of the wine and the quality of the cream. The sauce is spooned over the plate and the salmon laid on top: unheard of at the time, when tradition dictated that the sauce took precedence over the fish rather than letting it speak for itself.

To modern tastes this dish might taste distinctly unrevolutionary, as the techniques and flavours became a new normal. This is the story of a dish that was a turning point in French cuisine – from one code of practices to another – and also the story of how outside influences and inspiration helped make French cuisine what it is today. I present it here as close to the original as I can make it.

I will add a note here to say that nowadays I avoid farmed salmon altogether. Wild salmon is increasingly rare, but wild sea trout in season is a good option, or farmed trout (Chalk Stream Trout is an excellent producer if you're based in the UK), or wild sockeye salmon.

Recipe continues overleaf

Salmon & Sorrel Sauce continued

I	SHALLOT, FINELY DICED
IOOML/ 3½FL OZ/ SCANT ½ CUP	WHITE WINE (A SANCERRE WOULD BE LOVELY)
IOOML/ 3½FL OZ/ SCANT ½ CUP	GOOD FISH STOCK
IOOG/ 3½FL OZ/ ½ CUP	VERY GOOD-QUALITY THICK CRÈME FRAÎCHE
2	SALMON OR TROUT FILLETS, ABOUT 2CM/¾IN THICK, SKINNED
I BUNCH	SORREL, WASHED, STALKS TRIMMED
I5G/½OZ/ I TBSP	COLD UNSALTED BUTTER, CUBED
	LEMON JUICE
	SALT AND FRESHLY GROUND WHITE PEPPER

Put the diced shallot and wine in a saucepan and bring to the boil. Reduce until syrupy, then add the fish stock and bring back to a simmer. Reduce by half, then whisk in the crème fraîche. Season with salt and a little white pepper. Keep warm on a very low heat.

Slice the salmon fillets horizontally along the length to form two flat pieces about 1–1.5cm/½–⅝in thick. Put the pieces of salmon between two pieces of baking parchment and flatten slightly to an even thickness with a flat heavy implement.

Get a non-stick pan hot – one big enough to fit the four slices of salmon comfortably. Add no fat. Season the salmon fillets with salt and a touch of white pepper and lay them in the hot pan. The salmon will cook for no longer than 15 seconds on each side – it will be lightly seared on the outside and brightly pink within.

As soon as you put the salmon in the pan, rip the sorrel leaves in half and add to the sauce along with the cold butter. Shake the sauce rather than using a whisk to avoid breaking the sorrel. Cook the sauce, shaking the pan constantly, until the sorrel melts into it. After 30 seconds your salmon will be cooked pink and the sauce will be ready. Take the pan off the heat.

Taste the sauce for seasoning. It should be no thicker than double cream – any thicker and it will be cloying. Add a splash of water if you need to. Give it a little squeeze of lemon juice.

Spoon the sauce onto plates and arrange the sorrel so that it is nicely spaced out. Lay the cooked salmon over the top of the sauce and serve immediately. According to the Troisgros, the first bite should be taken about 20 seconds after the salmon hits the plate, so get your stop watch out.

Ensalada Rusa with Smoked Fish

SERVES 4

On my trip to the French-Spanish border I ate two versions of this salad. In France this is known as *macédoine* and is a mainstay of the *traiteurs* which offer a variety of prepared cooked items to take away. A *macédoine* really refers to the way that the salad is cut into little cubes before being dressed, but the most common is a mayonnaise-dressed number that most of us know as Russian salad or *salade Olivier*.

This is a salad that is made throughout Europe. I can't say that I think the French are that good at it, but the Spanish are massive fans, and they make this all over the country, most commonly with tuna. At a restaurant on the Catalonia coast I ate a spectacular version with smoked trout and trout roe on top. Here's an adaptation with smoked eel and avruga caviar, a caviar substitute made from smoked herring.

200G/ 7OZ	RED POTATOES, PEELED AND CUT INTO 1CM/½IN DICE
50G/ 1¾OZ	RADISHES, CUT INTO 1CM/½IN DICE
50G/ 1¾OZ	GREEN BEANS, CUT INTO 1CM/½IN DICE
1	BEETROOT, DICED FINELY
½	APPLE, CUT INTO 1CM/½IN DICE
20G/ ¾OZ	SHALLOTS, DICED FINELY
40G/ 1½OZ	CORNICHONS
100G/ 3½OZ	SMOKED EEL FILLET, CUT INTO 1CM/½IN DICE
	SALT AND FRESHLY GROUND BLACK PEPPER

FOR THE MAYONNAISE:

2	EGG YOLKS
2 TSP	MUSTARD
200ML/ 7FL OZ/ SCANT 1 CUP	OLIVE OIL
	JUICE OF ½ LEMON
1 TBSP	CRÈME FRAÎCHE

TO SERVE:

1	HARD-BOILED EGG, CHOPPED FINELY
4 TSP	AVRUGA CAVIAR
	FINELY CHOPPED CHIVES

Boil the potatoes, radishes and green beans in lightly salted water until soft but not mushy, then drain and leave to cool. Boil the beetroot in a separate pan of water, then drain, cool and keep separate.

Make the mayonnaise by whisking the egg yolks with the mustard and drizzling in the oil bit by bit. Season with salt and lemon juice, fold in the crème fraîche and thin slightly with water if necessary. Dress the beetroot with a little bit of the mayonnaise and set aside.

Mix the apple, shallots, cornichons and smoked eel with the cooled potato, green beans and radishes. Fold in enough mayonnaise to make a delicious mixture – not too thick, not too thin, and nicely lubricated. Season with salt and pepper.

To plate the salad, put a ring mould on each plate and fill with a layer of dressed beetroot. Spoon the potato/vegetable/eel salad on top of the beetroot. Thin the remaining mayonnaise slightly with some water. Spoon a little of the thinned mayonnaise on top of the salad. Top each portion with a little chopped boiled egg, a teaspoon of avruga caviar and some chopped chives. Remove the ring moulds carefully, *et voilà!*

Cassoulet

There is more fuss made in southwest France about how to cook *cassoulet* than there is about *bouillabaisse* in Marseille or paella in Valencia. *Cassoulet* is emblematic of the cuisine of this part of France and all its rustic charms but – despite its celebrity status – the dish is at heart a peasant one, with as many versions as there are cooks, although it must be said (or whispered) that it would seem that not all of these are good: I have eaten a few special *cassoulet*s and more than a few sorry ones. In the right hands this is one of the world's great dishes, but it does require an alchemy that not everyone possesses.

Observers have classified three main schools of *cassoulet*, from three towns in what has become known as the Cassoulet Belt: Toulouse, Castelnaudry and Carcassonne. Prosper Montagné, a famous chef of Carcassonne origin, and the creator of *Larousse Gastronomique*, described in his 1929 *Le Festin Occitan* a Holy Trinity of *cassoulet*: '… the *cassoulet* of Castelnaudry is God the Father, Carcassonne God the Son, and Toulouse the Holy Spirit.' For French food critic Maurice Curnonsky there were not three *cassoulet*s but four – like the musketeers: Castelnaudry with its *confit* goose or duck; Toulouse with its eponymous sausage, a little tomato and some mutton; Carcassonne with its pork ribs and partridge in season; and, further south in the Corbières, salted pig's ear and tails. In practice it seems that the most common constants are white beans, *confit* duck or goose, Toulouse sausages, pork rinds and some kind of pork, but the variations are myriad and all delicious if prepared with care.

In the right hands this is one of the world's great dishes, but it does require an alchemy that not everyone possesses.

This is a dish as rich in history as it is in animal fats. Most people interested in the origins of the dish have heard the story of the siege of Castelnaudry during the Hundred Years' War. Depleted of their reserves, surrounded by the Black Prince and the horrible English, the besieged townspeople cobbled together an enormous cauldron of what they had left: dried (broad) beans, sausages and salted and *confit* meats, and the first *cassoulet* was born. Nourished and inspired by their hearty creation, the defenders charged the panicked English and drove them from the city walls and the Lauragais region. This lovely story reminds me slightly of Asterix's village drinking the magic potion before attacking the Romans, which most probably has no real basis in fact, but it cannot be disputed that Castelnaudry is the spiritual home of the *cassoulet*.

The stew that might have ended the siege, however, would have been slightly different from the one we know today. White beans from the Americas did not reach Europe until the sixteenth century and dried broad beans would have been the main ingredient: a so-called *estofat*, *févoulade* or *févoulet* rather than a *cassoulet*. *Ragoûts* of fresh or dried broad beans, salted meats and sausages that would once have been common in this part of modern-day France display many similarities with the Catalan stews that are still called *estofats*, or with the famous *escudella*, a rich stew of various meats, sausages, chickpeas and sometimes pasta.

The word *cassoulet* itself comes from the earthenware pot that the stew is cooked in: the famous *cassole* from the town of Issel close to Castelnaudry. Some sources attribute its creation to a certain Jean Gabalda, a potter of Italian origin, in the year 1337. It is certainly possible that Monsieur Gabalda patented the distinctive truncated conical shape

I love the idea that a dish that has become world famous as a symbol of rustic French cuisine might well have much to do with a civilization from the other side of the Mediterranean.

that is the trademark of the *cassole d'Issel* to this day – a design which exposes more of the stew to the heat of the oven, encouraging the formation of a tasty crust. It would be simplistic to assume that no one before this date had thought to cook their broad bean estofat in some kind of earthenware vessel. The *estofat* became the *cassoulet* as people began to name the stew after the dish they cooked it in rather than the technique. The Occitan term *estofat*, like the Catalan, means 'to smother' – and was used to describe the technique of cooking a stew in a covered pot (elsewhere, the modern French Creole term *étouffée* is another example with the same origin).

The etymology of the word *cassole* (or indeed the English 'casserole') is slightly more complicated. Author and cook Clifford A. Wright makes a compelling argument for the word deriving from the medieval Spanish *cassa*, and in turn back to the Arabic *qas'at*, meaning a large shallow earthenware pot. To quote Wright: 'Apocrypha aside, a more appropriate historical question can be asked: Is the prototype of *cassoulet* the fava and mutton stews of the Arabs, as suggested by Julia Child and Paula Wolfert (but denied by Waverley Root)? Was the Languedoc the northern limit of the cooks, if not the commandos, of 'Abd al-Rahmān I [first caliph of Córdoba] …?' I find such theories hard to resist; I love the idea that a dish that has become world famous as a symbol of rustic French cuisine might well have much to do with a civilization from the other side of the Mediterranean, even if all the Arabs introduced was a style of cooking pot.

Yet Waverley Root, writing in *The Food of France*, is less convinced: 'It may be inquired, when it is suggested that Languedoc cooking stems from the Roman and the Arab schools, whether it not be more exact to describe it as coming from the European and African branches of Roman cooking; for it is a fair question to ask from what point the Arabs started. The universal *couscous* of North Africa, made from coarse flours cooked in steam, [and] the universal *polenta* of Italy, made from coarse flours cooked in water, [are] direct descendant[s] of the Roman *pulmentum*.' He makes the point that couscous, not beans, was the usual accompaniment to mutton, and that as sheep were indigenous to the Languedoc it is not necessary to stretch to a foreign land to explain the origins of the dish.

Root theorizes that 'originally [*cassoulet*] belonged to the family of farm-kitchen dishes, like *pot-au-feu*, which remain on the back of the stove indefinitely, serving as a sort of catch-all for anything edible that the cook may toss into the pot', and that French novelist Anatole France claimed that the *cassoulet* he used to eat in a favourite establishment in Paris had been cooking for twenty years. In this sense *cassoulet* has much in common with the Catalan *olla podrida* (literally 'rotten pot'), which dates back to the Middle Ages – to a point, perhaps, when much of Spain was under Arab rule. This was a deep stew of various meats, chickpeas or beans cooked in an earthenware vessel, that would tick over indefinitely on the fire. In the sense that *cassoulet* may well have started out as a kind of *pot-au-feu*, it would explain why there are so many variations: cooks used whatever they had to hand, and the only consistent ingredient was the beans.

In any case, *cassoulet* has slowly evolved over the centuries. Columbus's voyages to the Americas at the turn of the sixteenth century saw the introduction of white beans to Europe (although this fact is disputed by some, who insist that certain beans were indigenous to southwest France long before Columbus, and believe that Catherine de' Medici, who became Comtesse of the Lauragais, had a role to play.) Once white beans became available they quickly supplanted broad beans as the legume of choice for a *cassoulet*. Near Toulouse they opt for fat creamy *tarbais* beans and, further east, they tend to use the slimmer, slightly firmer local *haricots lingots du Lauragais*; both delicious.

Nowadays much fun can be had in arguing about the one 'true' recipe (one of my favourite pastimes). I shall not attempt to provide one myself, for I can do no better than Paula Wolfert, who writes with great verve about *cassoulet* in *The Cooking of South-West France*, and includes an impeccable recipe which is surely the definitive written word on the subject. The recipe is not one from any of the restaurant chefs she met along her journey, but from a home cook – Madame Pierrette Lejanou, the wife of a potato broker and descendant of an old Toulouse family – 'a charming woman, effervescent in her approach to food, generous in the tradition of the Languedoc, she feasted me and instructed me until I was overwhelmed. The secret of her *cassoulet*, I thought, was that it was *made with love.*'

> *A good cassoulet has a shimmering power to it, a glorious bubbling potential just underneath a perfect crust.*

Wolfert's observation is important. I mentioned earlier that a good *cassoulet* requires some degree of alchemy. Many arguments among *cassoulet* aficionados are about what meats should or should not be included, or what specific variety of bean is best; these arguments are all well and good, but many of the things that turn a *cassoulet* from merely good into something sublime are a little harder to articulate. A good *cassoulet* has a shimmering power to it, a glorious bubbling potential just underneath a perfect crust.

This is a matter of a million fine points of cookery. Of course, we should ensure that we are using a proper earthenware *cassole* (I hope you agree if you've read this far), but there are many other questions to answer: have you lined the pot with *couennes* (pork skins) and, if not, what are you afraid of? More to the point, how much fat has been left on the rinds, and how long have you boiled them before use? A *cassoulet* should be rich, of course, but also have enough aromatics to cut through and enough lightness that the eater can finish a hefty portion. What was the texture of the stock in which you have cooked the beans – did it have enough gloss, enough body, and did you skim sufficiently? Is your combination of meats harmonious, and how is the texture of your sausages? Have you timed the meats and beans correctly so that as the meats start to fall off the bone, the beans are creamy but hold their shape? Have you used breadcrumbs to help to form a crust, or are you relying on the beans to do the job? Are you breaking and reforming the crust, and if so, how many times? Has your crust coloured evenly, or have one or two beans coloured too darkly? Is the ratio of crust to bean correct? Is the bean broth wet enough? Is there just enough fat to make your lips smack? How is the acidity of the broth, and is it enough to balance the richness?

Thus *cassoulet* is a dish that is in a fine balance with itself. To make a really good one there are a lot of elements that must align; plenty of details that must be correct simultaneously, for, without balance, a *cassoulet* is just a pile of boiled meats and beans with breadcrumbs on top. There is no one true recipe, of course, for a rustic dish like this, but the humbleness of its origins can be transcended through careful attention to detail – a big part of what we cooks like to call 'cooking with love'. I think that a proper cook should interrogate their cooking to the extent that they realize that this kind of perfection is near unattainable. Can the perfect *cassoulet* really exist? In theory yes, perhaps, and on the pages of a book, certainly. In practice, merely gathering all the requisite ingredients in perfect health requires a degree of determination, let alone cooking the blooming thing.

I've cooked a lot of *cassoulet*s, and honestly, I can say that I've never really come close, although that is not to say that I don't enjoy trying. I've been a restaurant cook for more than a decade, but professional experience matters little for this kind of cooking: in my experience making a dish like a *cassoulet* in a restaurant setting only makes things more difficult. This is *real* country cooking, and should not be attempted in stainless steel kitchens, for the soul of thing resides elsewhere. In a farmhouse somewhere, lost in time, sits an enormous heavy clay pot, bubbling slowly over a scratchy wood fire, the plump beans rich with melting pork skin, bursting with joints of pork, *confit* goose and fat garlicky sausages.

Broad Bean Cassoulet (*Févoulet or Févoulade*)

SERVES 4

The precursor to a *cassoulet* was most probably made with broad beans. For much of the year, these would have been dried, but in the springtime comes this seasonal treat; a *cassoulet* made with *fresh* broad beans, *confit* duck and pork belly.

The cooking of this dish is quicker and a little deal lighter than a *cassoulet* proper (I said a *little* lighter).

I've adapted this recipe from the work of Paula Wolfert and André Daguin so credit must go to them.

2KG/ 4LB 8OZ	FRESH UNPODDED BROAD BEANS
200G/ 7OZ	PEARL OR BUTTON ONIONS, OR 2 BUNCHES OF SPRING ONIONS WITH LARGE BULBS (BULBS ONLY)
400G/ 14OZ	BONELESS PORK BELLY IN A PIECE, WITH SKIN
4 TBSP	DUCK FAT
6	GARLIC CLOVES
I TBSP	SUGAR

I	PEELED TOMATO, EITHER FRESH IF RIPE ENOUGH OR A GOOD ONE FROM A CAN
I	THIN LEEK
I	CELERY STICK
I	SPRIG OF THYME OR WINTER SAVORY
I LITRE/ 1¾ PINTS/ 4 CUPS	GOOD LIGHT HOMEMADE CHICKEN STOCK (WELL SKIMMED OF FAT)
4 PIECES	*CONFIT* DUCK (2 LEGS, CUT IN HALF), EXCESS FAT REMOVED
	SALT AND FRESHLY GROUND BLACK PEPPER

Pod the broad beans, then double-pod half of them. This will take ages, so get yourself someone to talk to at the table while you do it. To peel the onions, cut off the root and boil for 30 seconds, then put them straight into iced water. The skins will slip off. Let the onions dry for a while.

Remove the skin of the pork belly in one piece, then roll it into a tight cylinder and tie with kitchen string. Cut the pork belly into 2.5-cm/1-in pieces, season with salt, and fry in the duck fat in a big pot until golden brown on all sides.

Remove the pork belly and put the peeled onions into the fat with a pinch of salt. Lightly brown them, then add the garlic and the sugar. Fry gently until slightly softened, then season with black pepper. Add the double-podded broad beans and stir into the hot fat. Cover with a lid and cook all of this together for 5 minutes.

Squish the tomato with your fingers into small pieces and stir into the pot. Tie the leek and celery and thyme or savory together into a bundle

(tie it tightly – this will be removed later). Add this, the roll of pork skin, the browned pork belly and the rest of the broad beans to the ensemble.

Cover with chicken stock, bring to the boil, skim and simmer for 1 hour. Top up with chicken stock if the pot gets dry – the dish will bake in the oven later, so at this stage feel free to keep it quite wet. Add the pieces of *confit* duck and continue to simmer for another 15 minutes.

Meanwhile, preheat the oven to 170°C fan/190°C/375°F/gas mark 5.

Skim the pot again of excess fat, remove the leek and celery bundle, then transfer the meats and beans to an ovenproof dish – earthenware if possible. Pour over enough of the cooking broth to cover (save the rest of the broth to make a tasty soup), then bake in the oven, covered with foil, for around 30 minutes, until the meats are tender, then remove the foil for another 20 minutes and cook until the broad beans have formed a crust.

Salmis of Wood Pigeon

SERVES 2

A *salmis* is a classical preparation for game – roast a bird, flambé with cognac, and carve before reheating in a rich red wine sauce made with the chopped bones. Here the sauce is finished with dark chocolate – something I had previously only ever seen done in Catalan cookery – but this recipe, from a Basque cookbook, specifies the local chocolate from Bayonne. Jewish chocolate-makers, fleeing the Inquisition in Spain and Portugal, brought their recipes with them to Bayonne, and the tradition here has continued for 500 years.

This simple dish is best served with little triangles of fried bread (one edge dipped in finely chopped parsley – very smart), or some plain potatoes: boiled, peeled, buttered.

2	WOOD PIGEONS, CLEANED, GUTTED, NECK AND FEET REMOVED
2 TBSP	DUCK FAT
25ML/ 1 FL OZ/ 2 TBSP	COGNAC
30G/1 OZ/ 2 TBSP	UNSALTED BUTTER
1	SHALLOT, HALVED
1	SMALL CARROT, ROUGHLY CHOPPED
1	CELERY STICK, ROUGHLY CHOPPED
6	BLACK PEPPERCORNS
1	BAY LEAF
1	LARGE GLASS OF RED WINE
2	SLICES OF BAYONNE HAM OR PROSCIUTTO
6	PEARL ONIONS
8	BUTTON MUSHROOMS
	SPRIG OF THYME
1	SMALL SQUARE OF BITTER DARK CHOCOLATE
	SALT AND FRESHLY GROUND BLACK PEPPER

Preheat the oven to 200°C fan/220°C/425°F/ gas mark 7.

Season the pigeons with salt and pepper. Using an ovenproof sauté pan, brown the birds in the duck fat until golden brown all over. Transfer the pan to the hot oven (if your pan doesn't go in the oven, transfer to a snug roasting tin) and roast for 10 minutes.

Remove from the oven and pour off the excess fat (reserve a tablespoon for later). Deglaze the pan over a medium-high heat, first with a few tablespoons of water and then add the cognac and carefully light it: flambé! What fun. Watch your eyebrows…

Turn off the heat and allow the pigeon to rest in the pan for 5 minutes. Remove the legs and the breasts of the pigeons and set aside (at this stage they should be undercooked). Be careful to keep all resting juices to finish the sauce later.

Chop up the carcasses with a heavy knife or a cleaver. Put them in a deep-sided pan with 1 tablespoon of butter. Fry gently to give them a little colour, then add the shallot, carrot, celery, peppercorns and bay leaf, followed by the red wine. Top up with water to cover the bones (or, even better, use chicken stock if you have some lying around). Bring to the boil, skim well, then cook at a fast simmer for 30 minutes, until it has reduced by half and tastes rich and full. Strain through a fine sieve.

Meanwhile, cut the ham into small pieces and sauté in a large pan using the reserved rendered fat. Add the onions, button mushrooms and thyme, 1 tablespoon of butter with a pinch of salt. Cook until everything is golden coloured and slightly softened, then add the pieces of pigeon,

Serve the pieces of wood pigeon covered in the hot sauce. Eat with peeled, boiled and buttered potatoes.

Poulet Basquaise

Here's an excellent Basque way with chicken. It's a simple, tasty stew of chicken, ham, peppers and tomatoes flavoured with *piment d'espelette*, the mild chilli grown in the French Basque Country. Recipes are many and varied: I like a lot of garlic, and paprika as well as the espelette pepper, for a little smoke and ruddy colour. This is delicious with crusty bread, sautéed potatoes or a simple rice pilaf.

	OLIVE OIL
I	ONION, SLICED INTO HALF-MOONS
I TBSP	DICED CURED HAM (PROSCIUTTO)
4	FAT GARLIC CLOVES, SLICED
I	BAY LEAF
I	SPRIG OF THYME
I TSP	*PIMENT D'ESPELETTE*
½ TSP	SMOKED PAPRIKA
I	RED PEPPER, DESEEDED AND SLICED
I	GREEN PEPPER, DESEEDED AND SLICED
4	RIPE TOMATOES, PEELED, DESEEDED AND CHOPPED, OR 400G/14OZ PEELED PLUM TOMATOES, SQUISHED IN YOUR HAND INTO THE PAN
	A SPLASH OF WHITE WINE
2	CHICKEN LEGS, CUT IN HALF, OR 4 THIGHS
	SALT AND FRESHLY GROUND BLACK PEPPER
	CHOPPED PARSLEY, TO SERVE

Heat a good amount of olive oil in a large frying pan. Add the onion and diced ham with a pinch of salt and gently fry until the onion is soft with a little colour, then add the garlic and herbs. Fry for a few minutes longer over a low heat, then add the *piment d'espelette* and the paprika. Stir, cook the spice slowly in the fat, then add the peppers. Give everything a good stir to coat the peppers in the fat. Continue to fry slowly until they begin to soften slightly, then add the tomatoes, the wine and salt. Bring to a simmer, cover and cook for 30–40 minutes, until the peppers have fully softened into the sauce. Taste for salt. This is a *sauce Basquaise* that can now also be used to make a *Pipérade* (see page 58).

Meanwhile, season the chicken with salt, and brown in a separate pan. Pour off any excess fat (although a little of it will add flavour), then add the stewed vegetables. Cook for about 30 minutes, half covering the pan with a lid, until the chicken is cooked through. Add a little water if the sauce threatens to dry out. Adjust the seasoning, finish with chopped parsley and serve with your accompaniment of choice.

Poule au Pot Henri IV

SERVES 4

A dish named for a king. Henri IV, who was born in the Béarn city of Pau, reportedly expressed a wish to see every ploughman in his kingdom able to put a chicken in their pot. Whether or not the king really did care for the living conditions of the rural peasant class in seventeenth-century France I shall leave to the real historians. We are much more interested in this delicious recipe for a stuffed poached chicken. This is a kind of *pot-au-feu*, served with vegetables cooked in the broth and a pot of sauce to pass around – excellent for Sunday lunch.

There are many versions of Henri's namesake recipe. The most common, and perhaps most traditional in the Béarn region, is a stuffing of giblets, bread and cured ham, bound with egg yolks and seasoned with pepper and nutmeg. This is jolly good, but another angle of attack uses sausagemeat for extra oomph. An author with the pen name Babet wrote in 1892 a remarkable treatise on boiled beef which includes as an aside a recipe for this chicken. Babet recommended a version with chestnuts and truffles, and so here we are with my contribution. I like to mix some veal in with the pork for the stuffing, and a bit of boiled smoked sausage is excellent. I won't hold it against you if you don't have any fresh truffle to hand. The stuffing, bound as it is with egg and breadcrumbs, will firm up as it poaches, and can be sliced into thick pieces.

Recipes for *poule au pot* often recommend serving the dish with a thin tomato sauce, but as we have some delicious mellow earthy flavours going on I think it's nicer to make something less spiky to go with it: a dab of mustard, mixed *fines herbes*, concentrated *bouillon* (broth) and a few spoonfuls of cream.

I	LARGE WHOLE CHICKEN (APPROX. 1.6KG/ 3LB 8OZ)

FOR THE STUFFING:

	A HANDFUL OF FRESH BREADCRUMBS
50ML/ 2FL OZ/ SCANT ¼ CUP	MILK
150G/ 5½OZ	VEAL MINCE
150G/ 5½OZ	PORK MINCE
100G/ 3½OZ	COOKED SMOKED SAUSAGE – MORTEAU, MONTBÉLIARD OR POLISH SMOKED ŚLASKA KIELBASA, CHOPPED INTO 1CM/½IN CHUNKS (ALTERNATIVELY 50G/1¾OZ CURED HAM, FINELY CHOPPED)
200G/ 7OZ	COOKED VACUUM-PACKED CHESTNUTS, SEPARATED
10G/ ¼OZ	FRESH BLACK TRUFFLE, JULIENNED (OPTIONAL)
I	SPRIG OF THYME, LEAVES PICKED AND CHOPPED
I	WHOLE EGG, BEATEN
	SALT, FRESHLY GROUND BLACK PEPPER AND NUTMEG

FOR THE BROTH:

I	ONION, UNPEELED, HALVED, STUDDED WITH 2 CLOVES
I	CELERY STICK
I	CARROT
½	LEEK, LEFT IN ONE PIECE
I	BAY LEAF
	A FEW PARSLEY STALKS
IO	BLACK PEPPERCORNS
2	GARLIC CLOVES, UNPEELED
2	POTATOES, CUT INTO CHUNKS
2	TURNIPS, CUT INTO CHUNKS
2	LEEKS, CUT INTO THICK ROUNDS

FOR THE SAUCE:

1	EGG YOLK
4 TBSP	CRÈME FRAÎCHE
1 TBSP	DIJON MUSTARD
2 TBSP	FINELY CHOPPED FRESH *FINES HERBES* – A MIX OF PARSLEY, CHIVES AND CHERVIL IS GOOD
	A SQUEEZE OF LEMON JUICE
	A DASH OF HIGH-QUALITY COGNAC

To make the stuffing, soak the breadcrumbs in enough of the milk to cover. Leave for 15 minutes or longer, then squeeze well. Mix all the stuffing ingredients together and season with salt, pepper and nutmeg.

Season the cavity of your chicken with salt then fill it completely with stuffing. (Any excess stuffing can be wrapped in blanched cabbage leaves and poached with the chicken or in the leftover broth the following day, or even just formed into patties and fried.) Use a few cocktail sticks to hold the chicken together and prevent the stuffing from escaping.

Place the chicken in a large stockpot and cover with cold water and a couple of tablespoons of salt. Add the clove-studded onion, celery, carrot, the half leek, bay leaf, parsley stalks, black peppercorns and garlic. Bring slowly to the boil, skimming frequently, then reduce to a low simmer – the broth should 'blip-blip-blip' rather than bubble.

Taste the broth as it cooks – it should taste salty enough to flavour the chicken but be aware that it will reduce as it cooks, intensifying the salt. Keep skimming until no more scum forms. Continue to cook at a low simmer. After 50 minutes, remove and discard all the cooked vegetables, then add the potatoes and turnips to the pot then, 10 minutes after, add the sliced leeks. Check the chicken after about 1 hour 15 minutes of total cooking time; it should be nicely

cooked but do make sure – insert a skewer into the chicken where the breast meets the thigh, and the juices should run clear. When done, remove the chicken and vegetables to a large plate; keep covered and warm.

Strain the broth well, measure off 200ml/7fl oz/scant 1 cup of broth then season the rest with salt. This time it should taste seasoned enough to eat on its own. Leave over the heat while you make the sauce.

Pour the measured unseasoned broth into a small pan. Place over a medium heat and reduce by three-quarters – only about 3 tablespoons should remain in the pan. Allow to cool while you assemble the other sauce ingredients. Whisk together the egg yolk, crème fraîche and mustard in a bowl, then add the herbs, a little lemon juice, a dash of cognac and salt and pepper to taste. Whisk in some of the warm reduced broth, taste and adjust the seasoning once more. Keep adding broth until you are happy with the consistency of the sauce.

Address the chicken: remove the legs first and cut in half on the bone. Slip out the stuffing from the cavity and slice into thick pieces. (Note: sometimes the stuffing, although piping hot in the middle, can remain a bit pink. If this bothers you, briefly pan-fry the slices, or pop them in a hot oven for a few minutes.) Take the breast off the bone and cut in two.

To serve — Ensure each portion has one piece of breast, one piece of leg and a slice of stuffing. Serve the meat with the warm vegetables, and a little of the hot broth poured over on the plate to keep it moist and glistening. Serve the sauce on the side, warm or at room temperature, with a little pot of flaky salt for people to sprinkle over.

Duck Leg Daube with Dried Ceps, Prunes & Fried Cornmeal Cakes

SERVES 2

Duck is highly esteemed in southwest France. If you get sick of duck breasts grilled pink or crisp hot *confit*, this *daube* with red wine is the way to go. *Daube* is traditionally made with beef, but the process can be followed with virtually any meat; there is a recipe for turkey *daube* dating back to 1688, and civets enriched with blood and liver are a common treatment for furred and feathered game.

Ceps, prunes and duck is a classic combination. I am a bit funny about fruit with meat but, used judiciously, prunes help to cut through the earthy rich sauce. In the southwest they often use strips of cured ham in the base of their stews, but bacon or pancetta work just as well.

Cornmeal, or *millas* as they say throughout the southwest, was the starch of the southern poor. Paula Wolfert heartily recommended serving red wine-based stews such as this with little cakes of fried cornmeal, which are called *armottes* in the Périgord, and the recipe for these is hers.

2	DUCK LEGS
2 TBSP	OLIVE OIL OR DUCK FAT
2 TBSP	DICED CURED HAM OR BACON
I	ONION, SLICED INTO HALF-MOONS
6	WHOLE GARLIC CLOVES
I	BAY LEAF
I	SPRIG OF THYME
8	NICE SLICES OF DRIED CEP (PORCINI), SOAKED AND DRAINED (RESERVE THE SOAKING WATER)
½ TSP	FLOUR
	A SPLASH OF ARMAGNAC OR BRANDY
I	GLASS OF FULL-BODIED RED WINE
4	PRUNES, STONED
	CHOPPED PARSLEY, TO SERVE
	SALT AND FRESHLY GROUND BLACK PEPPER

FOR THE FRIED CORNMEAL CAKES (*ARMOTTES*):	
50G/ 1¾OZ/ ⅓ CUP	FINE POLENTA OR CORNMEAL
4 TSP	PLAIN FLOUR
	A PINCH OF SALT
2 TBSP	OIL, DUCK FAT OR BACON FAT, FOR FRYING

Preheat the oven to 160°C fan/180°C/350°F/ gas mark 4.

Season the duck legs with salt and pepper. Heat the oil or duck fat in a lidded ovenproof pan or casserole dish big enough to fit the duck legs, and brown them, skin side first, then add the ham or bacon. Fry until golden, then add the onion, garlic and herbs.

Cook until the onion is soft and starting to colour, then introduce the mushrooms. Fry them with the onions for a minute, then add the flour and stir well. Add the Armagnac, bubble for a second or two, then pour in the wine and pop in the prunes. Add the mushroom soaking water and a little fresh water or light poultry stock if you have some. Bring the assembly to the boil, then put a lid on the pan and put it in the oven.

Cook for around 2½ hours, turning the duck halfway through, until the duck is falling apart. The sauce should be slightly thickened, but add a splash of water if it looks like it needs it. Finish the stew with chopped parsley and serve with the cornmeal cakes.

To make the cornmeal cakes, mix the polenta or cornmeal and flour together in a small pan and whisk in 150ml/5fl oz/¾ cup of lukewarm water – make sure there are no lumps. Bring 300ml/10fl oz/1¼ cups of water to the boil and add the salt. Whisk the boiling water into the cornmeal, bring to a gloopy bubble, and cook over a medium heat for 15 minutes, stirring all the while.

Reduce the heat to very low and cook, stirring periodically, for a further 30–40 minutes, until the cornmeal is very thick but will still drop off your spoon. Lightly grease a baking tray or dish and pour the cornmeal into it – ideally it will be around 2cm/¾in thick. Smooth the top with a wet implement. Allow to cool and then refrigerate fully to set before using.

When fully set, cut into 5cm/2in circles. Fry the cakes in the oil, duck fat or bacon fat. Wolfert advises us to start the cakes off in cold fat so that they absorb less of it. When golden brown and crisp, serve with the hot stew.

Pictured overleaf

Braised Pig's Cheeks & Wild Mushrooms   SERVES 2

Midway through a trip to the Ariège we decided one day to drive up into the Pyrénées and into Andorra for a spot of retail therapy – cheap fags and booze, flick knives, electronic goods; we even visited an assault rifle shop. While I would not necessarily recommend Andorra la Vella as a summer holiday destination, we did stop for lunch at a charming little restaurant up in the hills above the town, with a wood-carved sign over the door, and a chalk board promising in Catalan 'Typical Andorran Homemade Cooking à la Carte'.

Restaurant Lydia is a family-run place; Lydia and her daughter work the floor, her husband is in the kitchen, and their granddaughter is behind the bar. Lydia is an imposing presence, short, squat, her hair in curlers like my grandma used to do, a pair of magnificent octagonal glasses, and a notepad and pen at the ready. My friend Guillaume asked me to make the booking, because he thought maybe an English accent was more likely to secure the booking than a French one. Lydia, he explained, was a tricky character. I think we caught her on a good day – I think she might have smiled, and she even spoke French (on Guillaume's previous visit, he explained, she categorically did *not*).

The service is brusque but, to be fair, very efficient. Lydia reads out the starters; we don't dare to ask her to repeat. Cannelloni, ham and melon, prawn cocktail with pineapple served in half an avocado (!) … she seems pleased with my order of snails with chorizo. Lydia passes the order to her husband in the kitchen, then comes back to read out the main courses. Civet of venison? Pig's trotters with snails? Steak and chips? Duck breast grilled over charcoal? I'll have the pig's cheek with wild mushrooms please.

While you wait there are little pots of *aïoli* sweetened with quince to dip bread into, and I can report this was also delicious stirred into the red wine and chorizo broth that my snails were sitting in. The pig's cheek came on the bone, beautifully cooked: you could eat it with a spoon. The wild mushrooms I had at Lydia's I'm not sure I could identify, but this would be excellent with girolles in the summer, or even better, fresh chanterelles or ceps in the autumn. This was served with some roast tomatoes with breadcrumbs (known as *tomates Catalanes* on this side of the border, but *tomates Provençales* on the other) and some deep-fried sliced potatoes. White beans would also be great.

This is a very simple recipe in terms of ingredients, but one that requires some real soul. Be patient with the cheeks and cook them nice and slow until they are almost falling apart.

Recipe continues overleaf

Braised Pig's Cheeks & Wild Mushrooms continued

6	PIG'S CHEEKS
	FLOUR, FOR DUSTING
3 TBSP	DUCK FAT OR OLIVE OIL
1	YELLOW ONION, THINLY SLICED INTO HALF-MOONS
8	GARLIC CLOVES, UNPEELED
1	SPRIG OF ROSEMARY
1	BAY LEAF
2	GLASSES OF WHITE WINE
	A BIG HANDFUL OF WILD MUSHROOMS – CEPS (PORCINI), CHANTERELLES, GIROLLES, HEDGEHOG MUSHROOMS ETC
	UNSALTED BUTTER, FOR FRYING
	SALT AND FRESHLY GROUND BLACK PEPPER

Preheat the oven to 150°C fan/170°C/340°F/ gas mark 3½.

Lightly flour the cheeks and season them with salt. Heat the duck fat in a large, lidded ovenproof pan or casserole and brown the cheeks. Remove, add the sliced onion with a pinch of salt, and lower the heat. Cook until the onions have begun to soften, then add the garlic and herbs. Cook for a further few minutes, then reintroduce the cheeks and pour over the white wine. Top up the pan with water so that the cheeks are covered.

Bring to the boil, cover with a lid, then place in the *hot oven*. The cheeks and their liquid should blip-blip-blip over the course of several hours – I think 3 hours should do the trick, after which the cheeks should be on the verge of collapse. Remove from the oven and taste the braising juices. If needs be, put the pan back on the hob and reduce the juices to concentrate them, while taking care not to overcook the cheeks.

Clean the mushrooms, slice thickly and add to a frying pan with some butter. Season with salt and fry until cooked. Add the mushrooms to the casserole, stir, then serve, with white beans and some buttery mashed potato, or some rustic fried potatoes like at Lydia's.

Fricot de Barques

This recipe, for a boatman's *ragoût*, is a long-simmered stew, remarkable in that it contains no liquid apart from what's already in your ingredients – they stew in oil and their own steam to give a concentrated result. A *barque*, in case you were wondering, is an old-style wooden boat used to ferry goods up and down the waterways of the Rhône and its delta. The boatmen would evidently sit for hours in their vessels, simmering strips of the excellent local beef with onions and salted anchovies.

There are many recipes for this kind of stew; a *broufade* is much the same but with the addition of capers, and other variants include a little white wine in a marinade for the beef. Elizabeth David calls her recipe a 'Grillade de Mariniers de Rhône'; the recipe is a good one.

As I write this introduction I am two hours into the cooking time; I haven't taken a peek inside the pot yet, as it's best to leave all the juices inside, but at this stage the scent has well and truly permeated the room, and has started to smell sweet, like cookies. I know, however, that the end result will be deeply savoury, demanding starch, so I have popped a couple of potatoes in the oven too. A mustardy salad makes an excellent addition to the meal.

	GOOD OLIVE OIL
I	ONION, SLICED INTO HALF-MOONS
500G/ 1LB 2OZ	BEEF – TOPSIDE OR CHUCK – CUT INTO SLICES 1CM/½IN THICK
2	GARLIC CLOVES, FINELY SLICED
4	SALTED ANCHOVY FILLETS
I TBSP	RED WINE VINEGAR
2	BAKING POTATOES, SKINS SCRUBBED AND SPRINKLED WITH SALT
	UNSALTED BUTTER
	SALT AND FRESHLY GROUND BLACK PEPPER
	GREEN SALAD, TO SERVE

Preheat the oven to 130°C fan/150°C/300°F/ gas mark 2.

Drizzle olive oil into a large, heavy-based lidded ovenproof pan or casserole dish. Add a layer of onion slices, followed by a layer of sliced beef. Season with salt and pepper, then add the garlic and anchovies, followed by another layer of onion. Repeat until all the ingredients are used up. Glug in the vinegar. Drizzle more olive oil over the top – be generous – then cover tightly with a piece of baking paper. This step is important, because if too much steam escapes the *ragoût* will dry out. Cover the pot with a lid and cook in the oven for 2½–3 hours.

After 1 hour put the potatoes into the oven. I like to splash the potatoes with water so that the fine salt sticks to their skins as they bake. At this stage it's not a bad idea to check on your *ragoût* – ensure that things are still nice and steamy, and, if not, add a splash of water.

Remove the potatoes, cut into them and stuff with cold butter. Have ready also a nice green salad with a mustardy dressing to serve with the *fricot*.

La Macaronade Sètoise

The bustling port town of Sète on the Languedoc coast has a remarkable food tradition heavy with southern Italian influences, including a number of dishes that immigrant sailors brought with them. *Macaronade* is very close to a Neapolitan-style *ragù* – known to Italian-Americans as 'Sunday gravy' – of mixed meats simmered for hours in tomato sauce. This is not something to be cobbled together quickly: the sauce should blip-burp-blip on the hob all day while everyone is driven mad by the slowly deepening aroma.

The Sète-style of *macaronade* is made with the classic combination of pork ribs, sausage and special beef rolls, or *brageoles*. These delicious little morsels, known as *braciole* in Italy, crop up in other places too: Sicily has its *involtini* stuffed with pine kernels; they are known in traditional Provençal cuisine as '*alouettes sans tête*', and in Belgium they are braised in beer. Ask the butcher for an escalope cut from the featherblade for a piece of meat that won't fall apart during the long cooking.

In Naples (or New York) the dish is often served in two parts: first in a plate of pasta mixed with the rich sauce, then the cooked meats are plonked on the table for everyone to attack, perhaps with a side of greens. In Sète, however, the meats, sauce and pasta are usually served together. Remember that the dish takes its name from the Italian *maccheroni* rather than the Italian-American equivalent, so use a short, tubular shape like ziti, penne or rigatoni.

FOR THE *BRAGEOLES*:	
4	THIN SLICES OF FEATHERBLADE, OR FAILING THAT, CHUCK STEAK
2	SLICES OF CURED HAM (ANY PROSCIUTTO OR A *JUS*), HALVED
1	GARLIC CLOVE, FINELY CHOPPED
1 TBSP	FINELY CHOPPED PARSLEY
1 TBSP	GRATED PARMESAN CHEESE
	SALT AND FRESHLY GROUND BLACK PEPPER

4	MEATY PORK RIBS
	OLIVE OIL
4	TOULOUSE OR FAT ITALIAN-STYLE SAUSAGES
1	ONION, FINELY DICED
6	GARLIC CLOVES, FINELY SLICED
1	BAY LEAF
1 TSP	FENNEL SEEDS, POUNDED TO A POWDER
2 TBSP	TOMATO CONCENTRATE
400G/ 14OZ	CANNED PEELED PLUM TOMATOES, BLITZED BRIEFLY IN A BLENDER
	A FEW BASIL LEAVES
2	GLASSES OF RED WINE
	PASTA OF YOUR CHOICE, TO SERVE
	PARMESAN OR PECORINO CHEESE (OR, EVEN BETTER, BOTH), TO SERVE

First, make the *brageoles*. If the slices of meat are too thick, bash them flat between sheets of baking paper, taking care not to smash straight through – they should be about 2mm/⅛in thick. Season the beef lightly with salt on both sides. Lay half a slice of prosciutto on each slice, then top them with the chopped garlic and parsley and the grated Parmesan cheese. Roll up the slices to form stubby little rolls. Secure with a cocktail stick or tie with kitchen string.

Season the pork ribs with salt. Heat a glug of olive oil in a large, heavy-bottomed pan and, working in batches to avoid overcrowding the pot, brown first the ribs, then the sausages, then the *brageoles*, removing each batch before introducing the next. Remove the last batch of meats, lower the heat slightly, and add the onion and a pinch of salt. Fry until soft and lightly golden, then add the garlic. Add a glug more olive oil and reduce the heat if the onion is catching a little.

Fry for a further couple of minutes then add the bay leaf and the powdered fennel seeds. Stir well, then blob in the tomato concentrate.

Cook over a low heat for a few minutes, stirring all the while to make sure it doesn't stick, then add the blitzed plum tomatoes, basil leaves, red wine, salt and plenty of black pepper. Bring to the boil, reduce to a simmer, pop the ribs and *brageoles* back into the pot and half-cover with a lid. Keep the browned sausages in the refrigerator until later.

Cook at a bare simmer for 5 or 6 hours; add the sausages back into the pot for the final 1½ hours of cooking. Add water if it threatens to dry out. The pan will need stirring from time to time so that the sauce doesn't stick (heed the advice of Henry from *Goodfellas*). After 6 hours the sauce will be silky with rendered fat, and all the meats at the point of collapse.

To serve, boil your pasta of choice in lightly salted water until *al dente*. Dress the cooked pasta with a few spoons of sauce, then plate the pasta and spoon the meats and more sauce over the top: one sausage, one pork rib and one *brageole* per person. A feast! Serve with grated Parmesan, pecorino or a mixture of the two cheeses.

Garbure

Garbure is *the* symbol of Béarnaise cookery, but it is also eaten in other parts of southwest France: the rest of Gascony, the Landes and the Basque Country. The word *garbure* is close to the old Spanish *garbias*, a word for stew. Regardless of this etymology, this style of soup-stew is common on both sides of the Pyrénées. The peasant staples of cabbage, beans and salted meats have been boiled up together in this part of Europe since the Middle Ages. *Garbure* is little known outside France – and even outside the regions of its origin – but Curnonsky, the most famous food writer of the early twentieth century and a champion of regional French cookery, proclaimed *garbure* to be one of best dishes in France.

Garbure is a meal in itself, albeit sometimes in two parts. Meats and broth are often served separately: first a bowl of the rich liquid, then a plate of the boiled meats, sometimes with pickled gherkins, pickled chillies or a vinaigrette: acid and heat to cut through the fat. Many say that a *garbure* must be so thick that you can stand the ladle up in it.

As far as specific recipes go, there are an abundance. This is a dish that is eaten all year round. In autumn some cooks add chestnuts, in summer it may be red peppers. In the Basque Country the stock is often enriched with the end piece of a cured ham (unfortunately always slightly thin on the ground where I live). Some cook it like a gratin, layered with bread and cheese like the Alpine *panade*; others put a slice of bread or toast in the bottom of the bowl. Swiss chard is a delicious addition, making the soup more luscious.

Meats are also up for debate. Sometimes there are boiled sausages (and why not!) and often the broth is made with a ham bone or duck stock, but there really must be some kind of delicious pork. An everyday *garbure* might once have contained very little meat at all. Scraps of salted fat, finely chopped with parsley and garlic to make *un hachi*, would be stirred into the pot for a deeper flavour when little else was available. Times are no longer quite so hard for most, and the *garbure* we are most interested in contains a little of all the above. The 'Sunday best' version, for weekends or high holidays, contains not only a good chunk of salted pork but also the crowning glory – the *lou trebuc* – *confit* of goose or duck.

The essential ingredients, most would agree, include white beans, cabbage, pork and *confit* duck, usually bolstered by a supporting cast of seasonal vegetables: potatoes, of course, but also turnips, leeks, chard, pumpkin … Feel free to add or omit according to what you have to hand or like best.

Recipe continues overleaf

Garbure continued

Put the ham in your biggest stockpot and cover with cold water. Bring to the boil; skim well. Meanwhile, drain and wash the soaked beans. Bring them to the boil in a separate pan of cold water; skim well. Boil the beans for 5 minutes, then drain and pop them in with the ham. Set the ham and beans to simmer.

Meanwhile, heat the duck fat in a roomy pan and fry the onions, celery and leeks until soft, season with lots of ground black pepper and a little grated nutmeg then tip the lot into the ham and beans. Add a bouquet garni made from the bay, thyme and parsley stalks. Simmer the assembly for 2–3 hours, until the ham is showing signs of getting soft. Top the water up if it gets low but try not to drown the ingredients with too much water – keep the mixture thick. Add no salt at this stage, as although the ham might not taste it at the beginning, sometimes after a few hours of boiling the broth can get a bit salty.

Add the chopped vegetables to the pot, bring back to a simmer, and cook for 15 minutes, until the vegetables are starting to soften.

Blitz, or very finely chop together, the ham fat, garlic and parsley, and stir the resulting paste into the broth. Finally, add the *confit* duck legs along with a little of the fat that is clinging to them. Simmer for a further 20 minutes or so.

The vegetables should be soft and the ham should be at the stage that it falls apart when prodded. Adjust the seasoning and add salt if needed. The *garbure* should be thick enough that you can stand a ladle up in the pot.

At this stage you have two options. Either keep the meats in whole pieces and serve a bowl of the vegetable-laden broth first – atop a slice of toasted sourdough, if you fancy – followed by a communal plate of delicious boiled gubbins (this method requires a little pile of cornichons, maybe a dab or two of mustard, or a mustardy vinaigrette). Otherwise, stir the contents of the pot to break up the meats into large pieces and serve all in a hot jumble together.

1	UNSMOKED HAM HOCK, OR 250G/9OZ GAMMON (SKIN ON), WASHED
250G/ 9OZ/ ABOUT 2 CUPS	DRIED WHITE BEANS, SOAKED OVERNIGHT
6 TBSP	DUCK FAT
2	ONIONS, CHOPPED
½	HEAD CELERY, CHOPPED
1	LEEK, SLICED
2	BAY LEAVES
1	SPRIG OF THYME OR WINTER SAVORY
	PARSLEY STALKS
2	TURNIPS, PEELED AND CHOPPED INTO 2.5-CM/1-IN PIECES
2	CARROTS, PEELED AND CHOPPED INTO 2.5-CM/1-IN PIECES
2	POTATOES, PEELED AND CHOPPED INTO 2.5-CM/1-IN PIECES (PICK A VARIETY THAT WON'T COMPLETELY FALL APART)
½	SAVOY CABBAGE, CORE REMOVED, CHOPPED INTO 5-CM/2-IN PIECES
25G/ 1 OZ	CURED HAM FAT (FROM THE ENDS OF A CURED HAM – ASK AT YOUR LOCAL DELI) OR GOOD FATTY BACON
2	GARLIC CLOVES
2 TBSP	CHOPPED PARSLEY
2	*CONFIT* DUCK LEGS
	SALT, FRESHLY GROUND BLACK PEPPER AND GRATED NUTMEG (AS ON PAGE 38)

Drunken Mutton à la Catalane (Pistache de Mouton)

SERVES 4–6

This has nothing to do with pistachios, but rather comes from the expression *avoir sa pistache*: to be drunk. It's traditionally a stew of mutton in the Catalan style, which according to *Larousse Gastronomique* could mean a number of things. Most recipes for mutton *à la Catalane* have one key ingredient in common: garlic. Elizabeth David's recipe has a modest twenty cloves, many call for more like fifty. Other common ingredients are dried orange peel, a favourite ingredient in the *daubes* of Provence and Languedoc, and dried ceps. The 'drunken' element of a *pistache* refers to the use of wine as a braising liquid. Recipes vary as to the preference for white, red or rosé – I'd say go with what your heart tells you.

Paula Wolfert's version, which she describes as a 'superb version of *cassoulet* … from the central Pyrénées', contains garlic sausages and white beans: a version closer to *cassoulet* than others. She also includes a piece of salt pork, tomatoes and the dried ceps typical of the mountains. The combination of lamb and beans is an ancient one, particularly favoured by the Arabs of the Maghreb who might well have introduced it to the south of France as early as the seventh century.

The following recipe is less of a *cassoulet* and more of a tasty *ragoût* of mutton and beans. A little orange peel adds a bit of fragrance, the dried mushrooms an earthiness, and garlic cooked in goose fat an unmistakable taste of the French Pyrénées. There's a lot of garlic, but with proper slow cooking it will mellow to a nice background hum.

Preheat the oven to 150°C fan/170°C/340°F/
gas mark 3½.

    Heat the olive oil in a large, heavy, lidded
ovenproof pan or casserole dish, big enough to
hold the shoulder. (If it won't quite fit in whole,
cut it into two or three big pieces.) Season the
shoulder well with salt and pepper, then brown
on all sides in the hot oil. Set the lamb aside and
discard the oil and any excess salt, but leave any
tasty brown scrapings, for they are full of flavour.

    Heat the goose fat in the same pot and
brown the bacon, then add the onions and garlic.
Fry them slowly with a small pinch of salt until
approaching softness, about 10 minutes. Add the
soaked porcini, the orange peel and herbs, give
everything a stir, then add the tomatoes, squishing
them well with your hands as you add them to the
pot. Cook the tomatoes for 30 seconds, then nestle
the lamb on top and pour in the wine and enough
water to come about two-thirds of the way up the
lamb. Bring the liquid to the boil, then reduce to
a low simmer. Drain your soaked beans and stir
them in. Make sure the beans are well covered, as
they will dry out and burn if the liquid level drops
below them. Add more water if necessary.

    Cover the lamb with a piece of baking
paper, put the lid on, then slide the pan into the
hot oven. Cook for at least 4 hours, or until the
lamb is very tender. You'll need to check that the
stew isn't drying out too much – top up with water
if needed. When the lamb is spoon-tender and the
beans are cooked through, remove from the oven.
Add a little water if you think it is looking a bit
too thick, and adjust the seasoning with salt and
black pepper. Eat on its own, or with crusty bread
and a lively salad on the side.

I TBSP	OLIVE OIL
I	SHOULDER OF LAMB, HOGGET OR MUTTON, BONED BUT OTHERWISE WHOLE (TOTAL WEIGHT SHOULD BE ABOUT 2KG/4LB 8OZ; IF YOU'RE USING HOGGET OR MUTTON A WHOLE SHOULDER MIGHT BE A BIT TOO BIG)
I TBSP	GOOSE FAT
I TBSP	PANCETTA OR SMOKED FRENCH SLAB BACON, CUT INTO 1.5CM/¾IN CHUNKS
2	ONIONS, FINELY SLICED INTO HALF-MOONS
40	GARLIC CLOVES (APPROX. 4 HEADS), PEELED IF YOU CAN BE BOTHERED
I TBSP	DRIED CEPS (PORCINI), SOAKED IN HOT WATER AND DRAINED
I	PIECE OF ORANGE PEEL
2	BAY LEAVES
I	SPRIG OF THYME
2	CANNED PEELED TOMATOES
250G/ 9OZ/ 2 CUPS	YOUR FAVOURITE DRIED WHITE BEANS, SOAKED OVERNIGHT
2	GLASSES OF WHITE WINE
	SALT AND FRESHLY GROUND BLACK PEPPER

Pipérade

Piper means pepper in the Gascon and Basque languages and *pipérade* is the French Basque country's best-known way with eggs. It's a spicy vegetable stew with eggs cooked in the heat of the sauce. Judging not least from my own preconceptions, this dish has been done many injustices over the years. Many people make this in the same way as scrambled eggs or an omelette, or even with eggs cracked in like a *shakshuka*, but the real deal is something much smoother; rather subtle and interesting to eat.

First, make a *sauce Basquaise* (see page 36). This sauce must be simmered for long enough that the vegetables collapse into a smooth oily sauce rather than a chunky sauté, and the eggs should be stirred in at the last minute over a low heat, moved around with a spoon to form a fine, frothy liasion of egg and sauce. The colour will turn from ruddy red to a lovely muted orange.

Pipérade crops up as an accompaniment to many Basque dishes. Elizabeth David, who knew what's what, writes that 'Brochettes of calf's liver are sometimes served with the *Pipérade* and a very good combination it is'. It is excellent at any time of day, and assuming you have the sauce already made, makes a very good quick breakfast: piled onto buttered toast, and served with a traditional topping of crispy fried ham.

2 SLICES	CURED HAM (*JUS* WOULD BE TRADITIONAL)
	OLIVE OIL
	SAUCE BASQUAISE (SEE THE RECIPE FOR *POULET BASQUAISE* ON PAGE 36 – WITHOUT THE CHICKEN)
4	EGGS
2 PIECES	HOT BUTTERED TOAST

Heat a deep-sided frying pan and slowly fry the cured ham in a little oil until crispy. Break into shards and reserve. Heat the sauce Basquaise in the same pan and bring it to a slow simmer.

Beat the eggs, then pour them into the pan. Immediately stir the eggs and sauce together and continue to stir over a low heat. Remove the pan from the heat if the eggs seem to be cooking too quickly – the idea is to keep the dish as smooth as possible. Cook, stirring, until you are happy with the consistency – the eggs must be cooked but still creamy. Serve with hot buttered toast and the crispy ham on top.

Grilled Pepper & Salted Anchovy Salad (Anchois à la Catalane)

SERVES 2

A simple preparation from French Catalonia via the town of Collioure, just 20 kilometres/ 12 miles from the Spanish border. The anchovy fishing tradition based around this coastal town goes back to the Middle Ages, when it was also known for salting tuna. This is a tasty little salad, sometimes referred to as an *assiette catalane*: a plate of grilled peppers, salted anchovies, black olives and egg. This is hardly a recipe, and not much of a starter, but more of a reminder that grilled peppers are very good with anchovies, and that to eat simply is to eat well.

A Catalan salad, as noted by Colman Andrews in his superb book *Catalan Cuisine*, should never be mixed together, and 'each ingredient holds its counsel'. It is in this spirit that this plate of food comes together. The peppers are grilled, skinned and marinated, the anchovies laid in strips alongside adding saline depth.

An excellent start to a summer's meal outdoors, this, with a glass or two of cold wine. If you can grill the peppers over a wood fire then all the better. I find it particularly satisfying to eat: the peppers drip and droop when fished up with a fork. Come armed also with crusty bread to sweep through the plate of oily juices.

I	I LARGE RED PEPPER
	OLIVE OIL
	RED WINE VINEGAR
I	GARLIC CLOVE, VERY FINELY SLICED
I TBSP	FINELY CHOPPED PARSLEY
6	SALTED ANCHOVY FILLETS (FROM COLLIOURE IF POSSIBLE)
	A FEW BLACK OLIVES, PITTED
I	EGG, HARD-BOILED, PEELED AND QUARTERED
	SALT

Grill the pepper hard over charcoal and/or wood until the skin is blackened all over. Put it into a bowl and cover with clingfilm until cool enough to handle. Peel the pepper with your hands, then deseed and slice into 1cm/½in strips. On the plate you will be serving them on, marinate the peppers for a while in a good amount of olive oil, a splash of red wine vinegar, some salt (go easy), and the finely sliced garlic.

Split the anchovy fillets lengthways in two to form two thin strips. Rearrange the slices of peppers side by side on the plate with strips of anchovy fillet interspersed. Pop the olives and quarters of boiled egg on the side of the assembly – remember: no mixing! Season the egg with a little salt. Sprinkle the peppers and anchovies with a line of chopped parsley and eat.

Chapter Two

North
Africa

North Africa

At first glance inclusion of this chapter might seem incongruous. You may be wondering: why a chapter on food from a different continent? Well, it is less about the food of North Africa (no one could do justice to North African cuisine in one chapter with a dozen recipes), and more about the sharing of ideas, and to some extent a shared history. It is about France as part of the Mediterranean, and hopefully my collection of recipes illustrates the point.

Outside influences on French cuisine have come from many angles, but an obvious centre for trade over the millennia was the port city of Marseille, formerly the Greek colony of Massilia or Massalia. Many new ingredients flowed through Marseille – among them salt cod, spices, saffron, pasta and beans along with tomatoes and other vegetables from the New World – that now typify French cuisine, particularly that of the south. Today Marseille is a multicultural wonder where the food is just as likely to be Tunisian or Algerian as Armenian or Italian. Is the food in Marseille French? Yes and no. Is the food of the south of France originally North African? This is obviously too simplistic, and we cannot discount the historical influences that the other peoples of the Mediterranean have had on French cuisine. Marseille was a vital conduit for the movement of goods, people and ideas into mainland France – ideas or ingredients that have gone on to become famous the whole country over – and Marseille itself has evolved its own cuisine which is truly mixed and truly modern. Marseille, I think it can be argued, is a true border town.

In the same way that fish and chips, a product of Eastern European and Jewish immigration to Britain, has become one of the nation's favourite things to eat, many French consider couscous to be one of their national dishes. Jean-Baptiste Reboul's book *La Cuisinière Provençale* is a collection of more than 1,000 Provençal recipes and 365 menus. Published in 1897 it remains a key resource for cooks interested in learning about the Provençal canon. It includes the curiosity of a recipe for '*LE COUSCOUSS*', of which he writes that although this dish is essentially Arabic, Provence is too closely linked with the North African regions to resist the request that has been repeatedly made to see this exotic dish appear in his book. Reboul's book was published long before the modern waves of emigration from North Africa to Europe. Links between Provence and North Africa are vastly older; both regions were part of the Roman Empire, and the movement of goods, people and ideas between the two has continued ever since.

Some of the following recipes are original, which is to say invented. Others are adaptations of traditional dishes from the southern side of the Mediterranean, and others still are recipes that are found in France but illustrate the link to North African cookery.

Poulet Antiboise (see page 102) comes from the famous resort on the Riviera, but the recipe is for chicken cooked smothered in onions, herbs and spices: add a cinnamon stick and it's basically a tagine. Aubergine *Bohémienne* (see page 79) might remind you a little of ratatouille – but add a few spices and the accent changes, just as for the Lamb, Aubergine & Tomato Tagine (see page 108). The recipes for Caldero or Fish Couscous (see pages 98 and 91) are patently not French, but I think the techniques have a lot in common with southern French fish stews, and the use of saffron, orange peel and spices makes the dishes shout just like a *bouillabaisse*. These are recipes that get me thinking about the food of the Mediterranean as a whole, about the part the south of France has to play in this story, and how the food from across the sea has helped to form the roots of the rich French cuisine we know today.

Provence and North Africa were part of the Roman Empire, and the movement of goods, people and ideas between the two has continued ever since.

Brik à l'Oeuf

Brik is found all over Tunisia. Tunisia was once a province of the Ottoman empire, which might explain the similarity between *brik* and the word *börek*, the Turkish twist on filo pastry, but then again it might not. *Brik* is at least 500 years old and is more likely the product of the Jews of southern Tunisia. The use of the French language in the name, *à l'oeuf*, is a relic of French colonization, but this is not to say that the French invented putting an egg in it.

A *brik* is a (usually) triangle-shaped, deep-fried pastry, like an exceedingly crisp fried wonton. Paper-thin pastry envelops a filling of tuna, capers, parsley and a raw egg, and is shallow or deep-fried until crisp. The egg yolk should definitely be runny. Eat it hot, with a squeeze of lemon and greasy fingers, positioning yourself in anticipation of the egg yolk spilling onto your plate below, only to be scooped back up later. A blob of harissa on the plate is a good idea: this way you can swipe and smoosh the harissa and egg yolk together to create an impromptu sauce. A fun thing to cook, and even more fun to eat.

I	TIN OF TUNA (150G/5½OZ), DRAINED
50G/ 1¾OZ/ ½ CUP	GRATED CHEDDAR CHEESE (AN ACCEPTABLE WESTERNIZATION I HOPE YOU'LL ALLOW ME)
2 TBSP	ROUGHLY CHOPPED PARSLEY
I TBSP	SALTED CAPERS, RINSED WELL
8	BRIK (*FEUILLES DE BRIK/BRICK*) PASTRY WRAPPERS, OR FILO PASTRY SHEETS
4	EGGS
	SUNFLOWER OR OLIVE OIL

TO SERVE:

	HARISSA
	LEMON WEDGES
	SALT AND FRESHLY GROUND BLACK PEPPER

Mix together the tuna, cheese, parsley and capers and season with salt and pepper. Brush two squares of *brik* pastry with water and stick them together. Put into a shallow bowl. Put 2–3 tablespoons of filling on the pastry sheets – slightly off centre towards one of the corners – then make a dent in the filling with the back of your spoon. Crack an egg into the dent. Brush the sides of the pastry with water, then carefully fold over into a triangle shape without breaking the egg yolk. Repeat with the remaining pastry sheets and filling to make another three parcels.

Pour in enough oil to come 2cm/¾in up the sides of a deep-sided frying pan. Heat until hot but not smoking. Carefully slide the parcels into the oil. Fry until it is golden brown and shatteringly crisp. Spoon hot oil over the top rather than turning it over – this will ensure even cooking, which should only take 1½ minutes. Drain briefly on kitchen paper, then eat with harissa and a squeeze of lemon.

Frites-Omelette

An excellent way of using up leftover fries (a rare occurrence, I know), this makes for a delicious quick lunch. Comparisons with the Spanish *tortilla* are welcome, but the technique is much more French, and the flavours unmistakably North African. Make *un sandwich frites-omelette*, the Algerian street-food staple, by stuffing the omelette into a buttered baguette spread liberally with harissa. Merguez sausages, squished into the already excellent sandwich, make for a thing of beauty, the *ne plus ultra*, for the holy trinity of sausage, egg and chips will then be complete.

	A HANDFUL OF LEFTOVER FRENCH FRIES (NOT FAT CHIP-SHOP CHIPS)
3	EGGS
I TBSP	OLIVE OIL
½	RED ONION, CHOPPED
½	MILDLY SPICY GREEN PEPPER OR MILD GREEN CHILLI
I TBSP	ROUGHLY CHOPPED PARSLEY AND/OR CORIANDER LEAVES
	A KNOB OF UNSALTED BUTTER
I TBSP	THICKLY GRATED CHEESE, ANYTHING YOU FANCY (I USE BOG-STANDARD CHEDDAR)
	SALT

TO SERVE:

	HARISSA (I LOVE THE LE CAP BON BRAND IN A TUBE)
	FRESH BAGUETTE AND SALTED BUTTER (OPTIONAL)
	MERGUEZ SAUSAGES, GRILLED (ALSO OPTIONAL, BUT PHWOAR)

Crisp up your leftover fries over a medium-low heat in your favourite omelette pan. Toss and shake the pan to ensure an even heat. Turn down the heat if they threaten to catch and darken. Once crisp, tip out onto a plate and keep warm.

Beat the eggs with a fork and season with salt. Add the oil to the pan and fry the onion and pepper for a minute or so. Throw in the chopped parsley or coriander, followed immediately by the knob of butter. Tip the pan around to spread the butter, then pour in the beaten eggs. Drag the eggs around and tip the pan as you would for any omelette. When still very runny, add the grated cheese and the fries. Press the fries into the egg as it sets, and cook for a minute or so, until the underneath is nicely browned but the middle still a little runny. Fold the omelette over and slide it out onto a plate. Eat with harissa.

Even better, butter a split crusty baguette well and spread a good teaspoonful of harissa on top. Fill with the omelette while it is still hot, which will melt the butter in the same way as the chips do in a chip butty. This is a good thing. Stuff in one or two grilled merguez sausages to achieve transcendence.

Brochettes

Chicken Thigh, Langoustine & Saffron Butter

SERVES 4

This might sound an unlikely combination but serving chicken with crayfish has a long history in Lyonnaise cuisine, back to the eighteenth century at least. The great chef Fernand Point, founder of the restaurant La Pyramide in Vienne, was a master of *la grande cuisine* and counted Paul Bocuse among his disciples. His book *Ma Gastronomie* is dotted with recipes for poultry and this one, chicken roasted in crayfish butter and garnished with their tails, is truly delicious!

In the UK we are forced to adapt, as fresh crayfish are impossible to source. Langoustines, thankfully, are an excellent substitute. I hope you will bear with me as we delve slightly into a convoluted process:

blanch the langoustines for a minute, shell, reserving the tails, and blitz the shells with butter to a pale pink paste. Cook the resultant mixture with a pinch of saffron to a pleasing shade of ochre and coral, strain, cool, and you have a saffron-spiked shellfish butter ready to use. This butter adds an excellent flourish to a classic *bisque* and would be a delicious topping to a grilled sole or a piece of roast turbot.

For our purposes we will roast some chicken thighs in the flavourful butter before threading them onto skewers with the langoustine tails. Brush the brochettes with more of the butter as they grill, and hey presto!

Bring a large pan of well-salted water to the boil. Drop in the langoustines and boil for a minute, then remove and cool. Shell the langoustines (reserving the shells) and keep the tails in the refrigerator for later.

Gather up all the shells and blitz with the butter in a heavy-duty mixer for a good 15 minutes. Alternatively, crush the shells as best you can before combining with the butter.

Transfer the shells and butter to a clean pan over a gentle heat and add the saffron. Cook the butter slowly for about 15 minutes, by which time the flavour and colour of the shells will have infused into the butter. Strain the butter through a fine sieve and set aside.

Preheat the oven to 180°C fan/200°C/ 400°F/gas mark 6.

Bone the chicken thighs, leaving the skin on. Cut each one in half, arrange in a roasting dish on a bed of thyme sprigs and drizzle lightly with olive oil. Roast for around 20 minutes, until the chicken is almost cooked, then drizzle over a few spoonfuls of the langoustine butter. Continue to roast for a further 5 minutes, then remove from the oven and allow to cool. Roll the pieces around in the butter so each piece is well coated.

Light the barbeque and have some melted langoustine butter at the ready. Thread the chicken thighs and langoustine tails onto skewers, alternating, so that there are four pieces of chicken thigh and four langoustine tails on each skewer. Grill the skewers over a medium-hot flame, brushing with the butter. (Use a sprig of thyme to brush for extra points.)

When the chicken skin is crisp and everything is hot through, the brochettes are ready. Serve seasoned with a squeeze of lemon and a crack of black pepper. These would be very delicious with *Aïoli* (see page 169).

Note — The preparation for this dish can be done the day ahead, as this is may be too much work for an impromptu barbeque.

16	LIVE LANGOUSTINES
250G/ 9OZ/ 2¼ CUPS	UNSALTED BUTTER
	A PINCH OF SAFFRON STRANDS
8	CHICKEN THIGHS, SKIN ON
	A FEW SPRIGS OF THYME
	OLIVE OIL
	LEMON JUICE
	FRESHLY GROUND BLACK PEPPER
4	LONG SKEWERS (IF USING WOODEN ONES, SOAK IN WATER FOR 10 MINUTES BEFORE USING)

Pictured overleaf, left

Brochettes

Scallops, Cucumbers & Dill with Coral Butter

SERVES 4

A typically idiosyncratic recipe from Richard Olney, this adapted from his book *Simple* *French Food*. This is absolutely worth the effort; a delicious combination.

16	SMALL–MEDIUM SCALLOPS, WITH THEIR CORAL
100G/ 3½OZ/ ½ CUP	SOFTENED UNSALTED BUTTER
I TSP	LEMON JUICE
4	SMALL, FIRM CUCUMBERS
	SALT AND FRESHLY GROUND BLACK PEPPER

FOR THE MARINADE:

I TBSP	CHOPPED DILL FRONDS
I TSP	LEMON ZEST
4 TBSP	OLIVE OIL
4	LONG SKEWERS (IF USING WOODEN ONES, SOAK IN WATER FOR 10 MINUTES BEFORE USING)

Remove the coral from the scallops, Pound using a pestle and mortar until you have a fine paste, then combine with the softened butter. Season the mixture with the lemon juice, salt and black pepper. Keep in the refrigerator for later – note that ideally the butter needs to be slightly softened when it is time to grill the brochettes.

Peel the cucumbers and cut into pieces roughly the same size as the scallops (if the cucumbers are large, halve lengthways and scoop out the seeds first). Boil the cucumbers for 1 minute in well-salted water, then drain and allow to cool.

Marinate the scallops and blanched cucumbers for an hour in the chopped dill, lemon zest and olive oil, adding a few cracks of black pepper.

Take the butter from the refrigerator and allow to come to room temperature. When you are ready to cook, season the scallops with salt, then thread the scallops and cucumbers alternately onto skewers. Grill over a lively flame for a few minutes, brushing once on each side with the softened coral butter, until the scallops are cooked. Transfer to a serving dish and brush liberally with more coral butter.

Pictured previous page, right

Brochettes

Duck Breast, Lamb's Kidney & Merguez

SERVES 4

All three meats are most delicious when grilled over charcoal, and the juices from the merguez will leak out and imbue the lot with fat and spice. The key here is to cut the ingredients to the right size – aim to keep the duck pink inside, but to give the sausage a good sizzling. Make sure your barbeque is fired up well in advance.

2	DUCK BREASTS
4	LAMB'S KIDNEYS
2	MERGUEZ SAUSAGES
	SALT
4	LONG SKEWERS (IF USING WOODEN ONES, SOAK IN WATER FOR 10 MINUTES BEFORE USING)

Score the fat of the duck breasts in a fine cross-hatch pattern – this will help to render the fat as they cook. Cut the breasts into chunky slices around 2.5cm/1in thick. Remove any fat and membrane from the lamb's kidneys and cut in half from top to bottom. Cut the merguez into 5-cm/2-in pieces. Season the duck breasts and kidneys with salt.

Thread the ingredients onto the skewers, alternating the meats. The merguez should be threaded on sideways rather than along the length.

Grill the brochettes over a medium flame, turning occasionally, until the duck breast has a soft bounce to it when poked, and the merguez are sizzling and their juices running. Rest for a few minutes before getting involved.

Pictured previous, centre

Avocado, Cedro Lemon, Pomegranate, Mint & Bottarga Salad

SERVES 2

I've seen *cedro* lemons bigger than my head. I am never usually able to find ones that big, but always seek out this special thing when in season in winter. *Cedro*, *cédrat* lemons, or simply *citron*, are the original lemon from which all other cultivars derived. They have much more pith than juice and a subtle flavour. They are delicious peeled, sliced thinly (thick pith and all) and tumbled through salads, and are make one of the very best candied fruits. They are also very good sliced a bit thicker, rubbed in oil, lightly grilled, and topped with a sliver of anchovy and a strand of mozzarella: elegant finger food.

Cedro lemon, mint and bottarga combine to an intriguing result, something reminiscent of Moorish Sicily, but also totally made up. This is one of my very favourite winter salads, full of things I love and plenty of festive colour. Avocado might seem unlikely here, but it is the perfect foil for these spiky flavours, and a little touch of cream in the dressing ties everything together.

I	AVOCADO, IN A STATE OF PERFECT RIPENESS — RIPE, OF COURSE, BUT JUST FIRM ENOUGH THAT IT DOESN'T SMUSH WHEN TUMBLED AROUND A BIT
⅛	*CEDRO* LEMON, PEELED (ROUGHLY 30G/1OZ) AND FINELY SLICED
	A HANDFUL OF ROCKET, WASHED
	A SPRIG OR TWO OF MINT, LEAVES PICKED
	OLIVE OIL
	LEMON JUICE
	BOTTARGA DI MUGGINE (GREY MULLET BOTTARGA)
I TBSP	POMEGRANATE SEEDS
I TSP	DOUBLE CREAM
	SALT

Halve, stone and scoop out the avocado. Slice into half-moons just less than 1cm/½in thick. Add to a salad bowl along with the sliced lemon, rocket and mint. Dress lightly with olive oil, lemon juice and salt, and fold gently with your hands to combine.

Using a swivel-head peeler, peel thin curled strips of bottarga over the salad, and sprinkle over the pomegranate seeds. Drizzle over the double cream using a teaspoon, and finish with another of olive oil.

Salade Tunisienne

Not quite the classic *salade Tunisienne*, but one that resembles more closely another famous *salade* from across the sea. At its simplest, the original is more along the lines of a tasty chopped salad with onion, cucumber, peppers, tuna and boiled egg. The version here is adapted from an aside in Robert Carrier's *A Taste of Morocco*: a salad 'inspired no doubt from its Mediterranean cousin, *Salade Niçoise*, or its Tunisian brother, *Salade Tunisienne*'.

This recipe might well, authentically speaking, be neither French, Moroccan nor indeed Tunisian, but is delicious all the same, and to me at least the similarities are enjoyable. A fresh salad of raw vegetables, anchovy, hot and sweet red peppers, and boiled egg: an idea that clearly bridges the gap. Here cooked green beans are included (heresy in a *salade Niçoise*), coriander seeds for an occasional orange-scented crunch, and a harissa dressing in case you thought we weren't being quite North African enough.

I	NICE RIPE FAT TOMATO
I OR 2	GREEN PEPPERS — THE SLIGHTLY PIQUANT TURKISH LONG PEPPERS WORK WELL HERE
	A SMALL HANDFUL OF GREEN BEANS, COOKED AND COOLED
	A FEW GREEN OLIVES, PITTED
	A SMALL HANDFUL OF BOTH PARSLEY AND CORIANDER, CHOPPED ROUGHLY
I	HARD-BOILED EGG, HALVED
	A FEW SALTED ANCHOVIES (OR SOME HIGH-QUALITY PRESERVED TUNA)
I TSP	FINELY DICED SHALLOT
I TSP	CORIANDER SEEDS, TOASTED IN A DRY PAN

FOR THE DRESSING:

I TSP	HARISSA PASTE
I TBSP	LEMON JUICE OR RED WINE VINEGAR
3 TBSP	OLIVE OIL
	SALT

Make the dressing by mixing together the harissa, lemon juice and olive oil; season with salt.

Cut the tomato into nice chunks or slices: I tend towards the chunkier (French) style rather than the fine dice of Tunisian preference. Deseed the peppers and slice finely. Mix the tomato, peppers, green beans, olives and chopped herbs together, and dress with the dressing, reserving a bit to drizzle on top. Arrange the boiled egg on top and drape over some salted anchovy fillets. Sprinkle the shallot and coriander seeds over the top, and drizzle with the reserved dressing.

Salade Juive

Jewish salad is a Pieds-Noirs import from North Africa. This is often cooked to a ratatouille-like mulch (add eggs and serve hot to make a shakshuka) but I prefer a little more distinction. This is an excellent salad for a barbeque, not least because you can grill the peppers over a real fire. Improvisation is welcome and well rewarded. Try the following add-ons: chopped red chillies or a sprinkle of hot paprika, roughly chopped parsley or coriander, flakes of grilled fish or poached salt cod, salted anchovy fillets, chopped hard-boiled eggs … just perhaps not all at the same time.

4	RED PEPPERS
4	GOOD-SIZED VERY RIPE TOMATOES
2 TSP	CUMIN SEEDS
I	FAT GARLIC CLOVE, VERY FINELY SLICED LENGTHWAYS
	OLIVE OIL
	LEMON JUICE, TO TASTE
	A HANDFUL OF BLACK OLIVES, PITTED
	SALT

Grill the red peppers on a barbeque (or under a grill in the oven) until collapsed and blistered black, then transfer to a covered bowl to let them steam. Meanwhile, peel the tomatoes (see page 143), core and cut them into quarters. Toast the cumin in a dry pan and lightly crush using a pestle and mortar.

When the peppers have cooled enough to handle, peel them, core them and cut into thick strips. While the peppers are still warm, toss them with the tomatoes, a four-fingered pinch of salt, the sliced garlic, a good glug of olive oil and some lemon juice. Arrange artfully on a big plate and scatter over the cumin. Dot the olives around the place and finish with a little more olive oil.

Bohémienne (Gratin Estrassaïre)

SERVES 4

This aubergine dish is related to ratatouille. Ratatouille is (most probably) originally from Nice but this variant comes from near Avignon, from what was formerly an enclave known as the Comtat Venaissin, a region once as famous for its cuisine as the Comté de Nice.

Bohémienne actually reminds me of a Moroccan dish called *zaalouk* – a cold salad of mashed roasted aubergine and stewed tomatoes. Absolutely delicious, particularly when the aubergine has been roasted and blackened over charcoal. In Morocco it's seasoned with garlic, cumin, coriander, paprika and olive oil, all mushed up to serve as a dip to eat with bread.

The *Provençal* equivalent is a little looser, seasoned with anchovy, and often baked as a breadcrumb-topped gratin. This last one is the version I prefer: excellent eaten hot with some roast lamb, say, or indeed cold the next day with a few other bits on the table. If eating hot as a gratin, I feel it's especially important to keep the texture on the rougher side, so don't stew everything down to a complete mush.

	OLIVE OIL, FOR FRYING
2	AUBERGINES, CUT INTO 2CM/¾IN CUBES
4	GARLIC CLOVES, FINELY SLICED
6	RIPE TOMATOES, PEELED AND CUT INTO PIECES (SEE PAGE 143)
I	SPRIG OF THYME, LEAVES PICKED
8	ANCHOVY FILLETS
25G/IOZ/ SCANT 2 TBSP	PLAIN FLOUR
IOOML/ 3½FL OZ/ ½ SCANT CUP	MILK
	PARMESAN CHEESE
	BREADCRUMBS

Preheat the oven to 180°C fan/200°C/400°F/ gas mark 6.

Heat a good glug of olive oil in a pan and fry the cubed aubergine until golden brown but not softened. Remove from the pan, add more oil, fry the garlic until it sticks together, then add the tomatoes and thyme. Cook down the tomatoes for a few minutes to a loose sauce then return the aubergine to the pan. Cook for 10 minutes or so until the aubergines have softened but not collapsed.

Meanwhile, crush the anchovies roughly using a pestle and mortar. In a separate small pan, fry the anchovies in 1 tablespoon of olive oil until they start to melt. Add the flour, stir well, then whisk in the milk.

Pour the resultant sauce over the vegetables and stir. Transfer everything to a gratin dish, grate over some Parmesan cheese and sprinkle with breadcrumbs. Bake in the *hot oven* for 20 minutes or so, until bubbling and golden brown on top.

Pasta and Chickpea Soup (Ciceri e Tria)

A slight diversion by way of Salento, part of Puglia in Italy's heel. *Ciceri e tria* is an ancient soup of chickpeas and both boiled and fried pasta, a relic from the Arab conquest of southern Italy: *tria* comes from the Arabic *itriyya*, a term for a dried semolina wheat noodle. The fried pasta topping is a good example of rustic innovation – adding a meaty flavour to an austere peasant dish. Everything here is wonderfully old-fashioned, and it's a study in khaki colour and deep starchy flavour.

FOR THE PASTA:

100G/ 3½OZ/ ⅔ CUP	DURUM WHEAT SEMOLINA FLOUR, PLUS EXTRA FOR DUSTING
55ML/ 2FL OZ/ ¼ CUP	WARM WATER
	OLIVE OIL

FOR THE SOUP:

	SMALL ONION, FINELY DICED
I	CELERY STICK, FINELY DICED
I	SMALL CARROT, FINELY DICED
I	GARLIC CLOVES, FINELY SLICED
2 X 400G	CANNED CHICKPEAS, RINSED
	PINCH OF DRIED CHILLI FLAKES
	CHOPPED PARSLEY
I TBSP	SALT

TO SERVE:

	GOOD OLIVE OIL, TO SERVE
	PARMESAN OR PECORINO CHEESE

First, make the pasta. Pour the flour in a pile onto the worktop, make a well in the middle and add the water. Using your fingertips, bring the flour gradually into the middle of the well, until a shaggy dough starts to form. Add a few drops of water if it looks too dry.

Knead for 5 minutes, until smooth. Wrap in clingfilm and allow to rest at room temperature for 30 minutes.

Use a rolling pin or a pasta machine to roll out the pasta to a 1mm/¹⁄₃₂ thickness. Cut into short strips about the width of tagliatelle (although the size is really down to preference). Don't be too fussed if your strips are slightly irregular. Sprinkle with semolina flour as you go to prevent the pieces of pasta sticking to each other. Set aside on a lightly semolina-floured plate.

Fry a quarter of the cut pasta in around 1cm/½in depth of olive oil. (You can of course reuse the oil for other delicious *fritti* purposes – strain it through a fine sieve, or better, muslin.) Stir the pasta frequently for an even browning. You are looking to achieve an even golden brown – no darker. Drain, season lightly with salt and set aside.

Recipe continues overleaf

Pasta & Chickpea Soup (Ciceri e Tria) continued

Meanwhile, in a separate pan, heat at least 2mm/⅛in depth of oil and slowly fry the onion, celery, carrot and garlic, adding a good pinch of salt, until soft – this should take at least 20 minutes to do properly. Don't be tempted to speed up the process; a long slow fry brings out an essential sweetness.

Once sweet and very soft, add the chickpeas, the chilli and another pinch of salt. Fry slowly for a few minutes, stirring well to coat the chickpeas in the flavourful oil. Add water to cover by 2cm/¾in, bring to the boil then reduce to a fast simmer. Cook for 30 minutes; top up the water if it dries out too much. Taste the chickpeas – they should be soft and full-flavoured – adding a little more salt if needed.

Bring a large pan of water to the boil, lightly salt it and add the remaining pasta. Boil for a minute only, until the pasta is *al dente*, then scoop it out of the water and into the chickpeas. A little of the pasta water into the chickpea pan is a good thing. Add the chopped parsley and stir well.

Some prefer a drier finish, but I like to keep the soup a bit brothy, so add a little water if you think it needs it. Turn off the heat and allow things to relax for a few minutes, then spoon the soup into waiting bowls. Top with your best olive oil, the fried pasta bits and some grated cheese.

Lablabi

This is a Tunisian staple: a simple chickpea broth spooned over stale bread with an array of tasty things on top. *Lablabi* shows us the potential that a modest bowl of chickpeas holds, and when fully garnished this is a bowlful of flavour.

A friend of mine recently described this soup as what would happen if someone came along and dumped the contents of a *pan bagnat* – Nice's most famous sandwich – in a simple Italian soup. Of course an outsider's observation, but I think one that sums *lablabi* up well. The chickpea soup itself is very similar to the way that it might be cooked in Italy or Provence, and the version in Jean-Baptiste Reboul's comprehensive *La Cuisinière Provençale* is simplicity itself: fried chopped leek, chickpeas and their broth, seasoned with salt and pepper, with fried croutons on top.

Garnishes for *lablabi* are the fun part, so do feel free to add or omit as it pleases you, but among the usual accompaniments are stale bread (toasted or fried, crouton-style, or just torn into the bottom of the bowl), boiled egg (hard-boiled and chopped, soft-boiled and halved, or soft-poached), ground cumin, chopped coriander, tuna, raw onion, olive oil, capers, pickles and of course plenty of harissa. Here's my version.

	A GOOD HANDFUL OF SOURDOUGH BREAD, TORN INTO 2.5-CM/1-IN PIECES
	OLIVE OIL
1	ONION, DICED
2	GARLIC CLOVES, CHOPPED
1	PLUM TOMATO FROM A CAN
1	JAR OF COOKED CHICKPEAS (660G/1LB 8OZ), WASHED WELL – LOOK FOR ONES IN GLASS JARS SOLD IN SPANISH DELIS OR TURKISH SUPERMARKETS
1 TBSP	CUMIN SEEDS
4	EGGS, SOFT-POACHED
	SALT

TO SERVE:

	A SMALL HANDFUL OF CORIANDER, CHOPPED
	SWEET ONION, FINELY DICED
150G/ 5½OZ	CANNED TUNA – THE STUFF IN OLIVE OIL IS THE BEST
	HARISSA
	OLIVES, PITTED

Preheat the oven to 170°C fan/190°C/375°F/ gas mark 5.

Put the torn bread into an ovenproof dish, drizzle with olive oil and bake in the oven until crisp but still a little chewy within. Alternatively, use a pan to fry the bread slowly in a small amount of olive oil until the same effect is achieved. Set aside.

Put a large saucepan over the heat and fry the onion and garlic in plenty of olive oil with a pinch of salt, until soft and lightly golden. Squish the tomato with your hands into the pan, then add the chickpeas. Stir well, then add water to cover everything by 2cm/¾in. Add salt, bring to the boil, and simmer for 30 minutes while you assemble the rest.

Toast the cumin seeds in a dry pan over a low heat for a few minutes, then grind to a powder using a pestle and mortar. Set aside.

It is time to prepare the eggs if you have not done so already. Poach until soft and set aside.

To assemble the soup: taste the chickpeas for salt, adding hot water if they look too dry. Blitz a ladleful of the soup to a purée in a blender and stir back in (or simply mash a little of the soup in the pan with a potato masher). Put the toasted bread into bowls. Ladle the chickpeas and broth over the bread in the bowls. Top the soup with a poached egg and season the egg with salt.

Arrange your other toppings alongside. I like to keep them all separate on top so I can have fun mixing them in according to whim: chopped coriander, a little finely diced raw sweet onion, tuna, a spoonful of harissa (or two, for extra spicy), olives, a little pinched pile of the ground toasted cumin and a liberal drizzle of olive oil.

Marseille

Jean-Claude Izzo was a writer born in Marseille to Italian and Spanish parents. He shot to fame with his crime novels, dubbed the Marseille Trilogy, detailing the exploits of a certain detective Fabio Montale. Izzo is widely credited as being the founder of the modern Mediterranean noir novel. Aside from crime fiction, in a lovely little book published in English under the title *Garlic, Mint & Sweet Basil* Izzo writes beautifully of the food and spirit of Marseille and its people: of their shared love of food, family and all that intertwines the two; of garlic, first kisses and 'the joys of bread rubbed in garlic and the spicy bodies of women'.

Izzo sees Marseille as a bridge to the rest of the Mediterranean Sea. A melting pot, of course, but perhaps also some sort of capital, where the life, food and music of the entire sea meet and are celebrated: 'I like to believe it will always be this way. On both shores of the Mediterranean. That our shores will still join together. And that they will remain without borders, as Louis Brauquier wrote in the *Cahiers du Sud* [a literary journal].' Izzo looks out across the sea to his Mediterranean cousins, and standing in a city that is more than 2,600 years old, feels a sense of community and belonging to something bigger.

Marseille has an unfair reputation for being 'rough', a particularly Parisian view of France's oldest city, and one awash with a fear of the Other. I suppose a better description might be 'rough around the edges', in a way that many cities are when they are overbrimming with life.

Living in Paris in my twenties I heard people talk of Marseille in a disparaging way. Dirty, dangerous, less French than African. Years later, talking to my Marseillais colleague, he explained that the people of Marseille feel Marseillais first, French second – the same way Sardinians or Sicilians identify themselves first and foremost, rather than Italian. One might argue that Marseille has always been at odds with France's idea of what it is to be French. The city that gave its name to the French national anthem – a terrifying, thrilling song of violent revolution – stands alone in its self-perception as a city of the outsider, a city apart. Emmanuel Macron, seeking his re-election as President, started and ended his campaign trial in Marseille, paid tribute to its multiculturalism: 'I see Armenians, Comorians, Italians, Algerians, Moroccans, Tunisians, Malians, Senegalese … But what do I see? I see citizens of Marseille, I see citizens of France.' At least certain sections of France's political classes recognize the importance of Marseille as a litmus test for a modern, multicultural France, but in the context of France's colonial history, Marseille poses a question: is France willing to accept, not just assimilate, the Outsider?

> *The city that gave its name to the French national anthem – a terrifying, thrilling song of violent revolution – stands alone in its self-perception as a city of the outsider, a city apart.*

Unlike Paris – where, as a general rule, the further from the centre and beyond the *périphérique* (ring road), the poorer neighbourhoods become, and the more diverse their populations – as writer, broadcaster and long-time Marseille resident Jonathan Meades expounds, 'Marseille is more like Britain in that the social housing is spread around, and there's no boundary outside of which to put poor people.' Marseille is and always has been a melting pot – Izzo's city of exiles or outsiders – where mainland France is confronted with its future. Izzo frames the struggle with reference to the Greek mariner, explorer and astronomer Pytheas of Massalia (the name for Marseille when it was a colony of the ancient Greeks): 'the new Italian-style ochre façades try to make everyone forget the ancient roots of the city, which are Greek, and therefore tragic, drowned now beneath tons of concrete to create shopping malls and parking garages, obliterating all maritime, Oriental and adventurous daydreams. Charles de Gaulle against Pytheas.'

> *Marseille is and always has been a melting pot where mainland France is confronted with its future.*

During the research for this book, I cooked lunch for Meades in London and, talking of Marseille, he explained that when his friends come to visit they ask for restaurant recommendations. *What kind of food? French of course!* But this reply puts Meades at a loss – when he eats out he doesn't eat French food; the restaurants he goes to are anything but: 'French or pan-French restaurants in Marseille are not part of the city's vernacular. They exist as something close to intruders. They are unremarkable – save when they have an Italian accent, which is often. That accent is generally southern. It was from Campania and Sicily and Puglia that people came seeking a livelihood …'

Marseille is the capital of Provence, but the food of the city is far from strictly *Provençal*. On the street there's *panisse*, a savoury chickpea pancake originally from Liguria, and another Italian import – *fritto misto* of baby squid, sprinkled with salt and doused in lemon, the oil seeping into the cone of paper these crispy fried morsels come in. There are *fricassées* – at first glance a short baguette, but on closer inspection a fried savoury doughnut stuffed with tuna, boiled egg, mashed potato, coriander and fiery harissa, topped with a fried pepper, rather like a *pan bagnat* from across the bay. Or the unlikely sounding *chapati*, more a cross between an Indian *roti* and an English muffin, stuffed with soft cheese, harissa, grated egg, meat or tuna and chopped onion.

Noailles market, in Marseille's central district a few hundred metres from the fishermen's boats and pleasure yachts of the old port, has a different flavour from the market in Aix-en-Provence and the village markets further inland on the massif of the Luberon. Noailles has overflowing, colourful displays of *Provençal* vegetables, sure, but also of North African fabrics, with the scents of spices and the sounds of spoken (and shouted) Arabic in the air. This market is enriched with North African and Middle Eastern exoticism: alongside tapenade, *anchoïade* and wood-fired pizza are olives drenched in harissa and sizzling cumin-scented sausages oozing lamb fat. Here it's freshly baked flatbreads – *m'semen* – dusted in semolina for breakfast instead of croissants, *mahjouba* not crêpes, and *raï* music plays, rather than French *chansons*.

The ultimate Marseille street food is a slice of thin, crisp, really good pizza, wood-fired in a small shop or in the back of a van, probably topped with the famous *moit-moit* (half and half): tomato, anchovy and raw garlic on one half, Emmental and olives on the other. The much-loved Noailles market institution Pizza Charly was opened sixty years ago by a Neapolitan-Algerian couple and has since been passed down from son to son (all called Charly, incidentally). There's the Armenienne, a *lahmacun*-inspired creation with spiced minced beef, peppers, tomato sauce and cheese, the Merguez (say no more), or a Sandwich Calentica, an Algerian-Spanish flan made with chickpea flour, like *panisse*'s fat, wobbly cousin, crammed into a crusty roll with a liberal smearing of harissa. At the rightly famous Chez Etienne in the Panier district, Etienne Cassaro turned the workers' canteen opened by his Sicilian father into a Marseille institution, and today Etienne's son Pascal keeps the flame burning. Pizza, of course (*moit-moit, s'il vous plaît*), but also lamb *brochettes* (kebabs) or fat *côtes de boeuf* sizzling from the white-hot wood oven, sprinkled with flaky salt and dried oregano, squid with parsley and (a lot of) garlic, aubergine gratin, gnocchi with tomato sauce and meatballs, spaghetti with *fruits de mer*, and *pieds et paquets* (stewed sheep's feet and stuffed tripe), little ravioli filled with spicy Italian sausage, and a perfect apple *tarte fine* with ice cream.

Meades writes to me: 'I don't know how to answer your question "Is there any real Marseillais cuisine?" The once Sicilian blends into the formerly Armenian (huge population from 1917) and mixes with the Levantine and of course with the Moroccan and the Algerian ... Mixété is the norm. The pizze are incidentally better than in Naples because they are French – approaching a tarte fine.' (The last comment is a strong claim from Mr Meades here, but one I'm sure many Marseillais would appreciate.)

Marseille is a city of pizza, of *bouillabaisse*, of *panisse*, *pastis* and *pieds et paquets*, but also, and maybe more so, of couscous, *lablabi, brik, figatellu, ojja, mahjouba*, harissa and merguez. Ultimately Marseille has started to

'I like to think – given that I grew up here – that Marseille, my city, is not a goal in itself but only a door open to the world, and to other people. A door that must remain open forever.'

found its own traditions separate from the *Provençal* repertoire that previously dominated. A vision of modern France? The chef and food historian Emmanuel Perrodin goes so far as to claim Marseille has a great role in informing French cuisine: 'Our national dish is couscous. Tajine is served in French schools. If you imagine French cuisine as a tree, the leaves are in Paris, but the roots reside in Marseille.' (A pithy line from Izzo also comes to mind: 'Paris is an attraction. Marseille is a passport.')

Marseille is as much a living, breathing frontier as one could hope to find. Perrodin, who was born in the Jura but found himself drawn irresistibly to Marseille, says '[Marseille] has a particular geography. My favourite Marseillais saying is "First you have the sea, then the city, and beyond that is another country called France" ... Marseille is a city as a portal to the other great ports of the Mediterranean – a lighthouse city as once was Alexandria. Here is a city that faces proudly out to sea, turning its back on the rest of France, towards its cousins on the horizon. The cuisine of Marseille, such as it is now, is not one of assimilation, but rather one of acceptance. In *Total Chaos*, the first of his Marseille Trilogy, Izzo writes that 'Marseille belongs to those who live here. Just a foot set on its soil, and a man can say, "I am home".'

Izzo's idea is one of Marseille as both literal port and imaginary portal to the other lands across the sea: 'I like to think – given that I grew up here – that Marseille, my city, is not a goal in itself but only a door open to the world, and to other people. A door that must remain open forever.' Here's hoping it does.

(Sort of) Sicilian Fish Couscous

SERVES 4

Sicily is famous for its fish couscous, a North African tradition that has long taken root on the island, which is itself a melting pot of mainland Italian, Norman French, Greek, Spanish and Arab influences. Dishes like this one reached Sicily's shores a thousand years ago and are still very popular on the west coast, where fishing fleets are crewed by Sicilian and Tunisan sailors alike.

I cannot resist a recipe that incorporates both North African and Italian tradition, and in the spirit of collaboration I offer an undoubtedly unauthentic method, but one that combines the best that the south of France has to offer on the subject of fish stews. This produces the most aromatic of broths, more heavily spiced than it would be on the north shores of the Med, but with plenty of the same spirit. Gurnard (which makes for a very tasty broth) and red mullet produce an excellent result, but this can be made with any fish you fancy – bream, red snapper, monkfish and so on – and the shellfish add a real depth of flavour.

I	MEDIUM SEA BASS, FILLETED AND PIN-BONED, HEAD AND BONES RESERVED
I	RED MULLET, FILLETED AND PIN-BONED, HEAD AND BONES RESERVED
	A BIG HANDFUL OF CLAMS OR MUSSELS, SHELLS DEBEARED AND WASHED
2	VERY FIRM COURGETTES, GREEN, YELLOW OR A MIXTURE
250G/ 9OZ/ 2 CUPS	COUSCOUS
	ORANGE JUICE AND LEMON JUICE, TO TASTE
15G/½OZ/ I TBSP	SOFTENED UNSALTED BUTTER

FOR THE BROTH:

	OLIVE OIL
I	ONION, DICED
½	FENNEL BULB, DICED
I	CELERY STICK, DICED
4	GARLIC CLOVES, FINELY SLICED
	A FEW PARSLEY AND CORIANDER STALKS, WASHED
2	BAY LEAVES
	A LONG STRIP OF ORANGE PEEL
	A NICE PINCH OF SAFFRON STRANDS
I TSP	FENNEL SEEDS

2.5-CM/ I-IN	LENGTH OF CINNAMON STICK
I TSP	CORIANDER SEEDS
I TSP	CUMIN SEEDS
IO	BLACK PEPPERCORNS
½ TSP	ANISEED
	A SMALL PINCH OF SWEET PAPRIKA
	A PINCH OF GROUND CAYENNE PEPPER
4	CANNED PLUM TOMATOES OR 4 RIPE FRESH TOMATOES, PEELED, DESEEDED AND ROUGHLY CHOPPED
I	GLASS OF WHITE WINE
	SALT

TO SERVE:

	A HANDFUL OF SKINNED ALMONDS, ROASTED UNTIL GOLDEN, THEN ROUGHLY SLICED
	CHOPPED PARSLEY AND CORIANDER
	A PINCH OF *PIMENT D'ESPELETTE* OR TURKISH PUL BIBER (OPTIONAL)
	OLIVE OIL

Recipe continues overleaf

(Sort of) Sicilian Fish Couscous continued

Heat some olive oil in a large saucepan and slowly fry the onion with a good pinch of salt, the fennel, celery, garlic, herbs, orange peel and spices, until all is soft and sweet – this should take at least 20 minutes.

Meanwhile, clean the fish bones – take off the gills from the heads, scrape away any dark gunk or guts that cling to the bones, and wash well. With scissors, snip into shorter sections that will fit easily in the pan. Add the bones to the pan, followed by the tomatoes – squish them with your hands as they go in. Stir vigorously – the aim is to start to fry both the tomatoes and the bones without anything sticking to the bottom. Add salt.

Once the tomatoes have collapsed into a rough sauce, pour in the white wine. Bring to the boil, top up with water to cover the bones, and simmer slowly for 45 minutes. Skim the scum that collects at the surface.

Strain the broth through a fine sieve into a clean pan and taste for salt. Cut the courgettes in half lengthways, then into 5-cm/2-in pieces. Drop them into the broth and simmer until soft but not falling apart.

Meanwhile, put the couscous in a large bowl and sprinkle with olive oil and a pinch of salt. Rub the couscous between your hands to coat each grain in the oil, until no clumps remain.

Pour over boiling water to cover the grain and seal the bowl with clingfilm or a tight lid. Leave for 5 minutes, then fluff the couscous well with a fork – discard any that has clumped together. Keep warm.

Cut each fish fillet in half to give four pieces. Remove the courgettes from the broth and keep warm. Season the fish with salt and poach gently in the broth, covered by a lid, for 2–3 minutes. Towards the end of the cooking time throw in the clams and re-cover with a lid. When the fish can be pierced easily with a skewer, and the clams are open, it is ready. Squeeze a little orange and lemon juice into the broth, and drizzle in a little olive oil for good measure.

Add the butter to the couscous and re-fluff, then mound it on a serving platter and lay the cooked fish and courgettes on top (dunk the courgettes back in the hot broth for a moment if they have cooled too much). Bring the broth to a brief but rapid boil, then pour some of it over the dish, without drowning the couscous. You can keep the broth warm if you need more as you eat. Sprinkle with the roasted sliced almonds, the chopped parsley and coriander, *piment d'espelette* and a good drizzle of olive oil.

Roast Sardines with Green Figs & Cumin

A recipe inspired by a similar idea I found in Rolli Lucarotti's Recipes from Corsica. This is a lovely combination, which reminds me of the Sicilian dish sarde en beccafico, one of my favourites from that island. For this variation the butterflied sardines are rolled around a slice of fresh fig and a salted anchovy fillet, topped with breadcrumbs and chopped tomatoes, and roasted with their proud tails sticking up in the air. A sprinkling of cumin rather than fennel seeds moves the flavours a little further south. If I had a fig tree, I might use fig leaves to line the dish instead of bay, but this I will leave up to you.

8	LARGE SARDINES, BUTTERFLIED
2	GARLIC CLOVES, SLICED LENGTHWAYS
4	ANCHOVY FILLETS, HALVED LENGTHWAYS
2	FRESH GREEN FIGS, QUARTERED
4	FRESH BAY LEAVES
2 TBSP	OLIVE OIL
2	FRESH TOMATOES, PEELED (SEE PAGE 143)
I TBSP	ROUGHLY CHOPPED PARSLEY
I TSP	CUMIN SEEDS
2 TBSP	FRESH BREADCRUMBS
	SALT
	COCKTAIL STICKS, FOR SECURING THE FISH

Preheat the oven to 220°C fan/240°C/475°F/ gas mark 9.

Lay the sardines out skin side down on a board with the tails facing away from you. Season them lightly with salt. Lay onto each fillet a slice or two of garlic and half an anchovy fillet. Put on a quarter of a fig and roll up the sardines towards the tail. Secure with a cocktail stick.

Lay the bay leaves on a small but handsome baking dish and arrange the sardines on top, turned on their side so you can see the fig poking out of the top. Drizzle each roll lightly with half the olive oil.

Chop the skinned tomatoes roughly, season with salt, and scatter over the fish and into the dish along with the parsley and cumin seeds. Finally top each sardine roll with a good pinch of breadcrumbs and drizzle the whole lot with the remaining olive oil.

Roast in the hot oven for 5–10 minutes, or until the fig has softened and the sardines are cooked through. Test a sardine roll with a thin skewer – if the skewer slides through easily the fish is cooked. Remove from the oven, allow to cool slightly, then transfer the dish to your table and eat.

Sea Bass Grilled Over Wild Fennel

SERVES 2–4*

It always thrills me to see wild fennel growing by the side of the road. In the South of France it's everywhere, but I have seen it on these shores too: free flavour for those who know where to look. I can't pass a branch of it with picking a seed and tasting its spicy anise flavour, and at the right time of year the heads will let fly a small cloud of delicious pollen. The stalks of wild fennel are an excellent addition to *Bouillabaisse* (see pages 164–169) or a braise of pork shoulder, or as a bed for roasting a leg of lamb or chicken in the oven, or as here: strewn directly on the fire so that the flavoured smoke rises up to the grill.

A large fish like wild sea bass is a very special treat, and grilled simply over charcoal or wood is almost always the best way to do it. Outside, hopefully in the sun, your charcoal fire ripping hot, thick branches of the fennel smouldering and the wispy tips catching fire and infusing the air with their sweet smell. Hopefully the smoke will penetrate the flesh of the fish, but even if it doesn't, the aroma of burning aniseed in the air will make the meal taste better.

With an ice-cold *pastis* in your hand and a fennel flower behind your ear you could pretend that this is the cooking of Provence, but really this is the cooking of the whole Mediterranean. Honestly this is some of the best eating you can do: gathered around an outside table, carefully filleting the hot fish for the people holding out their plates, and a bottle of something cold and delicious to drink with it.

While I'm at it, I'll have salad with this, please: a mixed one of little leaves, ideally from the garden. Little soft lettuces, a touch of peppery rocket, lots of whole basil, maybe some sorrel; the rosemary flowers from the bush and a few of the fresh seeds from the wild fennel flowers, all dressed with the lightest of vinaigrettes. Maybe a green sauce as well, without mustard but heavy on the anchovy, to eat with the fish, and a tomato and basil salad to start. Little toasts spread with *anchoïade aux figues* (see page 93) with the apéritif. And warm grilled peaches with nougat ice cream to finish. There, lovely.

depending on the size of your fish and the scope of the meal

Recipe continues overleaf

Sea Bass Grilled Over Wild Fennel continued

I	LARGE SEA BASS, SCALED AND GUTTED
	OLIVE OIL
	A FEW BIG BRANCHES OF WILD FENNEL
	LEMON
	SALT
	FIRE
	PASTIS, ICE CUBES, COLD WATER (FOR YOUR APÉRITIF)

Light a charcoal fire; put some wood in there if you have any. Rub the fish with olive oil and season well with salt both inside and out. Take some of the seed heads of the wild fennel and tuck inside the fish along with a couple of half-moons of lemon.

When your fire is hot, lift up the grill briefly and shove in the branches of wild fennel. Once the fennel starts to smoulder, lay your fish on the hot bars of the grill. Don't touch it. Let the skin crisp and blister golden black, then carefully roll the fish over. Grill until the fish is cooked – when the flesh starts to come away from the bone, and you can insert a skewer into the flesh nearest the head without any resistance.

Remove the fish and put on a serving platter. Drizzle with your best olive oil, squeeze over more lemon, and eat it.

Caldero

SERVES 4

This brothy dish of rice and seafood is made both in Algeria and on the other side of the sea in Spain. *Caldero* takes its name from the Spanish for 'cauldron' and was traditionally prepared by fishermen both at sea and on the shore. As with many fish stews it might well have started life as a stew made to use up the fish the fishermen couldn't sell at market.

In Spain this dish is known as *Caldero Murciano*. Apart from the Arab rule of Spain in the Middle Ages, it's easy to imagine a long history of trade between the regions of Oran in Algeria and Murcia in Spain, and difficult to know which side of the Mediterranean this originated from. The Arabs brought rice to Murcia in the tenth century, but this dish could be even older than that. What interests me is the comparison with the famous fish stews of Provence; the use of saffron, tomatoes, garlic and orange peel is clearly not unique to the south of France, and hints at a heritage shared by fishermen on both northern and southern shores of the Mediterranean. In Spain this would be served with *alioli*, in Provence they have their *aïoli* or *rouille*, and in Algeria of course there is harissa.

Pieds-Noirs who moved from Oran to France insist that this recipe must include Anisette Cristal, a white *pastis* originally made by two Spanish brothers who emigrated from Alicante to Algeria. The brothers eventually relocated, and the Cristal Limiñana company is now based in Marseille. Failing authentic anisette, a splash of *pastis* or *ouzo* is delicious.

In Spain *arroz caldero* is sometimes served quite dry, more on the way to a paella, but I like to keep the dish fairly soupy, the swollen grains of rice lurking just under the surface.

200G/ 7OZ/ GENEROUS I CUP	CALASPARRA OR BOMBA RICE
2	BREAM OR SEABASS FILLETS (APPROX. 200G/7OZ)
2	LARGE GURNARD OR RED MULLET FILLETS (APPROX. 200G/7OZ)
8–12	LARGE PRAWNS (WHOLE, SHELL ON)
250G/ 9OZ	SQUID, CLEANED, CUT INTO THIN STRIPS OR RINGS

FOR THE BROTH:

4 TBSP	OLIVE OIL
2	ONIONS, DICED
I	FENNEL BULB, DICED
6	GARLIC CLOVES, LIGHTLY SMASHED
	A SMALL HANDFUL OF CELERY LEAVES, ROUGHLY CHOPPED
2	BAY LEAVES
2	LONG STRIPS OF ORANGE PEEL
2 OR 3	MILD DRIED CHILLIES, CHOPPED (SPANISH ÑORA PEPPERS ARE THE AUTHENTIC ONES, KASHMIRI CHILLIES WOULD WORK WELL, OTHERWISE USE A PINCH OF MILD CRUSHED CHILLI FLAKES)
I TSP	PAPRIKA
	FISH HEADS OR BONES, CLEANED (GILLS, ORGANS AND BLOOD REMOVED, WASHED WELL)
	A GOOD GLUG OF ANISETTE CRISTAL, *PASTIS* OR *OUZO*
400G/ I4OZ	PEELED PLUM TOMATOES, DRAINED OF THEIR JUICE AND CRUSHED
	A BIG PINCH OF SAFFRON STRANDS, SOAKED IN 2 TBSP HOT WATER
	SALT

FOR THE SAUCE:

6	FAT GARLIC CLOVES, OR 12 SKINNY ONES
1	EGG YOLK
2 TSP	HARISSA (LE CAP BON BRAND FOR PREFERENCE)
100ML/ 3½FL OZ/ SCANT ½ CUP	OLIVE OIL
	LEMON JUICE, TO TASTE

TO SERVE:

	JUICE OF ½ ORANGE OR LEMON (OR A COMBINATION OF BOTH)
	CHOPPED PARSLEY
	OLIVE OIL

First make the broth. Place a big heavy stockpot over a medium heat. Add the olive oil and fry the onions, fennel, garlic, celery leaves, bay leaves, orange peel and chillies with a big pinch of salt. Fry over a medium heat for about 20–30 minutes. The vegetables should soften without browning too much. Add the paprika and stir well. Heat gently for a minute or two to cook the paprika but not burn it. Once done, push everything to one side, tilt the pot so that the empty side collects the oil, and add the fish heads and/or bones to this side. Sauté the heads and bones for a few minutes, turning once. Continue to cook in the oil for a few minutes until the heads and bones have softened a little.

Increase the heat and add a confident splash of anisette. Wait a moment for the alcohol to cook off, then stir everything together. Add the crushed tomatoes and the saffron and its water. Cook over a high heat until the tomatoes have started to break down into a rough sauce, then top up with about 1 litre/1¾ pints/4 cups of water. Bring to the boil, skim, then reduce to a simmer and cook for 30 minutes.

Meanwhile, make the sauce: pound the peeled garlic cloves with a pinch of salt using a pestle and mortar. Add the egg yolk and the

harissa, emulsify, and begin to add the olive oil drop by drop. Drizzle the oil steadily into the emulsion as you stir with the pestle. Go slowly and add a drop of water if it looks too thick. Taste for salt and add a little squeeze of lemon. It should taste very garlicky and pretty hot. Set aside.

After about 30 minutes, strain the broth through a sieve, and return it to the pot over the heat. Taste for seasoning; it may need a little more salt. You should be left with about 750ml/1¼ pints/3 cups of liquid. Add the rice to the pot, bring back to the boil, then reduce to a simmer and cook for about 15–20 minutes, until the rice is just tender. Add more (hot) water if the rice absorbs too much of the liquid – the end result should, in my opinion, be quite soupy, although just how soupy is down to personal preference.

Taste again for salt, then it's time to add the fish. Season the fish, prawns and squid with salt. Make sure there is enough liquid in the pot; add more hot water if the soup looks too much like a risotto. Drop in the fish fillets and cover with a lid. Cook over a low heat for 2 minutes, then turn the fillets over and add the prawns and squid. Continue to cook over a low heat, covered, until the fish is cooked. Test a piece of fish by inserting a thin skewer through the flesh: if it slides through without resistance it is done. The prawns are ready as soon as they turn pink all the way through and the squid when it is opaque.

When ready to serve, squeeze in the orange or lemon juice, or a combination of both. Throw in the chopped parsley. Serve the fish with some rice and the broth in deep bowls, and drizzle with olive oil. Serve the sauce on the side, and encourage everyone to spoon some on and mix it in. The prawns will need peeling, which is a fun but messy business. The juices from the heads can either be sucked straight out or squished back into the broth, enriching it further.

Rabbit Grilled in Chermoula

Chermoula is a North African herb mixture most usually encountered slathered on fish as a marinade before it meets a hot charcoal grill; it is, incidentally, also excellent with meat and vegetables. The French have an affection for farmed rabbits, which are much meatier and milder-tasting than their wild equivalent – excellent on the rotisserie or grill. The herb marinade helps to keep the meat moist, and the smell of the *chermoula* as it sticks to the bars of the grill and flames in the rendering fat is a thing of wonder. This is also very good on chicken wings as well as the traditional sardines and mackerel.

4	RABBIT LEGS ON THE BONE

FOR THE *CHERMOULA*:

½	BUNCH CORIANDER
½	BUNCH PARSLEY
4	MILD GREEN CHILLIES
	PINCH OF SWEET PAPRIKA
½	RIPE TOMATO
I TSP	CUMIN SEEDS, LIGHTLY TOASTED IN A DRY PAN
I TSP	CARAWAY SEEDS, LIGHTLY TOASTED IN A DRY PAN
	SQUEEZE OF LEMON JUICE
2 TBSP	OLIVE OIL, PLUS EXTRA FOR DRIZZLING
	SALT

Score the rabbit legs deeply to allow the marinade to penetrate – this will also reduce the cooking time on the barbeque.

To make the *chermoula*, put the herbs, chillies, paprika and tomato in a blender and blitz to a fine paste. Lightly toast the cumin and caraway seeds in a dry pan then crush using a pestle and mortar and add to the blender. Season with lemon juice and salt, add the olive oil and blitz again.

Slather *chermoula* all over the rabbit legs, getting it inside the slashes you have made. Allow the rabbit to sit with the *chermoula* for at least 1 hour while you light the barbeque.

When the barbeque is medium-hot, season the rabbit legs with salt, drizzle with a little extra olive oil and grill over the charcoal for around 10 minutes on each side, or until the rabbit is no longer pink at the bone. The *chermoula* may catch slightly, stick and char on the grill, but a little of this is to be encouraged. I would like to eat this with a dish of broad beans, couscous and yogurt, but that's another story.

Poulet Antiboise

This is very simple and very good. A lovely recipe first seen (by me, at least) in Elizabeth David's debut *A Book of Mediterranean Food* for roast chicken nestled in a mound of melting onions, sprinkled with cayenne pepper and dotted with black olives.

There's no accompanying text with David's recipe, and it's unclear whether this is really a traditional recipe from Antibes. There's something about it that makes me think of the Moorish influence on Provence. A good quantity of sweet onions stewed in olive oil, a little hot spice and a few salty olives for balance: add a cinnamon stick or a preserved lemon and suddenly we cross over into tagine territory.

I	WHOLE CHICKEN, I.2–I.5KG/2LB IOOZ–3LB 5OZ
IOOML/3½FL OZ/ SCANT ½ CUP	OLIVE OIL
	A PINCH OF CAYENNE PEPPER
IKG/2LB 4OZ	YELLOW ONIONS, THINLY SLICED INTO HALF-MOONS
	A SPRIG OF THYME
	A HANDFUL OF PITTED BLACK OLIVES
	SALT AND FRESHLY GROUND BLACK PEPPER

SERVES 2–4

Preheat the oven to 180°C fan/200°C/400°F/ gas mark 6.

Rub the chicken with a little of the olive oil and season with salt, pepper and the cayenne. Lay the onions and thyme in a roasting tray, season with salt, black pepper and cayenne, and pour over the rest of the oil. Mix well, then lay the chicken on top.

The idea is for the onions to melt slowly without taking too much colour. The onions should be nestled under the chicken; if they are left exposed to the heat they might well burn. Cover the onions around the chicken with foil, but leave the chicken exposed. Roast in the hot oven for about 1 hour 15 minutes. If the chicken is cooked but the onions are not yet sweet and melting, remove the chicken, cover the onions loosely with foil, and continue to cook until happy. If the onions look very oily, scoop out some oil with a spoon and discard.

When the chicken is cooked, remove and cut into eight pieces. Add the black olives to the onions and stir. Scoop the onions and olives out of the tray (leaving the excess oil in roasting tray rather than putting on the plate) and put the chicken on top. Eat, not too hot, with crusty bread and a green salad.

Seven-hour Roasted Leg of Lamb, Spiced Like a Mechoui

SERVES 6–8

This recipe is the product of two traditional techniques; one French and one North African. Both countries have evolved clever ways to cook old lamb so that the flesh is tender – the French in a sealed pot, the North Africans on a slow spit or buried in the ground. The French have a real love of a *mechoui* – roasting a lamb or a pig slowly over an open fire. Here is a recipe adapted for someone who doesn't necessarily want to dig a huge pit in their garden. Whatever the method, what I am interested in is spiced meat, falling off the bone, brushed with butter and crisped up in a hot oven. This is something to eat as part of a spread: with pilaf rice, salads and bread to pile the meat into, brushed with the melting onions, smushed with softened garlic and doused in the spiced juices.

I TBSP	CUMIN SEEDS
I TBSP	CORIANDER SEEDS
I TSP	BLACK PEPPERCORNS
4	CARDAMOM PODS
I TSP	TURMERIC
I TSP	HOT PAPRIKA
½ TSP	GROUND GINGER
½ TSP	GROUND CINNAMON
	A GOOD GRATING OF NUTMEG
4	YELLOW ONIONS, SLICED INTO HALF-MOONS

I	LEG OF LAMB ON THE BONE
	OLIVE OIL
4	CLOVES OF GARLIC, SLICED
I	BUNCH OF THYME
2 TBSP	MELTED BUTTER
I TSP	GROUND CAYENNE PEPPER
	LEMON JUICE
	BIG SPRIGS OF ROSEMARY OR THYME, TIED TOGETHER TO USE AS A BRUSH
	SALT

Recipe continues overleaf

Preheat the oven to 130°C fan/150°C/300°F/ gas mark 2.

Crush all the whole spices – take the cardamom seeds out of the pods first – in the pestle and mortar, then add the ground spices.

Poke holes in your leg of lamb with a knife and drizzle the leg of lamb all over with olive oil, season with salt, and rub it all over with the spice mix, making sure to get some inside the incisions. Into these holes also push slices of garlic and little sprigs of thyme. Tie the lamb with butcher's string so that it will hold its shape after it has been cooked (in my experience it matters not how you tie it – don't worry about being professional).

Put the onions, the rest of the thyme on the sprig and the whole heads of garlic in the bottom of an oven tray that will fit the lamb fairly snugly. Drizzle with olive oil and sprinkle with salt, then put the lamb on top and pour in a 5-cm/2-in depth of water. Seal with two sheets of foil, crimping the edges well so that no steam can escape.

Roast the lamb in the oven for 6½ hours – the lamb should be falling off the bone – then remove the foil. Increase the heat of the oven to 200°C fan/220°C/425°F/gas mark 7. Mix the melted butter, cayenne and lemon juice together. Roast the lamb for a final 30 minutes, basting a few times with the spiced butter using the herb brush. Add more water to the bottom of the tray as the liquid reduces; don't let it dry out so that the sauce evaporates and the onions burn.

Remove the lamb from the oven and allow to rest for a few minutes. Carefully snip off the string and put the lamb onto a serving platter with the onions and sauce underneath.

Lamb, Aubergine & Tomato Tagine

SERVES 4

Here's an idea adapted from a Paula Wolfert recipe in *The Food of Morocco*, which she describes as 'a tagine with a true Mediterranean spirit'. It's true that the combination of lamb, aubergine, tomato and garlic is appreciated in North Africa and Southern Europe alike.

Cooking with my *Provençal* hat on, I have often served aubergine, tomato and lamb together: grilled lamb chops with ratatouille, for example, or roast leg of lamb with a gratin of aubergine, tomato, garlic, basil and cream. The flavours here are similar, albeit more exotically spiced –

with saffron, paprika, cayenne, ginger and cumin – and featuring fresh coriander rather than basil. That said, for this one I like to keep the spicing quite light.

Here the lamb is stewed slowly with grated onion, spices and masses of garlic before the cooked, mashed aubergine and tomato are added – a mixture reminiscent of the *Bohémienne* on page 79, or indeed the *zaalouk* mentioned there. This dish would be good served with couscous, or maybe a buttery rice pilaf, or just some cooked, dressed greens and crusty bread.

1 KG/ 2LB 4OZ	BONELESS LAMB SHOULDER, CUT INTO 4-CM/1½-IN PIECES
5 TBSP	OLIVE OIL, PLUS EXTRA TO SERVE
1	RED ONION, GRATED ON A BOX GRATER
3 TSP	CUMIN SEEDS
½ TSP	CRUSHED BLACK PEPPERCORNS
	A PINCH OF SAFFRON
	A PINCH OF TURMERIC
	A PINCH OF GROUND GINGER
6	GARLIC CLOVES, FINELY CHOPPED

2	AUBERGINES, TRIMMED
6	RIPE TOMATOES, PEELED AND DICED
1 TSP	SUGAR
	A PINCH OF CAYENNE PEPPER
	A PINCH OF SWEET PAPRIKA
2 TBSP	ROUGHLY CHOPPED PARSLEY
2 TBSP	ROUGHLY CHOPPED CORIANDER
	LEMON JUICE, TO TASTE
	SALT

Put the lamb into a deep heavy earthenware casserole with a lid, season with salt and brown it in 2 tablespoons of the olive oil. Add the grated onion, 2 tsp of the cumin seeds, the black peppercorns, saffron, turmeric, ground ginger and all but 1 tsp of the chopped garlic. Stir well, then add enough warm water to cover the lamb. Cover with a circle of baking paper and put on the lid. Cook slowly for around 2 or 3 hours on the hob, checking occasionally that the pot doesn't dry out – add more water if necessary – until the lamb is meltingly soft.

Meanwhile, preheat the oven to 200°C fan/220°C/425°F/gas mark 7. Cut each aubergine lengthways into four thick slices and place in a single layer in a roasting tin. Drizzle the aubergine with 2 tablespoons of olive oil, sprinkle with salt and the remaining 1 teaspoon of cumin seeds, then roast in the oven for about 20 minutes, until soft and only lightly coloured. Remove from the oven, allow to cool, then chop and squish the aubergine thoroughly until it is mashed. Fry the remaining 1 teaspoon of garlic in the remaining 1 tablespoon of olive oil and add the diced tomatoes with a good pinch of salt and the sugar. Cook them into a sauce – this should take about 15–20 minutes. Add the aubergine, the cayenne and paprika and half the chopped herbs. Cook for a further 5 minutes. Taste for salt and keep hot over a low heat.

Once the sauce is cooked, check the tagine, adding more water if it looks too dry, and bring back to a simmer. Season with salt and lemon juice to taste. Add a few spoons of the lamb juices to the sauce.

Transfer the lamb to a serving dish with a few generous spoonfuls of its juices, then mound the sauce on top. Scatter with the remaining parsley and coriander, drizzle with olive oil, and serve.

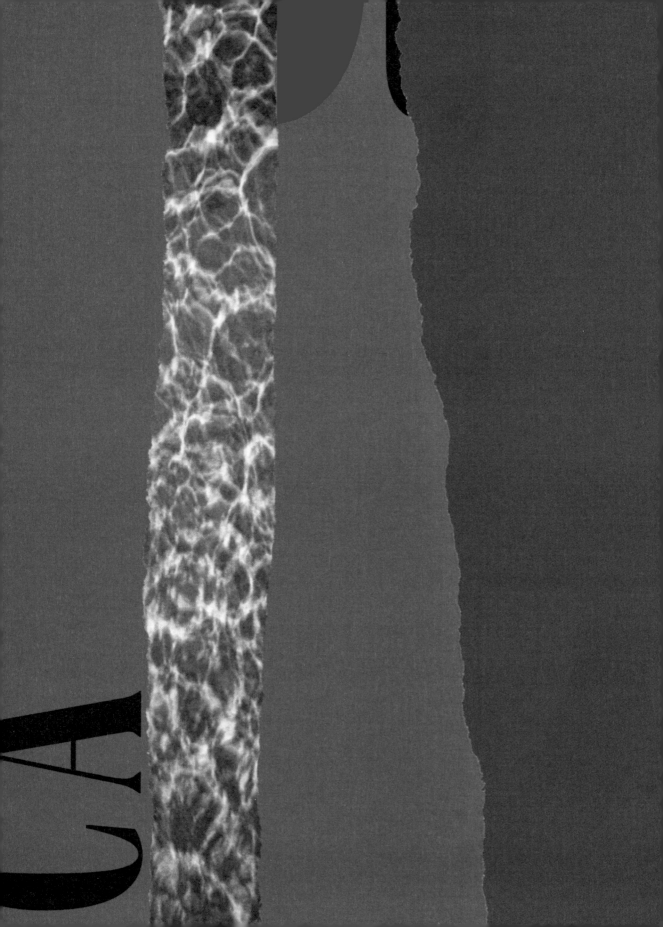

Chapter Three

The Riviera

The Riviera

Stéphen Liégeard, the French lawyer, writer and poet, was the man who first coined the term Côte d'Azur – the azure coast – for what we also know as the French Riviera. It is the French side of the coastal region that looms large in our imaginations, as a playground for the royal, the rich and the famous. But *Riviera* is an Italian word, and we must remember that the coastline doesn't stop at the border: the Riviera is both Provence and Liguria.

It is generally accepted that in its broadest definition the French Riviera stretches as far as Bandol or Cassis in the west all the way to the picturesque border town of Menton (Mentone in Italian). Once you cross the border the Italian Riviera runs clear all the way to La Spezia; to the Bay of Poets, or the end of the gulf of La Spezia, and the start of the Tuscan coast. It is not for me to lay out what would only be a potted history of this stretch of coastline, for the story is long and complicated, but what is of interest for the purposes of this book is shared culinary tradition. This is the longest chapter in the book, for which I offer no apologies but maybe a simple explanation: the food of the French and Italian Rivieras is so intertwined that there is a great deal to talk about.

For the past few years my interest in *Provençal* food has become a slight obsession. The more I read, the deeper the rabbit hole becomes; the cuisine is so rich in history, and the cooking so simple and soulful, that I can spend a long time cooking nothing but this. Maybe one day I should move to Provence. Anyway, what I initially found interesting about *Provençal* food is that it seems, to the outsider at least, so Italianate: with a focus on vegetables, seafood, garlic, herbs and olive oil that I used to associate not with France but its neighbour. Scratch the surface of Ligurian cuisine and you'll see that the two have much in common: Liguria has its *farinata* and *panissa* and Provence has its *socca* and *panisse*.

Part of what makes the cuisine of the Riviera so rich is simple geography: before the innovation of a coastal road, every indentation on the coastline was cut off from its neighbour by the mountains that ran into the sea on either side. Each little pocket therefore developed their own variation on the theme, ensuring a wealth of local specialities. But on either side of the border, and in every little bay or port, the food of the two Rivieras shares many characteristics. This stretch of coastline is a region where seafood is plentiful, but the fats of the land are few and hard-won: the steep hills that overlook the azure of the sea are hard to work, but the salty air, hot sun and rich soil form a microclimate that is ideal for growing olives, tomatoes and basil.

Olive oil is the cooking fat of choice here, and in both Provence and Liguria the olive is celebrated. From the wrinkly, soft, deep purple and powerful Tanche grown near Nyons, to the sweet, fruity and earthy Taggiasche from Taggia in Imperia, olives and olive oil form the basis of both Provençal and Ligurian cuisine. As well as olive oil, both cuisines swim in garlic, in fresh tomatoes, with basil and pine nuts, vegetables ripe with flavour, and fresh seafood of every type.

For centuries salt cod sustained Ligurian sailors who spent long periods at sea and used it to trade across the whole Mediterranean. The taste for it survives despite the ready availability of fresh seafood. Anchovies, both fresh and salted, are very popular – the fresh ones stuffed with Swiss chard, breadcrumbed and fried in olive oil (I have eaten identical versions in both Nice and Genoa), or the salted fillets used to flavour the famous sweet onion tart *pissaladière* or its Ligurian equivalent, a *focaccia* with tomatoes and salted fish called, incidentally, *pissalandrea*.

As well as olive oil, both cuisines swim in garlic, in fresh tomatoes, with basil and pine nuts, vegetables ripe with flavour, and fresh seafood of every type.

Nice is now the unofficial capital of the French Riviera, but over the centuries the city has been variously Ligure, Roman, Provençal, Savoyard, French under the First Republic, and Piedmont-Sardinian, until its eventual return to the French fold as recently as 1860, when it finally became Nice rather than Nizza. For hundreds of years Nice was neither French nor Italian, but its own; the capital of the Comté (county) de Nice, and a town that developed a cuisine with its own characteristics. Nowadays simple Niçois cuisine lives on just as traditional Genovese fare does in Genoa. Nice is a city with its own accent (and indeed its own language) where local ingenuity has made for a remarkably developed local repertoire, but the Italian influence is still obvious: there are queues outside the centuries-old ravioli shops, and the smell of wood-fired chickpea pancakes (*socca*) fills the streets of the old quarter.

What I hope to show here is that the most famous dishes from both sides of the border should be accepted as products of the same history. *Coniglio alla ligure* is a dish of rabbit cooked with garlic, wild thyme and olives from the hillsides. The same hillsides, the same rabbits and the same manner of thinking exist in parallel 30 kilometres/20 miles to the west of Ventimiglia. Many of the recipes that follow are traditional, but some elements are invented: one Englishman's amalgam of the philosophies of both side of the present border.

Raw Fish, Spring Vegetables, Almonds & Olive Oil

SERVES 2
as a starter, or 4 if piled onto toasts as a snack

Raw fish is delicious, and we should all eat more of it. You could call this a *crudo* if you like. I first made this with some wild bream, at the time of year when the spring vegetables are at their sweetest and best and needed no cooking at all. The vegetables and roasted almonds are chopped to a fine dice and dressed with good olive oil and good lemon. Lemon zest keeps it

fragrant, and a little rhubarb in the mix, if it's still in season, keeps things pleasantly astringent.

This recipe makes me think of Sicily, where raw fish is a real *thing*, but I see no reason why this would feel out of place anywhere on the Riviera. Sea bass is excellent here, but so is bream, and do try it with grey mullet.

I	FILLET OF SEA BASS, BREAM OR GREY MULLET (ROUGHLY 100–150G/3½–5½OZ OF FISH FOR 2 PEOPLE)
I TBSP	SKINLESS ALMONDS
	A HANDFUL OF PEAS IN THEIR PODS
	A HANDFUL OF BROAD BEANS IN THEIR PODS
2.5-CM/1-IN	STICK OF LATE-SEASON RHUBARB
I	SMALL, YOUNG, SNAPPY COURGETTE (NO LARGE WATERY ONES PLEASE)
	A SPRIG OF A NICE HERB – PARSLEY, TARRAGON OR WILD FENNEL ALL WORK WELL, FINELY CHOPPED
	ZEST AND JUICE FROM A TOP-DRAWER LEMON
	BEST-QUALITY OLIVE OIL
	SEA SALT AND FRESHLY GROUND BLACK PEPPER

Pin-bone the fish, skin it, and slice it as thinly as possible with your sharpest knife. (I am right-handed, and prefer to position the fillet with the tail on my left, skinned side down. Starting at the tail end, I slice towards the tail on an angle.) I always think that longer, thinner slices look more elegant and eat better. I am no sushi chef, and I leave thick sashimi-style slices to the experts. Put the sliced fish in the refrigerator while you prepare the rest.

Toast the almonds slowly in a pan on a very low heat, until a light golden brown, then allow to cool. Pod the peas and broad beans, peel the rhubarb and halve the courgette. Dice everything as finely and evenly as possible. Mix the chopped herbs, almonds, peas, beans, courgette and rhubarb, and dress with salt, pepper, lemon juice and olive oil.

Arrange the fish on a plate and season with flaky sea salt. Place a spoonful of vegetables in the middle of the plate. Top with grated lemon zest and drizzle heavily with your best olive oil.

Salted Sardines in Sweet Wine MAKES 20 SARDINES

A salted sardine is a handy thing to have in your fridge; more stridently fishy than its cousin the anchovy, it's an ingredient that makes its presence known. Salt some sardines when you next see some small specimens on the fisherman's slab, they don't cost much and are handy when conjuring up a quick snack or an off-the-cuff dinner. This process is a light cure, and these sardines will only keep for a week or two in oil, but to be honest it never takes me as long as that to work my way through them.

The recipe here is one that I like to serve as an *antipasto*. The salted fish has taken on a deeper flavour but retains some of the jellied texture of a raw fillet: the best of both worlds. This can be served as is, drenched in some of the oily marinade, with a wedge of lemon, or embellished with any combination of torn herbs, celery leaf, shredded chicory, little radicchios, capers, citrus, olives, fresh red chilli and so on. Cut up into smaller strips, these also taste excellent in a tomato and celery salad, or, even better, with a nice slice of ripe tomato atop a garlic-rubbed *crostino*. At the restaurant where I work we serve these splashed with sweet wine, which helps to counter some of the saltiness.

This recipe makes a decent-sized batch, but feel free to scale down (or up!). Here are quantities to give you an idea of how much of the ingredients to use.

20	SARDINE FILLETS, SCALED
	SEA SALT
I OR 2	GARLIC CLOVES, VERY FINELY SLICED
I TSP	CORIANDER SEEDS
I TSP	FENNEL SEEDS
I	SPRIG OF THYME
2	BAY LEAVES
½ TSP	ORANGE ZEST
½ TSP	LEMON ZEST
	PINCH OF DRIED RED CHILLI
	OLIVE OIL, TO COVER
TO SERVE:	
	A GLUG OF YOUR MOST DELICIOUS SWEET WINE
	PARSLEY, OREGANO OR FENNEL FRONDS
	WEDGES OF LEMON OR SOUR ORANGE

Trim the sardine fillets of all fins, including tail and that top bit. Make doubly sure that there are no scales left – any errant scale will ruin your future snack. Lay the fillets out in a single layer on a dish that will fit in your fridge. Scatter the top of the fillets with salt – use just shy of twice as much salt as you would use if you were cooking them fresh. Cover the dish with clingfilm and leave in the fridge overnight – 10 hours is usually perfect.

The next day, rinse the sardines well. Taste a little slice of raw salty sardine – if it tastes *wildly* salty to you, the sardines can be left to soak for an hour in cold water, but bear in mind that this will add unwanted water to the fish. Pat the sardines as dry as possible with kitchen paper.

Next, layer the sardines with all the dry ingredients in a snug plastic container with a tight-fitting lid. Pour over the olive oil to cover. Make sure no fillets are exposed to the air. Seal with the lid and place in the fridge overnight.

The sardines are ready to eat the next day. Remove from the marinade and lay on a plate. Spoon over a little of the oil. Pour a good glug of sweet wine over the top, cover with chopped herbs, and arrange some lemon or sour orange wedges around. Allow to macerate at room temperature for a while before you eat.

Roast Tomato Stuffed with Brandade & Egg

Brandade, a garlicky jumble of mashed salt cod and potato, is delicious on its own, or scooped up on little points of toast, but I love to stuff vegetables with it and serve the whole thing hot. Long peppers, artichokes, hollowed-out potatoes are all delicious, but in summer tomatoes are a lovely vehicle for this and have a great affinity with salt cod. Here is an embellishment pinched from my friends Alex Vines and Rob Shipley: lovely men and lovely cooks both. Vine tomatoes are stuffed with a rough, garlicky *brandade* then roasted, with a scattering of grated boiled egg, crisp breadcrumbs, capers and herbs to complete the picture. If you were to use cherry tomatoes, which would admittedly be a bit fiddly, what delicious little canapés they would make at a posh summer garden party (just saying!).

To salt the cod — The day before you need it, bury the fish in salt and leave for 3 hours in the fridge. Wash the cod, pat dry and return to the fridge overnight. The cod will keep like this for a good few days – if anything, the flavour will improve.

FOR THE *BRANDADE*:

200G/ 7OZ	THICK COD FILLET
	COARSE SEA SALT
4	GARLIC CLOVES, UNPEELED
3½ TBSP	OLIVE OIL, PLUS EXTRA FOR DRIZZLING
	MILK, FOR POACHING THE FISH AND BOILING THE POTATOES
200G/ 7OZ	FLOURY POTATOES, PEELED
4	DECENT-SIZED VINE TOMATOES
I	EGG
I TBSP	SALTED CAPERS, RINSED OF SALT AND SOAKED IN WATER
2 TBSP	CHOPPED PARSLEY AND TARRAGON
2 TBSP	FRIED BREADCRUMBS
	SALT AND PLENTY OF FRESHLY GROUND BLACK PEPPER

Preheat the oven to 200°C fan/220°C/425°F/ gas mark 7.

Crush the garlic cloves with the heel of your hand and fry very slowly in the olive oil to infuse it with their flavour. Scoop out the cloves, squeeze the soft flesh from the skins and reserve. Set the infused oil to one side.

Poach the cod gently in the milk for about 3–4 minutes or until the flesh is firm to the touch and opaque. Transfer the cod to a bowl, reserving the milk. Allow to cool, then skin the fish. Boil the potatoes in the reserved milk until soft, then scoop them into the same bowl, and roughly mash the fish and potatoes together. Add a splash of the cooking milk to bind, then beat in the garlicky olive oil and the garlic flesh itself. Season with salt if needed and add a splash more of the milk if it looks a little dry. The texture should be rough, and it should taste quite garlicky and fairly salty.

Cut the tops off the tomatoes and scoop out the seeds. Fill the cavities with the *brandade*, then drizzle with olive oil and roast in the hot oven for 15 minutes, or until the tomatoes are soft but not collapsing, and the *brandade* has browned slightly on top.

Meanwhile, hard-boil the egg, cool and shell. Grate the yolk and half the white, and sprinkle over the top of the tomatoes along with the capers, chopped herbs and fried breadcrumbs. Eat warm.

Anchoïade with Figs, Walnuts & Basil

Any southern French market worth its salt will have an eye-catching olive stand with myriad examples of the quintessential *Provençal* fruit: from fat, glistening green numbers to wizened and wrinkled indigenous black ones, either plain in a briny juice or tossed with aromatic herbs and swimming in their own oil. Alongside the buckets of olives, you will see a selection of tasty pastes of various shades, all with a deep flavour – *tapenades*, artichoke purées, smooth chickpea dips and *anchoïades*. Here is a delicious *Provençal* spread with a curious colour and an explosion of taste: anchovies, black figs, walnuts and basil blended to a smooth paste with garlic and olive oil. Make some little thin toasts and spread this on top to serve with your apéritif.

I (60G/ 2¼OZ/ GENEROUS ½ CUP)	JAR OF SALTED ANCHOVIES, DRAINED OF THEIR OIL AND BLOTTED DRY
I	FAT GARLIC CLOVE
4	RIPE FIGS, PREFERABLY BLACK *PROVENÇAL*
	A SMALL HANDFUL OF WALNUTS
½	BUNCH OF BASIL
IOOML/ 3½FL OZ/ SCANT ½ CUP	OLIVE OIL
	RED WINE VINEGAR, TO TASTE

Blend all the ingredients together. Adjust the seasoning – it will most likely need no more salt as the anchovies will have sorted this bit out but add just enough vinegar to cut through the oil and salt.

Stuffed Fried Sardines

SERVES 2

I've stuffed whole sardines before with a mixture of chopped chard, garlic and breadcrumbs, and the result is wonderful, with a loose tumble of stuffing spilling out of the belly of the fish as it roasts in the hot oven. Ordering stuffed sardines at the fantastic La Merenda in Nice's old town, they came not whole but butterflied (opened up flat), with a mound of deep-green stuffing squidged onto the fillets, and the whole assembly dipped into fine breadcrumbs before a trip into some hot olive oil. This ensures the juiciest result, as there is far more stuffing than fish.

Over the border into Liguria and to Genoa the same technique is employed, although sometimes for fresh anchovies rather than sardines, but always with Swiss chard.

La Merenda's version, which I approximate below, is a mixture of chard, parsley, Parmesan, smoked pancetta, bread soaked in milk and shallots softened in butter. Pan-fry in liberal amounts of olive oil, drain briefly, and serve them with lemon. Excellent.

6	FRESH SARDINES, CLEANED, SCALED AND BUTTERFLIED, FINS REMOVED BUT TAIL ON
1	BEATEN EGG, FOR DREDGING
	FRESH FINE BREADCRUMBS, FOR COATING
	OLIVE OIL
	LEMON WEDGES, TO SERVE

FOR THE STUFFING:

15G/ ½OZ/ 1 TBSP	UNSALTED BUTTER
1	SHALLOT, FINELY DICED
1 TBSP	FINELY DICED SMOKED PANCETTA
	A BUNCH OF SWISS CHARD, WASHED, STALKS SEPARATED FROM LEAVES
2 TBSP	FRESH BREADCRUMBS, SOAKED IN A LITTLE MILK
	A SMALL HANDFUL OF FLAT-LEAF PARSLEY, FINELY CHOPPED
25G/1OZ/ ¼ CUP	GRATED PARMESAN CHEESE
	SALT AND FRESHLY GROUND BLACK PEPPER

Melt the butter in a frying pan and slowly fry the shallots and pancetta until the shallot is soft and sweet. Meanwhile, boil the chard (stalks first, then leaves) in salted water until soft. Remove, cool, squeeze well and chop very finely. Squeeze the excess milk from the breadcrumbs, then mix with the shallots, pancetta, chard, parsley and Parmesan. Season to taste with salt and black pepper.

Lightly season the butterflied sardines with salt, lay them skin side down, then squidge a mound of stuffing onto the flesh – it should be about 1cm/½in thick. Dredge the assembly in beaten egg, then roll in the fine breadcrumbs. Set aside.

Heat a 5mm/¼in depth of olive oil in a deep-sided frying pan. Fry the sardines over a medium heat until coloured golden brown. Drain on kitchen paper and serve hot, with wedges of lemon.

Sardenaira

This savoury *focaccia* from Liguria, topped with tomatoes and salted sardines, is an interesting one. It goes by several different names – in Sanremo they call it *sardenaira* (or *sardenara*), most probably named for the sardines on top, but in Imperia it's known as *pissalandrea* (or *pizza all'Andrea*), supposedly named after a Genoese admiral who was a big fan of the dish.

Now, to me, this sounds suspiciously like the *pissaladière* we associate with Nice. Some of these names derive from the Niçard/old Ligurian dialect for salted fish – *peis salat* – which gives us the Niçois *pissala*, a tasty paste of fermented anchovies and

olive oil used to flavour the famous onion tart. Before tomatoes arrived in Italy this *foccacia* would most probably have been made with onions instead and would have closely resembled the Niçois version. There is some debate as to from which side of the border it originated, but as the modern French-Italian border is a relatively recent innovation, this point is moot.

I am a big fan of the thin Ligurian-style *focaccia*, all crisp crust, less oil-sodden crumb. This recipe will work well to achieve that if you omit the tomato and instead drench the dimpled dough with an emulsion of salt water and olive oil.

6G/⅛OZ	FRESH YEAST OR ½ TSP DRIED YEAST
200G/ 7OZ/SCANT 1½ CUPS	STRONG BREAD FLOUR
½ TSP	HONEY OR SUGAR
140ML/ 4½FL OZ/ SCANT ⅔ CUP	LUKEWARM WATER
½ TSP	FINE SALT
4 TSP	OLIVE OIL

FOR THE TOPPING:	
100G/ 3½OZ/ ½ CUP	POLPA DI POMODORO OR PASSATA, OR PEELED PLUM TOMATOES WITHOUT THEIR JUICE, BLITZED
	OLIVE OIL
2	GARLIC CLOVES, THICKLY SLICED (TOO THIN AND THE GARLIC WILL BURN)
	A SMALL HANDFUL OF PITTED BLACK OLIVES, TORN IN HALF
	A SCATTERING OF SALTED CAPERS, RINSED OF SALT AND SOAKED IN WATER
	DRIED OREGANO (OPTIONAL)
	A FEW FILLETS OF SALTED SARDINES OR ANCHOVIES
	SALT

Put the yeast, 3 tablespoons of the flour, the honey and 2 tablespoons of the water in a small bowl and leave to start proving. Meanwhile, mix the remaining flour with the salt in a large bowl and combine the rest of the water with the olive oil in a jug. After the yeasted mixture has started to bubble, make a well in the flour and pour in both the yeasted mixture and the oily water. Mix to combine until a dough forms, then knead this dough for 10–15 minutes, until smooth and very elastic. Leave to prove for 30 minutes.

With lightly wet hands, stretch and fold the dough back on itself, once from each edge, then leave to prove for another 30 minutes, before stretching and folding again. Leave for another 30 minutes.

Transfer the dough to an oiled heavy tray or large baking dish roughly 40 × 30cm/16 × 12in. Press and stretch the focaccia out using your hands and oiled fingertips until it is very thin – it should be no more than 5mm/¼ in depth. If you have too much dough for the size of your tray or dish, take some out and keep it in the refrigerator to bake tomorrow. If you are having trouble stretching the dough out, leave it for 10 minutes and come back to it.

At this stage, preheat the oven to its hottest setting. If you have a pizza stone, put it in the oven, and you can slide your tray on top – this is aiming to replicate a bake on the bottom of an oven.

Assemble the topping ingredients: season the tomato polpa or passata well with salt and mix in a good 2 tablespoons of olive oil. Now press your fingertips into the dough to form deep dimples roughly 1cm/½in apart – take care not to rip through the dough at the bottom. Spoon the tomato mixture onto the *focaccia*, right to the edge, spreading gently with the back of a spoon. It should be more than just a smearing of tomato. Scatter the other ingredients on top, drizzle with a little more olive oil, and allow to prove for a further 15 minutes.

Bake the *focaccia* in the hot oven for 15–20 minutes, until it is a crisp golden brown on the sides. Remove from the oven and cool on a wire rack to ensure that the bottom stays crisp.

Melon Salad with Purslane, Flat Beans, Basil, Almonds & Salted Ricotta

SERVES 2
*for a light lunch, or
4 as a small starter*

The sweet Charentais is a type of cantaloupe melon, brought to France most probably with the Popes of Avignon in the fourteenth century from Italy, and before that, perhaps from the Roman conquest of North Africa. Pope Paul II suffered a heart attack after gorging himself on delicious sweet melons, and the proximity of the papal seat in Avignon must go some way to explaining the excellent reputation that Provence has for the fruit.

Today melon madness continues in Cavaillon, Provence, home to the prestigious melon market and, since 1988, to the Confrérie des Chevaliers de l'Ordre du Melon – a robed order of melon knights dedicated to preserving the traditions and promoting the interests of all things melon. Each year there is a several-day orgy of melon loving: a melon festival! Bus tours of local melon farms, melon art, recipe competitions, melon-based buffets, insane processions and piles upon piles of the things: orbs heavy with nectar, their skins wizened under the summer sun, the flesh inside golden orange, dense, perfumed and sweet.

The melons are delicious on their own, of course, or served splashed with sweet wine as is traditional, but also come into their own in a salad. A little salty cheese works very well with the sweetness and, served very cold, this salad is one of the most refreshing, invigorating combinations I ate last summer.

Do try to seek out some decent salted ricotta or feta for this one; Parmesan or pecorino taste slightly too cheesy for the delicate fruit. Purslane is a great salad leaf for this salad, succulent and slightly sour, but something peppery like rocket would also work well. Raw beans add more freshness, roasted almonds provide much-needed crunch, and some torn basil a little added character.

	A SMALL HANDFUL OF SHELLED ALMONDS
I	DELICIOUS CHARENTAIS MELON, VERY COLD FROM THE FRIDGE
	LEMON JUICE
	GOOD OLIVE OIL
	A HANDFUL OF FLAT (STRINGLESS) FRENCH, RUNNER OR OTHER LONG BEANS
	A GOOD HANDFUL OF PURSLANE, ROCKET OR WATERCRESS
	A SMALL LUMP OF SALTED RICOTTA, OR 2 TBSP FETA CHEESE
	A FEW BASIL LEAVES
	SALT AND FRESHLY GROUND BLACK PEPPER

Toast the almonds slowly in a dry pan for about 5 minutes until an even golden brown. Sprinkle with salt while still hot. Set aside to cool, then cut lengthways into slivers with a sharp knife.

Halve the melon, scoop out the seeds, cut into wedges, then cut off the skin. Cut the pieces into nice chunks about 4cm/1½in thick. Put the melon in a bowl, dress with a bit of lemon juice, some olive oil and a few grains of salt, then transfer the melon to a nice big plate.

Wash the beans and slice into short lengths. Put the beans and salad leaves into the bowl and dress (more heavily this time) with salt, lemon and olive oil.

Arrange the salad leaves and beans on and around the melon, scatter with the salted almonds and grated ricotta or crumbled feta. Top with torn basil leaves, grind over some black pepper, drizzle with more olive oil and eat.

Mentonnais Christmas Salad

SERVES 4
as a side or starter

A Christmas salad from Menton, a town only *just* on the French side of the border, which is famous for its citrus fruit and a bonkers lemon festival, and also a few unique recipes. In December the black truffles are in season, and the famous *Provençal* olive oil has just been harvested and pressed, and along the Riviera good anchovies are always on hand.

This salad is a uniquely *Provençal* expression of the season, and I think this might be a rather elegant festive starter, or something to eat with any leftovers from a roast Christmas chicken or capon. There are very few elements to this salad, so it pays to make sure that all of them are absolutely tip-top.

2	CELERY HEARTS (NO STRINGY OUTER STUFF!)
	PARMESAN CHEESE
I	DELICIOUS LEMON
	NEW SEASON OLIVE OIL — *PROVENÇAL* IF YOU CAN GET IT
8	BEST-QUALITY SALTED ANCHOVY FILLETS
I	BLACK WINTER TRUFFLE
	SALT

Trim the base of the celery hearts and thinly slice on a slight angle. Include all the pale green and yellow leaves – keep them roughly chopped. Shave a small handful of Parmesan cheese with a truffle slicer. Dress the celery heart and Parmesan with (a little) salt, lemon juice and some of the olive oil. Arrange on your best big plate.

Cut the anchovy fillets in half lengthways. Toss gently with the salad. Shave over black truffle to your heart's (and wallet's) content. Drizzle over more of the green-gold oil and eat.

Barbajuans

Barbajuan means 'Uncle John' in Monégasque, the national language of Monaco. I'm not sure who Uncle John was, but apparently he had the brilliant idea of deep-frying his ravioli instead of boiling them. In Monaco, and over its borders to both east and west, these are sold as a snack on the street. The usual filling during the summer months is Swiss chard, but in Italy, and in winter, pumpkin is more common, and there's always a nice amount of ricotta in the mix too. These can be made into various different shapes. When I ate them at the lemon festival in Menton they were rough rectangles with a thick, uneven border, almost like fried *pierogi* (dumplings).

FOR THE DOUGH:

200G/ 7OZ/ 1½ CUPS	'OO' FLOUR, PLUS EXTRA FOR DUSTING
4 TSP	OLIVE OIL
50ML/ 2FL OZ/ SCANT ¼ CUP	WARM WATER
I	EGG
	PINCH OF SALT

FOR THE FILLING:

	OLIVE OR VEGETABLE OIL
½	YELLOW ONION, FINELY DICED
½	LEEK, WASHED, HALVED LENGTHWAYS AND THINLY SLICED
½	PUMPKIN OR BUTTERNUT SQUASH, ROASTED, FLESH SCOOPED OUT (APPROX. 200G/7OZ/1 CUP COOKED)
100G/ 3½OZ/ ½ CUP	RICOTTA
25G/1OZ/ ¼ CUP	GRATED PARMESAN CHEESE
1 TSP	CHOPPED MARJORAM LEAVES
	SALTED, FRESHLY GROUND BLACK PEPPER AND NUTMEG

Mix the ingredients for the dough in a large bowl and knead until smooth. Wrap in clingfilm and let it rest for an hour.

For the filling, heat a little olive oil in a small pan and sweat the onion and leek slowly with a pinch of salt. You want them soft and sweet with very little colour, but it's important that all the moisture is cooked out. Cool to room temperature. Combine the alliums with the cooked squash, the cheeses and the marjoram. Season with nutmeg, salt and pepper.

Lightly flour your work surface and roll out the dough to a thickness of 2mm/⅛in. Using a fluted wheeled pasta cutter, cut strips roughly 8cm/3¼in wide, then cut 6cm/2½in strips the other way to make rectangles. Put a spoon of filling in the middle of each rectangle, brush the edges with water and fold the dough over to make an elongated ravioli shape. Pinch the ends together (to resemble a sweet wrapper), then use the tines of a fork to seal the long edge. Don't worry if the result is a bit rough around the edges; this is to be encouraged. I prefer these dumplings when they look like little *pierogi*, and the borders are thick and uneven.

Heat a 2-3-cm/¾-1¼-in depth of oil in a wide, deep-sided pan – olive (better taste, more expensive) or vegetable (blander, cheaper). Get the oil medium-hot, and deep-fry the *barbajuans* in batches, turning once, for a few minutes on each side. They should be an attractive golden-brown colour, with the filling visible through the pasta coating. Drain on kitchen paper, sprinkle lightly with salt, and allow to cool slightly before eating, or else the filling will incinerate the inside of your mouth.

Raviolis à la Daube

A recipe from the Niçois repertoire for using up leftover *daube de boeuf,* or indeed the *Tocco* on page 130. Don't feel you have to make one specifically for this recipe, but if you do have any leftover beef stewed in red wine then this is a great way to stretch the leftovers, especially with the addition of some Swiss chard. Although making fresh pasta is a faff, this recipe is actually quite a clever, frugal bit of cooking.

Here the leftover beef and freshly cooked Swiss chard are finely chopped and re-moistened with some of the liquid from the *daube,* and I like to add a little ricotta, which lightens things a bit. I prefer to make these ravioli quite small, so they look almost like the ones you get out of a can, except much more tasty. The little ravioli are boiled briefly then dressed in a sauce made from more of the *daube* juices, enriched with a bit of butter.

FOR THE PASTA DOUGH:

200G/ 7OZ/ 1½ CUPS	'00' FLOUR, PLUS EXTRA FOR DUSTING
2	EGGS

FOR THE FILLING AND SAUCE:

1 TBSP	OLIVE OIL, PLUS EXTRA FOR DRIZZLING
	A BUNCH OF SWISS CHARD – LEAVES ONLY (KEEP THE STALKS FOR A GRATIN)
ABOUT 4 TBSP	LEFTOVER BEEF FROM A *DAUBE* (OR OTHER STEW), PLUS A SMALL LADLEFUL OF THE JUICES FOR THE SAUCE
2 TBSP	GRATED PARMESAN CHEESE, PLUS EXTRA TO SERVE
1 TBSP	RICOTTA
1	EGG YOLK
2 TBSP	UNSALTED BUTTER, CUBED
	SALT, FRESHLY GROUND BLACK PEPPER AND NUTMEG
	A HANDFUL OF CHOPPED PARSLEY, TO SERVE

First, make the pasta dough. Pour the flour onto a work surface, make a well in the centre and crack in the eggs. Whisk the eggs with a fork, then slowly incorporate the flour until a dough forms. Knead for 5–10 minutes until smooth and soft. If the dough seems a touch flaky and dry, add a few drops of water or moisten your hands. Equally, don't feel that you have to work all of the flour into the dough if it doesn't seem needed. Wrap in clingfilm and leave to rest at room temperature for an hour (or, if making ahead of time, refrigerate).

To make the filling, heat the oil in a pan, drop in the chard leaves and cover while they cook for a minute or two. Cool, then squeeze them very well and finely chop. Now finely chop the leftover meat, then mix with the chard (there should be as much chard as beef). Add the cheeses and egg yolk. Season with salt, pepper and nutmeg to taste, and mix well.

Cut the dough into two pieces. Using a pasta machine or a rolling pin, roll out the first piece of dough. For ravioli you want the pasta to be quite thin – you should be able to read a newspaper headline through it. Set aside the first strip of pasta on a lightly floured surface covered with a tea towel to prevent it drying out while you roll out the second.

When you have two even-sized strips of pasta, ensure that your surface is floured, then blob level teaspoonfuls of filling down one side of the first pasta strip, leaving roughly 2cm/¾in between each lump of filling. Repeat to create a second line of filling on the strip, leaving a 2cm/¾in gap between the two lines. Carefully lay the other strip of pasta over the top. Press very gently on each lump then, using your fingertips, press the pasta around the mounds of filling to seal. Squish well to ensure there are no big air pockets. Using a fluted wheeled cutter, cut between each parcel. Separate the ravioli and set aside on a floured surface.

Bring a large pan of salted water to the boil. In a separate pan (large enough to allow you to toss the ravioli once cooked), heat the remaining *daube* liquid, which is all the better if there are a few strands of meat left in it.

Drop the ravioli into the boiling salted water, in batches if necessary. Boil for a minute or so, until the ravioli float and the pasta is just cooked through (eat one to be sure!). Meanwhile, add the cubed butter to the hot *daube* sauce along with a spoonful or two of the pasta cooking water. When cooked, remove the ravioli with a slotted spoon and drop into the sauce. Toss the ravioli gently in the sauce: add more pasta water if it looks too dry.

Tip the sauced ravioli onto plates or a big serving platter. Top with finely chopped parsley and grated Parmesan. A nice drizzle of olive oil is a lovely touch to finish.

Tocco (Genoese Meat Sauce for Pasta) SERVES 4

After *pesto*, the second-favourite pasta sauce in Genoa is *tocco*. The word is Ligurian dialect for 'sauce', but *tocco* is synonymous with a specific one, namely a rich braise of beef or veal with dried ceps, pine kernels and wine. In a similar vein to the Neapolitan *ragù*, here the goal is to produce a rich, meat-flavoured sauce for pasta as a first course, with the meat itself served separately as a *secondo*. The idea is that the meat and its sauce blip away all day in a heavy pot until the meat has given up all its flavour and the sauce is reduced and full.

My interest here is the similarity between *tocco* and a *Provençal daube*, another wine-rich beef stew in which dried ceps are often used, and the sauce is also often thickened slightly using a *roux* – a technique nowadays associated closely with French cooking. In any case, this is delicious. I prefer to make it with veal, white wine and chicken stock in a bid to lighten it slightly, with cinnamon and nutmeg. Bone marrow is a traditional ingredient – I suggest using a thick piece of *osso bucco*, which will give lots of sticky flavour as the marrow melts into the sauce.

Tocco is often served with meat-stuffed ravioli: comparison with the Niçois *Raviolis à la Daube* (see page 128) is obvious. Both meat and vegetable stuffings are common – either with some of the meat from the braise, or with borage and a little ricotta. I would be especially pleased with the latter.

500G/ 1LB 2OZ	VEAL SHIN ON THE BONE (*OSSO BUCCO*) – IDEALLY IN ONE PIECE
	FLOUR, FOR DUSTING
2 TBSP	OIL
100G/ 3½OZ/ ½ CUP	UNSALTED BUTTER
1	YELLOW ONION, CHOPPED
2	CELERY STICKS, CHOPPED
1	CARROT, CHOPPED
2	GARLIC CLOVES, SLICED LENGTHWAYS
1 TBSP	PINE KERNELS
	A SHORT LENGTH OF CINNAMON STICK (OPTIONAL)
	GRATED NUTMEG, TO TASTE
2	BAY LEAVES
	A SMALL SPRIG OF ROSEMARY, CHOPPED
15G/ ½OZ	DRIED PORCINI, SOAKED IN HOT WATER
400G/ 14OZ	CANNED PEELED PLUM TOMATOES
½	BOTTLE OF WHITE WINE
500ML/ 18FL OZ/ 2 CUPS	GOOD CHICKEN STOCK
	SALT AND FRESHLY GROUND BLACK PEPPER

Season the veal well with salt and pepper and dust with flour. Heat the oil and half the butter in a large, heavy-bottomed pan then brown the veal until golden on all sides. Remove the meat, add the rest of the butter with the onion, celery, carrot, garlic and a pinch of salt.

Fry slowly in the fat until soft – around 20 minutes – then add the pine kernels, cinnamon (if using), nutmeg, bay, rosemary and porcini (reserve the soaking liquid) for 5 minutes, until aromatic. Add the tomatoes, mushroom soaking liquid, white wine and chicken stock. Bring to the boil, cover with a tight lid, and reduce to a very low simmer. Cook for 3–4 hours, turning the veal once, until the meat is spoon-tender and the sauce full-flavoured. Remove the veal and reserve.

To finish the sauce, adjust the seasoning with salt, and add a little more water if needed. Either pass the sauce through a food mill, or remove the bay and cinnamon and pulse-chop briefly in a blender.

Serve the sauce with pasta or ravioli. You can do several things with the cooked veal – chop and stuff some ravioli or vegetables, or serve as a main course with polenta or potato. I rather fancy a baked potato with butter, grated cheese and the veal would make a nice dinner.

Pasta with Salted Sardines (Bigoli in Salsa)

SERVES 2

You can use marinated sardines as you would fresh sardines in pasta, as the light cure means that they aren't too different from fresh. Here is a pasta dish from Venice called *bigoli in salsa*: a rich sauce of sweet melted onions and salted fatty fish to serve with a thick spaghetti. Now commonly made with anchovies, this used to be made with salted sardines. Bigoli are a delicious thick wholewheat spaghetti. If you can't track them down, use bucatini, spaghettoni or just spaghetti – wholewheat or otherwise.

4 TBSP	OLIVE OIL, PLUS EXTRA IF YOU THINK IT NEEDS IT
	A GOOD KNOB OF UNSALTED BUTTER
2	WHITE OR YELLOW ONIONS, SLICED AS FINELY AS POSSIBLE INTO HALF-MOONS
4	SALTED SARDINE FILLETS, OR 6 SALTED ANCHOVY FILLETS (OR A COMBINATION!)
½ GLASS	WHITE WINE
200G/ 7OZ	BIGOLI, BUCATINI OR OTHER THICK PASTA
2 TBSP	CHOPPED PARSLEY (OPTIONAL)
	SALT

Heat the olive oil in a deep pan, add the butter and chuck in the onions. Season lightly with salt to help them cook nicely but don't overdo it as the fish will add salt later. Cook the onions slowly, for at least 30 minutes, stirring occasionally, until very soft. They should be sweet and melting. If they threaten to dry out and take too much colour, cover them with a lid or add a small splash of water.

Chop the sardine fillets and mush them a bit with the flat of a knife – this will encourage them to melt into the sauce. Add the sardines to the pan with the onions and fry over a medium heat until the sardines start to break down – squish them with a wooden spoon to help them along. Add the white wine and bubble the sauce until the wine has evaporated.

Continue to cook over a low heat, adding a spash or two of water if the sauce threatens to dry out.

Meanwhile, boil the pasta in salted water until *al dente* then drain, reserving some of the pasta water. Toss the pasta with the sauce and add a little of the starchy pasta water. Add the parsley, if using, and drizzle in a little more olive oil if it needs it.

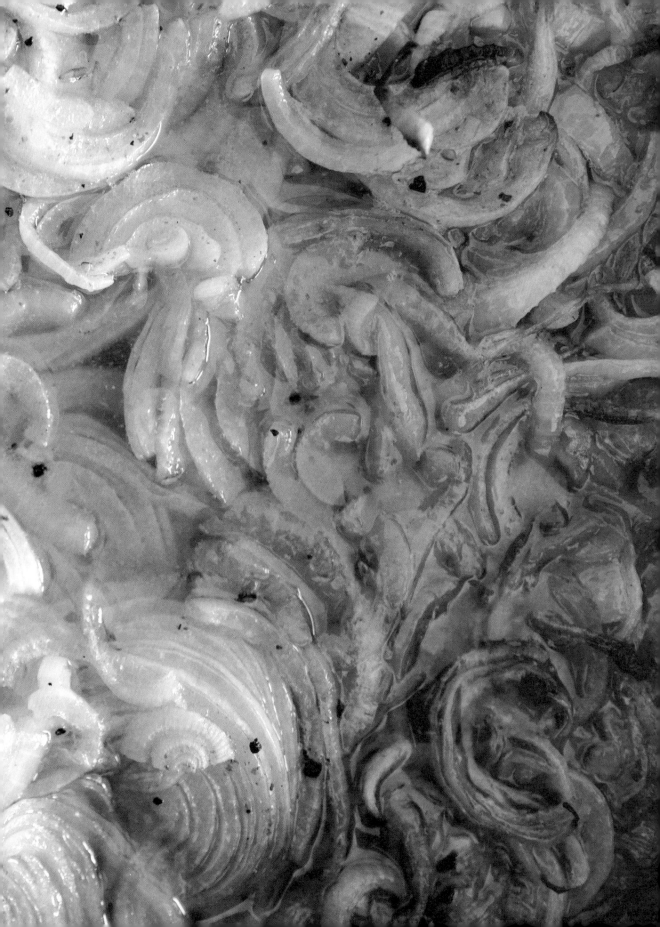

Pansoti & Walnut Sauce

Pansoti are Liguria's famous ravioli. The name comes from dialect for 'pot-bellied', and these fat little dumplings are stuffed with a mixture of wild edible greens called *preboggion*. Your selection can be as varied as what you forage from hedgerows, but should you be walking in a park or along a canal path instead of open countryside you can of course supplement your finds with some shop-bought greens.

I think an ideal mix will include at least some chard, nettles, borage and dandelion, but spinach is of course welcome too – the greens are boiled, squeezed and chopped finely, and the mixture lightened with ricotta (and maybe a spoon of soured cream, in an effort to imitate the local Genoese soft cheese *prescinsêua*).

Walnut sauce is the traditional accompaniment – crushed walnuts, garlic, marjoram and Parmesan, loosened with milk, olive oil and a little of the cooking water. When I ate this in Genoa the sauce was very loose, like a thin cream: subtle, earthy and most delicious.

FOR THE PASTA DOUGH:

250G/ 9OZ/ GENEROUS 2 CUPS	'OO' FLOUR
5	EGG YOLKS
I	WHOLE EGG
	SEMOLINA FLOUR, FOR DUSTING

FOR THE FILLING:

	A BUNCH OF SWISS CHARD
	A HANDFUL OF YOUNG NETTLES, LEAVES PICKED
	A HANDFUL OF DANDELION LEAVES
	A BUNCH OF BORAGE OR SPINACH
250G/ 9OZ/ I ½ CUPS	RICOTTA
I HEAPED TBSP	CRÈME FRAÎCHE
50G/ I ¾OZ/ ½ CUP	GRATED PARMESAN CHEESE, PLUS EXTRA TO SERVE
	SALT, FRESHLY GROUND BLACK PEPPER AND NUTMEG

FOR THE WALNUT SAUCE:

½	GARLIC CLOVE
	A SPRIG OF MARJORAM, LEAVES PICKED
50G/ I ¾OZ/ ½ CUP	SHELLED WALNUTS
I TBSP	PINE KERNELS
25G/I OZ/ ¼ CUP	GRATED PARMESAN CHEESE
50ML/ 2FL OZ/ SCANT ¼ CUP	WHOLE MILK
50ML/ 2FL OZ/ SCANT ¼ CUP	OLIVE OIL

Note — There are a few different ways to fold *pansoti*. Best to do it the way your Ligurian grandmother used to.

First, make the pasta dough. Pour the flour onto a work surface and make a well in the middle. Add the eggs and slowly whisk the flour into the middle. When you have a shaggy dough, knead it by hand until it comes together, then continue kneading for 5 minutes or so until smooth to the touch. Add a little sprinkle of water (or wet your hands as you knead) if the pasta feels a little dry. Wrap the dough in clingfilm and set aside for an hour.

Meanwhile, make the filling: wash the greens well then boil them briefly in salted water. Drain, cool, squeeze very well, then chop as finely as possible. Mix the greens with the ricotta, crème fraîche and Parmesan, then add salt, pepper and nutmeg to taste. Chill.

Use a pasta machine to roll out dough as thinly as possible, then cut the sheet into 8cm/3¼in squares – I like to use a fluted cutter. Put a heaped teaspoon of filling in the middle of each square. Brush the edges of the square lightly with water, then fold in half of diagonally to make a triangle shape. Squeeze the dough together to seal and exclude any air pockets too. With the base of the triangle towards you, push your thumb up into the 'belly' of the dumpling. This will make the edges of the triangle look like two little legs – squeeze the two legs together, tucking one slightly under the other as you squeeze.

Set the finished pasta on a tray lightly floured with semolina flour.

To make the sauce, crush the garlic, marjoram and a pinch of salt to a paste using a pestle and mortar. Add the walnuts and pine kernels and crush to a paste – don't worry about getting it too fine, as a little texture is quite nice. Add the Parmesan cheese, then the milk, followed by the olive oil, mixing with the pestle all the while. You might need to add a little extra milk or oil – aim for a loose sauce about the consistency of yogurt.

To finish, cook the *pansoti* for a minute or two in a large pan of salted fast-simmering water. Meanwhile, add the sauce to a sauté pan (one with curved edges) and let it down with a bit of the hot pasta water. No need to heat the pan. When the *pansoti* are cooked (eat one to check), scoop them out into the waiting sauce and mix. Add a little more of the pasta water if the sauce has thickened too much – it should be like double cream.

Serve the *pansoti* in the walnut sauce and grate over extra Parmesan at the table.

Swiss Chard Gnocchi (Merda de Can)

These little green gnocchi are known in Niçois as *merda de can*. Translation: dog poos. Not a particularly appetizing piece of information, but rest assured it's more down to the shape of the dumplings than the taste.

Swiss chard is ubiquitous in Niçois cooking, and here a roughly chopped purée of chard greens is mixed with potatoes, flour, a little egg and some nutmeg. These are delicious just with melted butter, sage and some Parmesan, with a simple, garlicky tomato sauce, or on a rainy day, a sauce made from Gorgonzola and cream. Traditional, and very tasty, is to serve them with the leftover juices from a beef *daube*, enriched with some butter.

Nice's former mayor Jacques Médecin recommends serving them with the juices from a roast chicken, which will also do nicely, thanks very much.

1 KG/ 2LB 4OZ	FLOURY POTATOES, UNPEELED
	SALT, FOR BAKING
	A BUNCH OF SWISS CHARD
2	EGG YOLKS
150G/ 5½ OZ/ 1 HEAPED CUP	PLAIN FLOUR, PLUS EXTRA FOR DUSTING
	NUTMEG
TO SERVE:	
50G/ 1¾OZ/ 3 TBSP	UNSALTED BUTTER
4	SAGE LEAVES
2 TBSP	GRATED PARMESAN CHEESE

Preheat the oven to 180°C fan/200°C/400°F/ gas mark 6.

Sit the potatoes on a bed of fine salt in a baking dish and bake them in the hot oven until cooked through and crisp. This will take about an hour, depending on the size of your potatoes. Meanwhile, separate the greens from the stalks of the chard. Reserve the chard stalks for another recipe – a gratin with anchovy, perhaps? – and wash the leaves well. Boil in salted water for a couple of minutes, then drain and allow to cool. When cool, squeeze every last drop of water out of the chard, then chop very well so that you end up with a fine green paste.

When the potatoes are cooked, and while they are still hot, cut them in half and scoop out the flesh. Pass the hot flesh through a potato ricer or a mouli-légumes (failing that, mash well with your trusty masher). Work quickly, now, as this works better if everything stays warm. Add the chard paste, egg yolks and a grating of nutmeg, and mix well. On a well-floured surface, spread out the potato mix and sprinkle with half the flour. Incorporate the flour into the potato using your hands like two shovels, or, even better, armed with a dough scraper.

Turn the mixture this way and that until it starts to come together, but use a light touch, and try not to work the potato mixture unnecessarily. Add the rest of the flour gradually but note that you might not need it all. Bring it together into a soft dough. I find that if I can press my finger into the dough without too much potato getting stuck to it – a bit like testing a cake with a skewer – I know my dough has enough flour and is ready to cut.

Cover the dough with a tea towel while you roll the gnocchi. Keep the surface lightly floured. Cut off a slice of dough and roll into a (chipolata) sausage. Cut this sausage into 3cm/1¼in lengths, or whatever looks most like a dog poo to you. Set aside.

Boil some water in a big pan and salt it until well seasoned, like a tasty soup. Warm a wide sauté pan, plop in the butter and sage, then scoop in a small ladleful of your cooking water. Shake to emulsify and keep warm. Don't let it dry out and start to fry again.

With the pan of water at a fast simmer, drop in your dumplings, in batches if necessary to avoid overcrowding the pan. When the gnocchi pop up and float at the surface, cook for 15 seconds more, then scoop out with a slotted spoon and drop into the sage butter. Toss around a bit and pour onto plates to serve, with grated Parmesan on top.

If serving with leftover beef *daube* instead of the sage butter, well done you: heat a bit of the juices, including some squished strands of meat, and when you drop in the cooked gnocchi toss with a generous knob of butter.

Minestrone al Pesto

The Ligurian sister of Provence's *soupe au pistou*. The two soups are made in almost identical fashion, the main difference being the use of either *pistou* or *pesto Genovese* – Ligurian *pesto* uses pine kernels, while the *Provençal pistou* sometimes has a little tomato. I can't decide which version I like more, although I'm sure millions on both sides of the border hold stronger opinions on the matter.

In a move sure to irritate countless more, here is a version of a *minestrone al pesto* I once made on a hot early summer's day; served slightly chilled, the texture thicker and smoother than usual. This is still substantial but most refreshing, a bowl of green heady with the flavour of basil.

500G/ 1LB 2OZ/ 3 ½ CUPS	FRESH PODDED PEAS, PODS RESERVED
	A BUNCH OF BASIL, LEAVES AND STALKS SEPARATED (RESERVE THE LEAVES FOR THE *PESTO*)
	OLIVE OIL
1	WHITE ONION, FINELY DICED
1	CELERY STICK, FINELY DICED
½	FENNEL BULB, FINELY DICED
½	LEEK, FINELY DICED
2	GARLIC CLOVES, FINELY SLICED
	A BUNCH OF GREEN ASPARAGUS, IF STILL IN SEASON
150G/ 5½OZ	FRENCH BEANS
4	SMALL SNAPPY COURGETTES
1	SMALL POTATO, PEELED
1 CAN (400G/ 4OZ)	COOKED WHITE BEANS, RINSED WELL
	SALT AND FRESHLY GROUND BLACK PEPPER

First make a bit of pea-flavoured stock. Put the pea pods and the basil stalks into a pan and cover with about 1 litre/1¾ pints/4 cups of cold water. Bring to the boil, then simmer for a good 30 minutes until the pea pods have given up their sweet flavour. Strain and set aside.

Meanwhile, heat a generous amount of olive oil in a large saucepan and gently fry the onion, celery, fennel, leek and garlic with a pinch of salt until everything is very soft and sweet, but with little colour. Chop the asparagus, French beans, courgettes and potato into small pieces – about 5mm/¼in. Add the vegetables, except the white beans, to the pan with a nice pinch of salt.

Cook slowly, half-covered with a lid, for about 20 minutes, until everything has softened. Do not be tempted to add the pea stock before this step.

Once the vegetables are soft, add the beans and enough pea stock to cover. Reserve any remaining stock if you have it – keep in the refrigerator for later. Cook slowly for a further 30 minutes, until everything is soft and tastes

Recipe continues overleaf

Minestrone al Pesto continued

FOR THE PESTO:

½	SMALL GARLIC CLOVE
2 TBSP	PINE KERNELS
25G/ 1 OZ/ ¼ CUP	GRATED PARMESAN OR PECORINO CHEESE
50ML/ 1 ¾OZ/ SCANT ¼ CUP	OLIVE OIL, PLUS EXTRA FOR DRIZZLING

harmonious. Season with salt and pepper. Blitz half the soup in a blender then mix back into the rest. Don't make the soup too thick – add more stock or some water if you think it looks too thick. Allow the soup to cool fully, then refrigerate until slightly chilled. Taste again for seasoning – it may well need a little more salt once it has cooled.

To make the *pesto*, smash the garlic with a pinch of salt using a pestle and mortar. Add the pine kernels, smash them to a paste, then add the reserved basil leaves. Smash to a smooth paste then add the grated Parmesan cheese. Mix well and drizzle in the olive oil to finish. Add a little splash of water to take the edge off things a bit.

Assess the texture of the soup – loosen slightly with the cold pea stock if it has thickened too much as it chilled. When you're happy, ladle into bowls and spoon over the *pesto*. Drizzle with your best olive oil. This is best eaten outside in the sun.

Spring Vegetable Soup with Eggs & Parmesan

SERVES 4

Nice and the rest of the Riviera are home to some delicious vegetable soups, not least Provence's famous *soupe au pistou* and the Ligurian equivalent, *minestrone al pesto* (see page 138), given bulk in season by the excellent fresh white beans of the region.

When the first spring vegetables arrive on the markets this is an excellent way to approach them: simmer in a light broth, then enrich with eggs, olive oil and Parmesan.

Similarities to the (modern) Roman soup *stracciatella* are obvious and to be encouraged. Feel free to add or omit vegetables according to what you can get. A little broken pasta here adds just enough bulk to make it lunch.

I LITRE/ I ¾ PINTS/ 4 CUPS	LIGHT CHICKEN STOCK OR WATER
	A HANDFUL OF PODDED BROAD BEANS (KEEP THE PODS AND ADD TO THE STOCK)
	A HANDFUL OF FRESH PODDED PEAS (KEEP THE PODS AND ADD TO THE STOCK)
2	GREEN ASPARAGUS SPEARS (SNAP OFF THE WOODY PART AND ADD TO THE STOCK)
	OLIVE OIL
½ BUNCH	SPRING ONIONS OR WHITE SALAD ONIONS, TRIMMED AND FINELY SLICED
I	FRESH GLOBE ARTICHOKE HEART, DE-CHOKED AND FINELY SLICED
2	NEW POTATOES, PEELED AND FINELY DICED
	SWISS CHARD TOPS, FINELY SHREDDED (OPTIONAL)
	A SMALL HANDFUL OF SMALL SOUP PASTA (STELLINE, ORZO OR SPAGHETTINI BROKEN INTO I CM/½IN LENGTHS)
2	EGGS
	A SMALL HANDFUL OF GRATED PARMESAN CHEESE
	SALT AND FRESHLY GROUND BLACK PEPPER

Heat the stock or water in a pan and add the broad bean and pea pods and asparagus stalks. Keep at a simmer while you start the soup. Heat some olive oil in a nice pan, and gently fry the spring onions for a minute or two with a pinch of salt. Add the artichoke and potato, stir around until slightly softened, then add the other vegetables, soup pasta and the strained stock. Season with salt, bring to the boil, simmer until the vegetables are done and the pasta is almost cooked (the pasta will continue to cook as the soup sits), and turn off the heat.

When you are ready to serve, and your guests are at table, reheat the soup. In a large bowl, whisk the eggs with the Parmesan and a drizzle of olive oil. Slowly pour in a ladle of hot soup, whisking furiously, until the mixture is smooth and fairly thick. Add the rest of the soup, more quickly this time, stirring with the whisk. Season well with black pepper and serve immediately.

Tuna-stuffed Tomatoes
(Tomates à l'Antiboise)

SERVES 4

During a trip to San Sebastian in the Spanish Basque Country I ate a gorgeous stuffed tomato: presented whole, peeled and glistening with oil. The tomato had been ingeniously stuffed from underneath so that you were none the wiser until you cut into it. Within lay a mixture of the finest *confit* tuna, and some other bits that I have sadly forgotten due to Txakoli-related reasons.

This recipe is from the Mediterranean, not the Atlantic, but both the Basques and the Provençaux seem to have understood that tuna is excellent with tomatoes. The Antibes style uses rice and mayonnaise, and it is easy to see how *tomates à l'antiboise* has become a very seventies dinner party kind of starter. We must embrace this retro appeal and run with it.

Try to resist the temptation to add too much mayonnaise or rice to the mix – keep the stuffing tasting fresh and this will be a success.

ABOUT 2 TBSP	HOMEMADE MAYONNAISE (MADE WITH I EGG YOLK, ½ TSP MUSTARD, IOOML/ 3½FL OZ/SCANT ½ CUP OLIVE OIL AND A SQUEEZE OF LEMON)
4	RIPE TOMATOES, THE SIZE OF A TENNIS BALL
I	ANCHOVY FILLET
I TBSP	PARSLEY
	A SMALL HANDFUL OF ANY TYPE OF COOKED RICE
I5OG/ 5½OZ	BEST-QUALITY LINE-CAUGHT TUNA, DRAINED
I TSP	SMALL SALTED CAPERS, RINSED OF SALT AND SOAKED IN WATER
	OLIVE OIL, FOR DRIZZLING
	LEMON JUICE
	SEA SALT FLAKES AND FRESHLY GROUND BLACK PEPPER

First, make the mayonnaise if you haven't already: whisk the egg yolk and mustard together, then drizzle in the oil slowly, whisking all the while, until the oil is used up and the sauce thickened. Season with salt and lemon juice. Thin with a sprinkle of water if necessary. Refrigerate until ready to use.

Peel the tomatoes: lightly criss-cross the top of the tomato (by the stalk) with a small knife, dunk them for 20 seconds in boiling water, and then leave under cold running water until cool enough to handle. Be careful not to score too deep – this might cause you structural problems later on! Peel the skins off. Cut 5mm/¼in off the top of the tomato and scoop out the seeds.

Chop the anchovy finely and the parsley a little less finely. Mix all the ingredients apart from the mayonnaise together. Add some mayonnaise, bit by bit, until you are happy with the consistency – don't make it too sloppy or it'll be gross. Season the mixture with salt, pepper and a good squeeze of lemon juice.

Season the inside of the tomato with salt. Stuff with the mixture, but don't overfill. Invert the stuffed tomato onto a serving plate so that it looks like it hasn't been tampered with. Drizzle with olive oil for added sheen, and sprinkle with flaky sea salt.

Courgette Flowers Stuffed with Mussel Rice, with Tomato Sauce & Bottarga

SERVES 2

At first glance this recipe might seem exclusively Italian, for these are ingredients that have long been associated with Italy. But at the markets in Provence shellfish is plentiful, courgette flowers are piled up and sold by the handful, the tomatoes are ripe and heavy, and bottarga (preserved grey mullet or tuna roe) is not unique to Sardinia.

Making bottarga (*boutargue* in French or *poutargue*, as the Provençaux call it) is an ancient tradition, first documented from the Nile Delta in 10BC. The roe is carefully extracted from the fish intact, salt-cured and air-dried, and sometimes encased in wax. In Provence production is now limited to the town of Martigues in the Camargue, but bottarga is found all over the Mediterranean, from Greece to North Africa and back to its northwestern shores.

Courgette flowers are often deep-fried in batter and the result is delicious, particularly when stuffed with fresh cheese, lemon zest and an anchovy fillet (yes please), but my favourite way with them is to stuff and bake; a lighter, more delicate thing. Here the flowers are stuffed with shelled mussels and rice cooked in their winey broth, before being baked briefly with a little tomato sauce to moisten; the bottarga adds a savoury depth to proceedings. I can't say that I've eaten this exact dish anywhere outside my own kitchen, but this is a recipe that could happily find itself speaking Italian, Greek or French: a product of the Mediterranean as a whole – or at least one cook's idea of it.

Recipe continues overleaf

Courgette Flowers Stuffed with Mussel Rice, with Tomato Sauce & Bottarga continued

Preheat the oven to 180°C fan/200°C/400°F/ gas mark 6.

Clean the mussels – debeard, wash well and discard any that are broken or that refuse to close when tapped hard on the edge of the sink.

Heat a large pan, drizzle in a little olive oil and add the mussels and white wine. Cover with a lid and steam for a couple of minutes until the mussel shells open – take care not to overcook. Strain the mussels through a fine sieve, reserving the broth, and allow to cool before shelling. Keep the mussels in the refrigerator until needed.

Meanwhile, heat a second large pan and sweat the shallot, 2 garlic cloves and the fennel seeds in some olive oil, with a pinch of salt, until very soft. Add the anchovy fillet and chilli flakes and stir until the anchovy has melted. Add the rice, stir well, and add a splash of white wine. Cook like a risotto, adding the reserved mussel broth in stages, only adding more liquid when the first lot is absorbed: use the fish stock or just-boiled water to continue cooking the rice when the mussel broth is finished. When the rice is cooked set it aside to cool.

While the rice is cooling, make a quick tomato sauce in a small pan: fry the remaining garlic clove in olive oil until sticky and lightly golden, then add the passata and a pinch of salt. Cook over a low heat for around 15–20 minutes. If the sauce dries out, add a splash of water – you don't want a sauce that is too thick or the finished dish won't be quite as luscious and light.

Once the rice is cool, fold through the shelled mussels and chopped herbs, and grate in a little lemon zest. Taste for seasoning. When happy, stuff the rice inside the courgette flowers until full to bursting. Spread the tomato sauce and a drizzle of olive oil in a baking dish in which the flowers fit snugly. Nestle in the flowers, drizzle over more olive oil and bake in the hot oven for 10 minutes. Spoon the flowers and the sauce onto plates, drizzle again with olive oil, grate a generous amount of bottarga on top and eat.

500G/ 1LB 2OZ	MUSSELS
	OLIVE OIL
1	SMALL GLASS OF WHITE WINE, PLUS ANOTHER SPLASH FOR THE RICE
1	SHALLOT, FINELY DICED
3	GARLIC CLOVES, FINELY SLICED
1 TSP	FENNEL SEEDS
1	SALTED ANCHOVY FILLET
	A LITTLE PINCH OF DRIED CHILLI FLAKES
100G/ 3½OZ/ ½ CUP	RISOTTO RICE (CARNAROLI FOR PREFERENCE)
ABOUT 250ML/ 9FL OZ/ GENEROUS 1 CUP	HOT FISH STOCK OR WATER
200ML/ 7FL OZ/ SCANT 1 CUP	PASSATA
2 TBSP	FINELY CHOPPED PARSLEY, DILL OR FENNEL FRONDS
	LEMON ZEST, A SMIDGEN
6	COURGETTE FLOWERS
	SALT AND FRESHLY GROUND BLACK PEPPER
	BOTTARGA, TO SERVE

Grilled Stuffed Mussels with Basil Butter (Moules Niçoises)

SERVES 2

This recipe is adapted from Elizabeth David's *French Country Cooking*. The mussels are stuffed with a *pistou* made not with the traditional olive oil but with butter; a French–Italian hybrid if ever there was one. Here we will include a little bit of tomato, as is the custom on the French side of the border. Ignore those who say that Parmesan should always be omitted when cooking fish, for a little Parmesan adds extra umami to the bubbling juices that fill the mussel shell.

This makes for an excellent snack to eat with an apéritif, and slices of crusty baguette will help to mop up any butter that spills out onto the plate. Mine's a glass of rosé please.

1 KG/ 2LB 4OZ	MUSSELS, SHELLS DE-BEARDED AND SCRUBBED
1	SMALL GLASS OF WHITE WINE
	CRUSTY BREAD, TO SERVE

FOR THE BASIL BUTTER:

1	GARLIC CLOVE
1	BUNCH OF BASIL
1	SMALL RIPE TOMATO
1 TBSP	FINELY GRATED PARMESAN CHEESE
100G/ 3½OZ/ ½ CUP	SOFTENED UNSALTED BUTTER
	SALT

Clean the mussels – debeard, wash well and discard any that are broken or that refuse to close when tapped hard on the edge of the sink.

Heat a lidded pan, add the mussels and pour in the wine. Cover with a tight lid and cook for a couple of minutes. Remove the mussels from the heat as soon as the shells open. (I often stand over the pan so I can fish out those that open first – thus ensuring that no mussel overcooks. Some might think this a faff, but I find it rather fun, so there.)

Once the mussels are open put them on a baking tray and leave them to cool. Simmer the resultant liquor in the pot until the alcohol has been cooked out (give it a quick taste) and the juices are powerful with flavour. Strain the liquor through a fine sieve to eliminate any grit, and reserve.

Once cool enough to handle, pull away one half of the shells of the mussels but leave them attached to the other half shell. Preheat the grill unless you have a barbeque lit.

To make the basil butter, crush the garlic and basil using a pestle and mortar with a good pinch of salt until you have a fine paste. Grate the tomato on a box grater and put the resultant pulp into a sieve for a minute to drain the excess water.

Add the tomato pulp to the garlic and basil and smash it around a bit. Next, add the Parmesan cheese, followed by the softened butter. Taste for balance; add a bit more cheese if you think it can take it. Add a tablespoon or two of the reduced juices from the mussels; better if they are warm, as it will melt the butter slightly, which will help the colour of the end result.

Blob a little of the butter on each mussel and grill hot for 30 seconds until all is bubbling and starting to colour. Have some bread on hand to dab up the juices that escape the shells and run onto the plate.

Pictured overleaf

Stuffed Cabbage from Grasse (Lou Fassum)

This recipe for *chou farci*, or stuffed cabbage, is from the town of Grasse in the hills above Cannes. The local way is to stuff a whole cabbage: boiled whole, opened up like a farty flower, stuffed with a rich forcemeat and re-formed into a glorious heavy orb. In Grasse it is wrapped in a string bag called a *fassumier* (although muslin will suffice for our purposes) before a slow poaching in stock.

Traditionally this would have formed part of a gargantuan *pot-au-feu*, to be served by the slice alongside the various meats. Alone, a whole cabbage will feed 4–6 people and, with some mashed potato and a little sauce to help it on its way, it is a very satisfying lunch. A bit of an operation, but this is an excellent way to spend a Sunday morning.

1	LARGE SAVOY CABBAGE
½	YELLOW ONION, FINELY DICED
45G/ 1½OZ/ 3 TBSP	UNSALTED BUTTER, PLUS EXTRA FOR FRYING
400G/ 14OZ	FATTY PORK MINCE
50G/ 1¾OZ	MINCED PANCETTA OR FINELY CHOPPED BACON
100G/ 3½OZ	PORK BELLY, CUT INTO SMALL DICE
250G/ 9OZ	SWISS CHARD, LEAVES ONLY, BLANCHED AND CHOPPED
4	GARLIC CLOVES, 3 CRUSHED AND 1 FINELY SLICED
	A SPRIG OF THYME, LEAVES PICKED AND CHOPPED
	A SPRIG OF WINTER SAVORY, LEAVES PICKED AND CHOPPED
	A HANDFUL OF FRESH BREADCRUMBS, SOAKED IN A LITTLE MILK
500ML/ 18FL OZ/ 2 CUPS	LIGHT CHICKEN STOCK OR WATER (OR HALF AND HALF)
1	BAY LEAF
	OLIVE OIL
200ML/ 7FL OZ/ SCANT 1 CUP	TOMATO PASSATA
	SALT, FRESHLY GROUND BLACK PEPPER AND NUTMEG
	PARMESAN CHEESE, TO SERVE
	A LARGE PIECE OF MUSLIN AND STRING

Trim the stalk of the cabbage slightly but keep it intact or the cabbage will fall apart later. Simmer the cabbage whole for 10–15 minutes in a large pan of lightly salted water, then drain through a colander and allow to cool slightly.

Meanwhile, make the stuffing. In a small pan fry the onion in the butter until soft then allow to cool. Combine the meats, cooked onion, chopped cooked chard, crushed garlic, herbs and the breadcrumbs, squeezed of the milk they have soaked in. Season well with salt, plenty of black pepper, and some grated nutmeg. Fry off a little flattened nugget of the stuffing and taste – it should be stridently seasoned.

Lay the muslin on your work surface. Trim the stalk of the cabbage again so that it sits flat and place it in the centre of the muslin. Carefully peel back the cabbage leaves, one at a time, until the cabbage is open, like a half-eaten artichoke. When you reach the heart of the cabbage, where the leaves remain firm, slice off the heart. Finely chop the cabbage heart and mix it into your stuffing.

Using about three-quarters of the stuffing, place a large ball of it in the centre of the flattened cabbage, and re-form the leaves around it into its original shape. As you re-form the cabbage around the ball of stuffing, place the remaining stuffing around the leaves that you fold over, until all the stuffing is used up and the cabbage is full. Gather up the edges of the muslin, wrapping the cabbage tightly to keep everything in place. Tie the muslin tightly with string.

Place the wrapped cabbage back in the pot and pour in the chicken stock or water. Season the stock lightly with salt and pop in the bay leaf. Bring the stock to the boil, then reduce to a slow simmer. Simmer the cabbage, making sure it is almost totally submerged, for around an hour.

Meanwhile, make a light tomato sauce: fry the sliced garlic clove in 1 tablespoon of both olive oil and butter, then add the tomato passata and some salt. Cook for around 20–30 minutes, moistening the sauce with the cabbage poaching liquid if it should threaten to dry out. The sauce should be glossy and loose.

Test the cabbage with a meat thermometer or a thin skewer – the stuffing should be hot at the centre. Fish out the cabbage in its muslin wrapping and allow to drain in a colander for a few minutes. Unwrap the cabbage and present it in all its steaming glory at the table. To serve, slice with a bread knife into thick wedges, and serve with mashed potato and the tomato sauce – spoon a little of the sauce onto each plate and place the sliced cabbage on top. Moisten each slice with a little of the leftover stock too and have Parmesan ready to grate at table.

Pictured overleaf

Roast Chicken Stuffed with Rice, Fresh Figs & Prosciutto

SERVES 4

A recipe adapted from a simpler idea in Jacques Médecin's *Cuisine Niçoise*. I am a bit funny about fruit with meat but I will make an exception for this luxurious summery number. This recipe is uniquely *Provençal*, I suppose, but there's also something very un-European about a chicken stuffed with rice, nuts and fruit. Omit the prosciutto, add a few crushed allspice berries to the buttery onions, and a drizzle of pomegranate molasses towards the end, and you would be well on the way to the Levant rather than the western Mediterranean. Anyway, I digress. This is delicious.

I	NICE FAT CHICKEN, WEIGHING APPROXIMATELY 2KG/4LB 8OZ
	OLIVE OIL
	A PINCH OF CAYENNE PEPPER
200G/ 7OZ/ I CUP	BASMATI RICE
50G/ 1¾ OZ/ 3 TBSP	UNSALTED BUTTER, PLUS A LITTLE EXTRA, SOFTENED, FOR BRUSHING
I	LARGE WHITE ONION, SLICED INTO HALF-MOONS
I	BAY LEAF
I	SPRIG OF THYME OR WINTER SAVORY
4	GARLIC CLOVES, UNPEELED
2 TBSP	PINE KERNELS
	A FIG LEAF, IF YOU HAVE ONE
8	FRESH FIGS (SMALL BLACK *PROVENÇAL* FIGS IF YOU CAN FIND THEM)
4	SLICES OF PROSCIUTTO
2 TBSP	PICKED PARSLEY LEAVES
½	LEMON
	SALT AND FRESHLY GROUND BLACK PEPPER

Take the chicken out of the fridge, place in a roasting tin, rub it with olive oil and the cayenne pepper, then sprinkle with salt all over. Set aside while you prepare the stuffing.

Preheat the oven to 200°C fan/220°C/ 425°F/gas mark 7.

To make the rice pilaf stuffing: carefully wash the rice in three changes of cold water, until the water runs almost clear. Soak the rice for 15 minutes in fresh cold water. Meanwhile, melt the butter in a large, lidded, heavy-bottomed saucepan and slowly cook the sliced onion, herbs and garlic, adding a good pinch of salt. When the onion is soft but without colour, add the pine kernels and cook until lightly golden.

Drain the rice well, being careful not to break the delicate grains. Add the rice to the pot, another pinch of salt, and pour over boiling water to cover by 5mm/¼in.

If you have a fig leaf, lay it over the rice, which will impart a wonderfully fragrant flavour, but it's not essential. Cover with a tight-fitting lid and cook for 2 minutes over a high heat, then turn down to the lowest possible heat and cook for another 4 minutes. Take the pan off the heat but leave the lid on for 10 minutes.

Recipe continues overleaf

Roast Chicken Stuffed with Rice, Fresh Figs & Prosciutto continued

Remove the lid and fig leaf and fluff the rice with a fork. The rice should be not quite cooked. Halve the figs, cut the prosciutto into strips, roughly chop the parsley and mix all into the rice. Stuff the rice mixture into the chicken, pressing with a spoon to fit more in. Leave any excess in the pan to reheat later when the chicken is ready. Squish the half lemon on top of the rice so that the stuffing stays inside.

Transfer the chicken to a tin and roast in the hot oven for about 1 hour 15 minutes in total. After 45 minutes, brush the chicken all over with softened butter. Continue to roast until the skin is golden brown and the juices run clear,

then remove the chicken from the tin and let it rest for 10 minutes. Meanwhile, put the roasting tin on the hob over a low heat and pour in about 200ml/7fl oz/scant 1 cup of water. Scrape the base of the tin and simmer the resulting juices briefly to make a thin gravy – here I suppose the word *jus* is permitted – that can be enriched by whisking in a little cold butter if so desired. Taste for salt (it probably won't need much) and season with black pepper.

Reheat any remaining pilaf gently in the pot. Remove the half lemon, spoon out the rice stuffing, and serve the chicken on top with the juices spooned over.

Courgette Gratin with Parmesan & Cream

For years I have struggled to find the right balance for a gratin of courgettes; caught in two minds between the Italian olive oil/tray-bake style and the heavier French sort of thing. I've read a great recipe for a kind of *Provençal tian* involving grated courgettes and rice, but I wanted something lighter and more Italianate.

Thus this recipe is a meeting of two schools of thought. The courgettes are sliced into coins and layered roughly with olive oil, basil, salt, pepper and Parmesan. A big drizzle of cream helps to bind it all, and the end result is aromatic, homely and delicious. I first made this during a heatwave, so I used basil and went lighter on the cream, but this would be equally delicious and more wintery with tarragon, made creamier and served hotter.

Courgette gratin is delicious on its own, of course, but I like to eat this the most with roast lamb.

SERVES 4–6

1KG/2LB 4OZ	SMALL, FIRM COURGETTES
2	GARLIC CLOVES, SLICED FINELY LENGTHWAYS
	OLIVE OIL
½	BUNCH OF BASIL, LEAVES PICKED
50G/1¾OZ/½ CUP	PARMESAN CHEESE, FINELY GRATED
3½ TBSP	WHITE WINE
100ML/3½FL OZ/ SCANT ½ CUP	DOUBLE CREAM
	A HANDFUL OF FRESH BREADCRUMBS
	SALT AND FRESHLY GROUND BLACK PEPPER

Preheat the oven to 180°C fan/200°C/400°F/gas mark 6.

Slice the courgettes into thin coins with a mandoline or a sharp knife. Toss the slices with the garlic, a good amount of salt and a little olive oil, then jumble a third of them into an oiled gratin dish to form a layer.

Crack over some black pepper, roughly tear over half the basil leaves, and sprinkle over some of the grated Parmesan. Add another third of the courgettes, and repeat the pepper, the rest of the basil and more Parmesan. Make a final layer with the remaining courgettes.

Pour over the wine and the cream, then top with the remaining Parmesan, sprinkle with the breadcrumbs and drizzle with olive oil. Bake in the *hot oven* for 40–45 minutes, until soft within and golden brown on top.

Bouillabaisse

Bouillabaisse is one of the Mediterranean's most revered dishes, and in a sea of fish stews, it somehow stands apart. We find examples all over France and other parts of the Med: Brittany's *cotriade*; Corsica's *aziminu*; *bourride*, another Provençal fish stew, not to be confused with *burrida* from Liguria; *caccuicco* from the Tuscan coast; the Catalan *zarzuela*; or the Basque *ttoro*. All these versions are delicious in their own right, but for many are only mere cousins of *bouillabaisse*, the gold standard, and a dish as food writer Richard Olney puts it of mythical reputation.

If you are in Marseille, France's second city, they will tell you that that is where *bouillabaisse* originated, although US journalist and writer Waverley Root observed more than sixty years ago that 'Marseille is a city of tall stories'. Pots of *bouillabaisse* can be found everywhere along the coast east of Marseille, each locality boasting its own variation, and individual cooks their little variation on the local method: there are as many *bouillabaisses* as there are cooks. One thing everyone can agree on is that *bouillabaisse* was born out of necessity. The fishermen's catch that was too small, too bony, too spiny or too ugly to sit on the slab was boiled up in a pot instead. As Jean-Claude Izzo, a native of Marseille, put it in *Garlic, Mint & Sweet Basil*: 'That was how *bouillabaisse* was born: out of the ugly looking, inedible, unsellable scorpion fish … A poor man's cuisine, yes, but one whose genius still delights us.'

All good recipes agree that a collection of little rockfish is ideal for the base of the soup, but many seek to define further what constitutes a proper one. The Bouillabaisse Charter, created in the 1980s by a group of Marseillais restaurateurs (who might possibly have had a racket going), stipulates that the composition should include at least weever, red mullet, conger eel and scorpion fish, with optional extras including John Dory, monkfish, spiny lobsters and slipper lobsters. The charter goes further: 'One essential fact that remains for the quality of a *Bouillabaisse* is the extreme freshness of fish, the primordial condition of its success.' One fish is mentioned in almost every recipe I've read: the spiny, bony scorpion fish (*rascasse*), but the others, it seems, are all up for debate. Gurnard, sea bass, red mullet, *langouste* (spiny lobster), dentex (me neither), bream, whiting, conger eel, John Dory, little crabs, sea urchins for the rouille … the list goes on.

Bouillabaisse is always served with *rouille*, a rust-coloured sauce spicy with chilli and masses of garlic, either to eat with bites of fish, or to spread on a crouton and dunk into the hot broth. I like to soak bread in the broth and whizz it with anchovies, garlic and fiery cayenne pepper, before adding eggs and mounting the sauce with olive oil. But the best *rouilles* are intense affairs; enriched with poached, mashed monkfish liver or the briny roe of a sea urchin.

As for the other components of *bouillabaisse*, the soup is flavoured with the characteristic ingredients of the region: olive oil, garlic, tomatoes, saffron, orange peel and wild fennel, but arguably the first ingredient here is most important. Olive oil hallmarks the cuisine of Provence, but it also crucial to the technique involved in making the soup. The name *bouillabaisse*, or to use the Provençal, *bolhabaissa*, comes from two words: *bolhir*, meaning 'to boil', and *abaissar*, meaning 'to reduce heat' or 'to simmer'. This should give us a clue as to how to cook the dish – boiling the broth creates an emulsion of the gelatine in the fish heads and the olive oil, thickening the liquid, making it silky and glistening. In his classic work *The Food of France* Root disparages the Parisian habit of thickening the broth with butter – what he calls 'committing treason to the olive oil'. Olive oil is the element that binds the soup together, both in texture and as a conduit for flavour. A good amount of olive oil, suspended and bound in the broth, will carry the flavour of the aromatics and create something powerful: what Provençal food writer Jean-Noël Escudier called 'the magical synthesis'.

Is it this magic that sets *bouillabaisse* apart from the rest? Perhaps. But there's more magic than that which lies in the cauldron. *Bouillabaisse* is more than an emulsion of fat and gelatine, or a clever combination of orange peel, fennel and saffron. It is also a story: of how the humble fisherman created a pot of magic from a net of spiny fish that no one else wanted. The story is an old one. Modern Greek food writers have laid claim to what they say is bouillabaisse's precursor. *Kakavia* is a Greek fisherman's stew of small fish and their heads, tomatoes, celery, potatoes, bay and olive oil, which certainly is a soup in the same spirit, and may be one of the oldest existing recipes in the Mediterranean. The Greeks brought olive oil to Marseille, but the dish we know today is a product of a larger human story. Ultimately it would be foolish to try to attribute a single location as a point of origin, for the technique of boiling fish in seawater with olive oil is as old as the olive tree and the fishing boat.

> *Bouillabaisse and aïoli are mythical dishes. The words, themselves, are magic – musical and salivating as the liquid syllables roll round one's tongue – and, to all the world, they symbolise the exuberance of Provence, its bright colours and white light, its sky as blue as the Mediterranean.*
>
> Richard Olney, *Lulu's Provençal Table*

French chef Raymond Oliver, author of *The French at Table*, attempts to trace the dish's history through the ages: 'To start with, *bouillabaisse* was a fish soup, consisting mostly of *rascasse* with olive oil, garlic, leek, onion, and sea water. Later, in Greco-Roman times, herbs and spices were added; then after Arab supremacy, saffron; and after the discovery of America, tomatoes and potatoes.' He goes on: 'The rules for *bouillabaisse* as we know it were laid down in the sixteenth century, and its new cradle was Marseille. Perhaps indeed, it was invented by the Catalans living there since it was they who brought saffron with them.' Thus a picture emerges of a dish that has been shaped by many influences and formed over thousands of years. *Bouillabaisse* is an emblem of Marseillais, Provençal and, by extension, French cuisine, but the pieces that make up the jigsaw are Phoenician, ancient Greek, Roman, Arab and Catalan.

In *Lulu's Provençal Table* Olney writes, as ever, romantically on the subject. A table set on the long terrace in front of the old house above the vineyard at Domaine Tempier, toasts spread with tapenade, a glass of rosé in everyone's hand, and the scene is set. An antique copper-plated cauldron dragged onto a fire built with fruitwood – 'gleaming inside, blackened on the outside from the smoke of a hundred *bouillabaisse* fires … a caress of wood smoke, a memory of the original fisherman's *bouillabaisse* cooked over a driftwood fire at the seaside'. The family and guests wait, wine in hand, surrounding the fire, as the ritual unfolds before them. For *bouillabaisse* is just this; a ritual, as imbued with romance as Provence is itself, and marinated in the history of the entire Mediterranean.

The restaurateurs of Marseille can keep their charter, or boil it up with fish heads and saffron for all I care. It is my feeling that arguments as to the one true *bouillabaisse* – what fish to include or exclude, whether or not it can be made outside the Bay of Marseille and so on – are moot. *Bouillabaisse* can and will be made wherever a sensitive cook attempts it, whether or not there is a *rascasse* to hand to put in your pot. As to what recipe might be the definitive one, Izzo has this to say: 'these days people argue over the thousand and one ways to prepare *Bouillabaisse*. In order not to upset anyone, I'll only say it's best to prepare it yourself.'

One of the tall stories told by the Marseillais is that *bouillabaisse* was given by Venus to her husband Vulcan to send him to sleep while she consorted with her lover Mars. Rumours persist that saffron is soporific and that *bouillabaisse* is an aphrodisiac. I suppose it depends who you are making it for, but I might venture to say that cooking a pot of *bouillabaisse* is just as much about ritual and mythical romanticism as it is about flavour. *This* is what we cooks must strive to capture, and worry not about where to source fresh weever. So let us build a wood fire on a beach or in a garden, set a young red Bandol to cool in buckets of ice, pound garlic, fish livers and hot peppers into the *rouille*, and marinate the sparkling fish with a spice more expensive than gold. Whether or not our pot is lined with copper, as long as the table is set and the breeze caresses us with the scent of wood smoke and saffron all will be well.

Egg Bouillabaisse (Bouillabaisse Borgne)   SERVES 4

This vegetarian variation on a theme is less well known outside Marseille than its fishy cousin, but while not quite as glamorous, this is simple and very good. If you wish to try your hand at the traditional fish bouillabaisse, you can find the recipe in my first book *Provençal*.

A 'poor man's bouillabaisse' is a delicious vegetable stew with all the flavours of the famous fish version. Make a soup with the usual *Provençal* aromatics – dried orange peel, wild fennel, onion, garlic, tomato and saffron, throw in some potatoes, then stew in some spinach or poach some eggs in the broth.

A spinach bouillabaisse is delicious with garlic-rubbed toast drizzled with an extravagant amount of olive oil. Or, even better, smear the toast thickly with homemade *aïoli*. For a further variation, omit the spinach and concentrate on poaching a perfect egg to nestle in the middle of the soup bowl – *voilà une bouillabaisse borgne* (one-eyed bouillabaisse).

	OLIVE OIL
2	YELLOW ONIONS, DICED
2	CELERY STICKS, DICED
4	GARLIC CLOVES, SMASHED
I	SPRIG OF THYME
I	BAY LEAF
5CM/2IN	LENGTH OF ORANGE PEEL
I TBSP	FENNEL SEEDS
I	SPRIG OF WILD FENNEL FRONDS AND A BIT OF THE STALK (OPTIONAL, BUT IF YOU CAN GET IT, THIS GIVES THE SOUP A FANTASTIC FLAVOUR)
I	DRIED CHILLI
	A NICE PINCH OF SAFFRON
400G/14OZ	CANNED PEELED PLUM TOMATOES
2	MEDIUM POTATOES (NOT TOO FLOURY, SOMETHING THAT WON'T FALL APART IN THE BROTH), SLICED INTO 2CM/¾IN COINS
I	SMALL GLASS OF WHITE WINE

Heat a good amount of olive oil in a large frying pan and fry the onion, celery, garlic, herbs and chilli. Add a big pinch of salt at the start. Cook slowly, stirring occasionally, for a good 20–30 minutes, or until the vegetables have softened and taste sweet. Add the saffron, stir into the veg, then add the tomatoes and squish them well with your spoon or a fork.

Turn up the heat so that the tomato starts to cook into a sauce. Add the sliced potatoes, followed by the white wine and some water to cover (not too much; you can always add more water, but adding too much at the start is a mistake). Bring back to the boil then reduce to a simmer. Cook at a simmer for 30 minutes or so, until the potatoes are cooked. At this point, add a little more water to loosen the sauce if you think it needs it.

Meanwhile, make the *aïoli*, if using. Crush the garlic with some salt to form a fine white paste then combine with the egg yolks in a bowl. Drizzle in the olive oil – drop by drop at first, then in a steady thin stream – to make a wobbly mayonnaise. Season with salt, lemon juice and a little water if you want to thin it without adding more acid. Keep in the fridge if it's a hot day.

When ready to serve, poach the eggs in a separate pan and toast the sourdough. Have the *aïoli* waiting on the table. Check the soup for seasoning, and sprinkle with the chopped parsley.

To eat, there are two approaches: either put a slice of toast in the bottom of wide bowls, top with a poached egg, then pour the rest over (soggy and satisfying) or serve the soup with an egg in it and keep the toast on the side. I usually prefer the second option and attack the dish with a spoon in one hand, and *aïoli*-spread toast in the other. This presents ample opportunities for dunking but also for topping your toast precariously with bits from the soup. Serve extra *aïoli* on the side for those who would like to stir some into their broth.

FOR THE *AÏOLI*:	
2	EGG YOLKS
150ML/ ¾ CUP	OLIVE OIL
2	FAT GARLIC CLOVES
	LEMON JUICE
	SALT

TO SERVE:	
4	EGGS, FOR POACHING
	SLICES OF SOURDOUGH
	CHOPPED PARSLEY

Pictured page 167

Burrida of Cuttlefish & Peas

SERVES 2

Liguria's *burrida* is surely some relation of Provence's *bourride*: in Genoese dialect *burrida* refers to 'pieces' rather than whole fish, which may be one explanation or, more likely, in Occitan the same word means 'boiled'. A *burrida* can be made with any number of fish, but I particularly like this simple cuttlefish stew with peas.

I have seen a few recipes that contain saffron – no doubt delicious here, and more along the lines of a *Provençal* fish stew, but I am more interested in one flavoured intriguingly with pine kernels, anchovies and dried mushrooms – a combination that has its roots on opposite North African shores.

Once upon a time this would have always been served with ship's biscuits, *galette del marinaio*, the Ligurian sailor's hardtack that was a long-time staple. It is just about possible to buy these biscuits through specialist suppliers at your local posh deli, but I think that toast is an acceptable replacement.

500G/ 1LB 2OZ	CUTTLEFISH OR SQUID, CLEANED
4	SLICES OF DRIED CEP (PORCINI)
	OLIVE OIL
1	SMALL TO MEDIUM ONION, DICED
1	CELERY STICK, DICED
4	GARLIC CLOVES, FINELY SLICED
1 TBSP	PINE KERNELS
2	SALTED ANCHOVY FILLETS
2	RIPE TOMATOES, PEELED, CORED AND CHOPPED
1	SMALL GLASS OF WHITE WINE
2	BIG HANDFULS OF PODDED PEAS (FRESH OR FROZEN)
	SALT AND FRESHLY GROUND BLACK PEPPER

TO SERVE:

	SLICED SOURDOUGH
1	GARLIC CLOVE, HALVED
1 TBSP	CHOPPED PARSLEY

Cut the cuttlefish body into thin short strips – approximately 1cm/½in by 3cm/1¼in feels right to me but go with what your heart tells you. Tentacle sections can be quartered depending on size, or else cut them into individual tentacles.

Soak the dried cep in a small amount of boiled water. Gently heat a good glug of olive oil in a large, heavy-bottomed pot and fry the onion, celery and garlic slowly with a pinch of salt, until all is soft and sweet. Add the pine kernels; stir until lightly browned. Drain and chop the dried cep and add to the pot with the anchovies. Cook, stirring, until the anchovies have melted and everything smells amazing. Stir in the cuttlefish and cook over a medium heat for a few minutes, stirring well.

Next, add the tomatoes, the white wine and some salt and pepper to taste. Bring to the boil, then reduce to a simmer and cook for 45 minutes. Top up with a little water if it looks too thick. When the cuttlefish is soft and delicious, chuck in the peas and cook at a simmer for a few minutes. Taste for seasoning.

Toast the sourdough slices, rub lightly with garlic and drizzle with olive oil. Put the slices in the bottom of wide bowls and spoon the *burrida* on top. Sprinkle with finely chopped parsley and drizzle with more olive oil.

Salt Cod Ragoût (L'Estocaficada)

SERVES 2

Jacques Médecin writes in *La Cuisine Niçoise* that *l'estocaficada* is 'a stew that has become the symbol of authentic Niçois gastronomy'. It takes its name from stockfish, the salted and air-dried cod that Médecin reckons is more typically Niçois than any other preserved fish. Stockfish, dried as hard as wood, needs attacking with a saw or hammer, followed by a good week of soaking and a thorough boiling until it is again recognizable as food.

At the risk of offending any staunch Niçois traditionalists, I think that a delicious dish can be made in the same spirit with homemade salted cod – a couple of days immersed in salt, followed by an overnight soak, will produce a tasty, fresher result, albeit with only a little of the famous pungency associated with the real deal. We shall perhaps also omit the stockfish guts that tradition prescribes.

So if not a real *estocaficada*, here we have a *ragoût de morue à la niçoise*. It should be served wet, with plenty of juice for the potatoes to mop up, and with a good drizzle of your best olive oil.

2	150-G/5½-OZ FILLETS OF SALT COD, SOAKED OVERNIGHT (TO MAKE YOUR OWN SALT COD, PACK FILLETS OF FRESH COD IN SALT FOR A MINIMUM OF 2 DAYS AND UP TO 2 WEEKS. WASH WELL AND SOAK OVERNIGHT IN FRESH WATER BEFORE USING)
	OLIVE OIL
1	ONION, DICED
3	FAT GARLIC CLOVES, SLICED
	A BOUQUET GARNI OF PARSLEY, BAY, THYME, WINTER SAVORY, WILD FENNEL AND MARJORAM
1	RED PEPPER, ROUGHLY CHOPPED
1	GREEN PEPPER, ROUGHLY CHOPPED
2	LARGE RIPE TOMATOES, PEELED (SEE PAGE 143) AND DICED
	A SPLASH OF *GRAPPA, MARC DE PROVENCE* OR *EAU-DE-VIE*
4-6	POTATOES, DEPENDING ON SIZE, QUARTERED
	A HANDFUL OF BLACK OLIVES
	SALT AND FRESHLY GROUND BLACK PEPPER
	GOOD OLIVE OIL, TO SERVE

Remember to soak your salt cod overnight. Heat a generous amount of olive oil in a heavy-bottomed pan. Cook the onion and garlic for around 30 minutes, until soft and golden. Add the bouquet garni and the red and green peppers. Stir until beginning to soften, then add the diced tomatoes and a good glug of your chosen alcohol. Season lightly with salt (remember, both the salt cod and olives are salty) then add enough water to cover by 2.5cm/1in, cover with a lid, and cook for 30 minutes.

Slip the pieces of cod, skin side up, the quartered potatoes and the black olives into the stew and season with black pepper. Make sure the potatoes are submerged and cover with a lid. Cook at a simmer for 20–30 minutes, until the potatoes are soft. Remove the lid, peel off the skin from the cod, and stir gently to break up the fillets into flakes. Taste for salt and add a little more water if the sauce is too thick. Spoon into bowls and drizzle your best olive oil over to finish.

Salt Cod in Wine Sauce (Morue en Raïto)

Christmas Eve in Provence is the time of the *Gros Souper* (Great Supper). In accordance with the Catholic faith, no meats or animal fat are eaten and the meal begins with a procession of traditional dishes. There'll be blanched cardoon in white sauce (or with a *bagna cauda*), often *aïoli* with snails and vegetables, and maybe a cabbage or garlic soup, before a table of the famous 'thirteen desserts' – nougats, nuts, fruits and sweetened *fougasse* among them. A mainstay of the *Gros Souper* is this dish of salt cod, first floured and fried in olive oil, then simmered with tomatoes, capers and red wine.

This sauce, a *raïto* or *raïte*, is older than the Catholic faith, brought most probably by the Phoenicians from ancient Greece to the trading post they called Massalia, today the city of Marseille. Some recipes use vinegar (a little harsh for my taste) and in the Var department of Provence people sometimes use *vin cuit*, a sweet wine made by cooking grape juice until sweet and syrupy, before fermenting it in barrels: delicious, and particularly festive, but I prefer this version using red wine; its tannin helps to give body to the sauce and adds a particular savoury richness. A little sweet fortified wine in the mix is a nice optional extra – *Banyuls* is perfect.

250G/9OZ PIECE OF FRESH COD, SKINNED
COARSE SEA SALT
PLAIN FLOUR, FOR FLOURING THE FISH
OLIVE OIL, FOR FRYING

First, salt the cod. Bury the cod in coarse sea salt and leave it to sit in the fridge uncovered for 3 hours. After 3 hours, wash the fish and dry it well. Leave it uncovered in the fridge to dry out further while you make the sauce.

Recipe continues overleaf

Salt Cod in Wine Sauce (Morue en Raïto) continued

FOR THE SAUCE:

4 TBSP	OLIVE OIL
I	MEDIUM YELLOW ONION, FINELY DICED
4	GARLIC CLOVES, FINELY SLICED
	A PINCH OF DRIED OREGANO
	A BOUQUET GARNI, USING AS MANY AS YOU HAVE AVAILABLE OF THE FOLLOWING — THYME, BAY, PARSLEY STALKS, LOVAGE LEAVES, CELERY LEAVES, LEEK TOPS — TIED TIGHTLY WITH STRING
400G/ 14OZ	CANNED PEELED PLUM TOMATOES, RINSED OF THEIR JUICE
I	LARGE GLASS OF RED WINE
	A SPLASH OF *BANYULS* OR OTHER SWEET WINE (OPTIONAL)
I TBSP	SALTED FINE CAPERS, RINSED OF SALT AND SOAKED IN WATER
I TBSP	PITTED BLACK OLIVES
I TBSP	CHOPPED PARSLEY
	SALT AND FRESHLY GROUND BLACK PEPPER

Heat the olive oil in a large pan and slowly fry the onion and garlic with a little pinch of salt. They should be very soft but take on little colour. Add the dried oregano, the bouquet garni, then the tomatoes, squished up with your hands as you add them to the pan. Cook until the tomatoes start to turn to sauce, squishing and smashing them with your spoon, then add the red wine and sweet wine, if using. Bring to the boil then cook at a simmer for at least an hour, until the sauce has thickened and the tomatoes no longer taste raw. Discard the bouquet garni. Season (lightly) with salt and black pepper and add the soaked capers and black olives. Add a little water if the sauce starts to dry out.

Heat some olive oil in a deep-sided frying pan. Flour the fish and fry it until nicely golden brown on each side, then drain on kitchen paper.

If the sauce has thickened too much, add a little water and reheat until just bubbling, then gently lower in the fried fish and poach slowly, without turning, for a few minutes until it is cooked through. Sprinkle with the parsley. Serve the sauce on a big platter with the fish on in the middle on top. Put it in the middle of the table for everyone to attack. Eat with some crusty bread.

Braised Rabbit with Anchovies, Bacon, Button Onions & White Wine

SERVES 4

The combination of bacon and anchovies might seem unnatural at first, but what's not to like? A dusting of Parmesan over the finished dish adds even more umami. This would be good served with boiled, dressed greens, with some cooked lentils or beans laced through it. This recipe feels like one of those points where Italy meets France – anchovies and tomatoes simmered into a sauce is *molto Italiano*, but bacon, wine and button onions is very *coq au vin*. Incidentally, I have seen a recipe like this entitled *lapin à la mentonnaise*, meaning from the town of Menton, which is just on the French side of the border with Italy.

20	BUTTON ONIONS
I	RABBIT, JOINTED, OR 4 RABBIT LEGS
	OLIVE OIL
50G/ 1¾OZ	PANCETTA, DICED
2	BAY LEAVES
10	SALTED ANCHOVY FILLETS
6	SOFT RIPE TOMATOES, PEELED AND ROUGHLY CHOPPED, OR 400G/14OZ CANNED PEELED PLUM TOMATOES, RINSED OF THEIR JUICE
I	LARGE GLASS OF DRY WHITE WINE
	SALT AND FRESHLY GROUND BLACK PEPPER
	PARMESAN CHEESE, GRATED, TO SERVE

To peel the button onions, blanch for 1 minute in boiling water. Cool, then slice off the sprout end and slip off the skins.

Season the rabbit with salt and pepper. Heat some oil in a nice big pot and brown the rabbit all over, then add the diced pancetta, the bay leaves and the peeled onions to the pot, with a drizzle more olive oil if needed. Allow everything to colour slowly in the hot fat.

Add the anchovy fillets to the pot and stir as they melt into the fat, then tip in the tomatoes. Cook until the tomatoes turn into a rough sauce, then add the white wine. Bring to the boil then reduce to a slow simmer. Cook slowly, half-covered with a lid, for around 45 minutes, turning the rabbit occasionally. If the sauce threatens to dry out add a splash of water.

When the meat is soft enough that it falls off the bone, take off the heat. Serve the rabbit in the sauce with a scant grating of Parmesan and a good drizzle of olive oil. Eat with greens and lentils.

Richard Olney's Chicken Pilaf Provençal

The French love *riz au pilaf*. Most often their rice pilafs are simple affairs of onions cooked slowly in butter, long-grain rice and sometimes stock for a fuller-flavoured result, and this basic way with pilafs makes a wonderful accompaniment to meat or fish.

This recipe, adapted from Richard Olney, incorporates more ingredients into the rice pot; leaning more towards the pilafs that you might find in eastern Mediterranean countries. Here is a one-pot dish with all the flavours of southern France and some of the technique from further afield. When the rice is cooked with chicken on the bone, the flavour penetrates deeply into the pilaf.

I usually cook chicken pilaf in the style of the Indian subcontinent, but here the spicing is much more restrained, and the sweet herbs you might encounter in the Levant replaced by Provence's favourite herb: basil. Olney includes saffron flowers – perhaps referring to safflowers – but anyway this is not something I have ever seen in my local corner shop. I suggest using a mixture of whatever edible flowers you can find, be it those from herbs or something a little more flamboyant.

4	HANDFULS OF BASMATI RICE (APPROX. 300G/10½OZ/1½ CUPS)
	OLIVE OIL
4	CHICKEN LEGS, HALVED INTO THIGHS AND DRUMSTICKS
3	MEDIUM YELLOW OR WHITE ONIONS, SLICED INTO HALF-MOONS
2	BAY LEAVES
100G/ 3½OZ/ ½ CUP	UNSALTED BUTTER
2	COURGETTES, CUT INTO COINS 1.5CM/⅝IN THICK
8	GARLIC CLOVES, UNPEELED
	A LARGE SPRIG OF FRESH OREGANO OR MARJORAM
	A SMALL PINCH OF CAYENNE PEPPER
500ML/ 18FL OZ/ 2 CUPS	GOOD (LIGHT) CHICKEN STOCK OR WATER
	A NICE PINCH OF SAFFRON
4	RIPE TOMATOES, PEELED AND QUARTERED
1	SMALL RED PEPPER, GRILLED UNTIL BLACKENED, COOLED, SKINNED, TORN INTO STRIPS
	A SCATTERING OF PITTED BLACK OLIVES
½	BUNCH OF BASIL, LEAVES PICKED
	HERB FLOWERS, OR OTHER EDIBLE FLOWERS, FOR FLAVOUR BUT ALSO FOR EFFECT
	SALT, FRESHLY GROUND BLACK PEPPER AND SUGAR

First, wash and soak the rice. Wash the rice three times in cold water, stirring gently with your fingers, until the water runs almost clear. Take care not to bash the delicate rice about too much as it will break the grains. Cover with fresh cold water and leave to soak for 30 minutes.

Season the chicken with salt and pepper. Heat a little oil in a large, heavy-bottomed pot with a lid and slowly fry the chicken, skin side down first, until golden brown all over. Remove to a plate (leave the chicken fat in the pot), add the sliced onion, bay leaves and 30g/1oz/2 tablespoons of the butter. Fry the onions slowly, adding a pinch of salt to help soften, until they are properly soft, sweet and only lightly golden. Transfer the onions to the plate with the chicken. Add a further knob of butter if the pot looks a bit dry and put in the courgettes and garlic. Fry gently, until the courgettes are lightly coloured and just beginning to soften, but don't overcook or they will collapse to a mush later. Season lightly with salt, throw in the sprig of oregano or marjoram and add the cayenne.

Drain the rice well and put into the pot with a nice pinch of salt. Stir gently with a wooden spoon to coat the rice with butter but take care not to break the grains. Return the chicken and onions to the pot, stir once or twice, then increase the heat, and pour over the hot chicken stock or water to cover by 1cm/½in. Cover with a tight-fitting lid. Without removing the lid – no peeking! – cook the rice on high for 3 minutes, then reduce the heat to very low and continue to cook for another 7 minutes. Turn off the heat but leave the lid on.

While the rice is cooking, heat the remaining butter in a frying pan. Add the saffron, stir over a low heat for 30 seconds, then add the tomatoes, roasted pepper and olives. Stew for a few minutes, until softened but not yet disintegrated into a sauce, then season with salt, pepper and perhaps a little pinch of sugar. After the rice has cooked for 10 minutes, turn off the heat, lift off the lid, and without disturbing the rice, pour in the stewed vegetables with their saffron juices, before quickly replacing the lid.

Let the covered rice pot stand for a further 10–15 minutes, then transfer it to the table. Fluff the rice, half-mixing the saffronned tomatoes, peppers and olives through the rice as you do so. Spoon the pilaf onto waiting plates, tear the basil leaves and the flowers over the top and tuck in.

Lamb Shoulder with Artichokes, Broad Beans & Ham

Something to celebrate the springtime when the first artichokes and broad beans pop up at the market (even if before you get to the butcher's shop it starts to rain and doesn't let up all weekend). With many of the flavours of a Roman *vignole* – spring vegetable stew – this dish is cooked together with the lamb and a good amount of tasty sauce. The ham to use is a nice one from Bayonne or Parma, here shredded thinly and mixed through the vegetables just before serving.

Preheat the oven to 200°C fan/220°C/425°F/gas mark 7.

Season the lamb with salt and black pepper. Set it in a small roasting tin (just big enough to accommodate the lamb) on the hob, pour in a little olive oil and slowly brown the lamb on all sides. Throw in the onions, garlic and thyme, and nestle underneath the lamb. Pour in the wine and enough water to come half-way up the lamb. Cover the tin with foil and crimp the edges to form a seal.

Roast the lamb in the *hot oven* for 30 minutes then turn the temperature down to 150°C fan/170°C/340°F/gas mark 3½ and cook for 2 hours.

Meanwhile, prepare the artichokes: remove the tough outer leaves, trim the stalk of dark green bits, cut in half and remove the choke. Keep in a bowl of lemon water until ready to use. Pod the broad beans.

After 2 hours, remove the foil and poke the lamb – the meat should be approaching softness and can be coaxed off the bone. Add more water if the roasting tin is drying out, skim off a little of the fat, then throw in the artichokes and beans. Re-cover the tin with foil and cook for a further 20 minutes.

I	LAMB SHOULDER, ABOUT 1.5KG/3LB 5OZ
	OLIVE OIL
2	WHITE ONIONS, SLICED INTO HALF-MOONS
6	GARLIC CLOVES, UNPEELED
I	SPRIG OF THYME
I	LARGE GLASS OF WHITE WINE
8	SMALL GLOBE ARTICHOKES, OR 4 BIG ONES
I	JUICE OF LEMON (TO ACIDULATE THE WATER FOR THE ARTICHOKES)
2KG/ 4LB 8OZ	BROAD BEANS IN THEIR PODS (YIELDS ABOUT 600G/1LB 7OZ SHELLED BEANS)
I	SLICE OF PROSCIUTTO HAM, SHREDDED THINLY
I TBSP	CHOPPED MINT LEAVES
	SALT AND FRESHLY GROUND BLACK PEPPER

When the lamb is spoon-tender and the artichokes and beans are cooked, it is ready. Squish the garlics from their skins into the sauce, add the shredded ham to the vegetables and mix through. Serve the lamb on a big dish and spoon the vegetables and cooking juices over the top. Scatter with chopped mint and drizzle over some olive oil. Some tiny new potatoes boiled in their skins would go well with this if you fancy a bit more bulk.

Chapter Four

The Alps

The Alps

The mountains of eastern France form a natural border: a barrier to travel, trade and the march of armies. It is no coincidence that the frontiers of France, Switzerland and Italy meet at the highest peaks in Western Europe. As the height of the mountains rises and the passes become more inaccessible, the food becomes less nuanced and more direct. Mountain cookery is first and foremost about fuel. Monotonous, perhaps, but honest, simple and extremely tasty. Up here the larder is restricted, for the soils are thin and sparse, but the pasture is excellent, the potatoes are good and the cheeses delicious. In a region where access is difficult the need to make cheese becomes greater – easier to transport than milk, and a perfect way to preserve protein through the cold winters.

Although the shopping basket is limited, the French Alps are home to some delicious dishes; far more than fondue or *tartiflette*, but why not? Cooks here have learnt to work with what they have: lake trout and char, crayfish, feathered game in season, wild mushrooms, potatoes, cabbages, chestnuts, smoked salted pork and sausages, rich cream and some of the world's best cheeses. The people of the mountains, isolated in their high valleys, have created their culinary traditions with little outside influence; perhaps a traveller or trader from over the pass brings an ingredient, a different tradition, or word of a recipe or two, but otherwise these folk quietly get on with tending their herds, making their cheeses and cooking the hearty food they love. I find it fascinating that the traditions on both sides of the French–Italian border have evolved in parallel – pasta made with buckwheat or chestnut flours, soups of wild mushrooms, smoked pork or wild greens, gratins of turnips, potatoes or pumpkin, thick baked soups with cabbages, bread and beef stock, and hearty stews of furred or feathered game flavoured with red wine or the local liqueur: Chartreuse.

The recipes in this section are for the most part uncomplicated, not because the food of the French Alps is always basic, but there is plenty to enjoy in cooking something humble, old, quiet and good, whether or not you are in a wood hut up a mountain.

Baked Eggs Florentine

Florentine means from Florence and for the French cook, that denotes spinach in a recipe. It is said that when the young Catherine de' Medici, a native of Florence, crossed the Alps to marry Henri II of France, among her retinue were Italian chefs who introduced both spinach and the white sauce they called *besciamella* to the French court from where its fame spread. Whether or not Catherine can take the credit, this simple dish is a lovely reminder of how useful and delicious *béchamel* is.

Soft-boil the eggs in a saucepan of simmering water for about 4–5 minutes, then cool in cold running water. Peel and set aside.

4	EGGS
2	BUNCHES OF SPINACH
	A GOOD HANDFUL OF GRATED GRUYÈRE CHEESE
	A NUGGET OF PARMESAN CHEESE, GRATED

FOR THE *BÉCHAMEL*:

30G/ 1 OZ/ 2 TBSP	UNSALTED BUTTER, PLUS AN EXTRA KNOB
2 TBSP	FLOUR
225ML/ 8FL OZ/ 1 CUP	MILK
	SALT, FRESHLY GROUND BLACK PEPPER AND NUTMEG

Meanwhile, make the *béchamel*: melt the butter in another pan, whisk in the flour and cook for a few minutes over a low heat, whisking all the while. Gradually add the milk, whisking vigorously to eliminate lumps. Cook the sauce for 10 minutes at a low simmer. Season with salt and a touch of nutmeg, then set aside. The sauce should not be too thick; it must drape over and coat the eggs when spooned on top. Loosen with a splash more milk if necessary.

Heat a large, lidded pan. Wash the spinach and put it, still wet, into the hot pan. Cover with the lid and cook over a medium heat for a minute. Drain the spinach, squeeze it well, chop through once or twice (if using large-leaf spinach), then return it to the pan with a good knob of butter. Sauté briefly, turning around in the butter, then season with salt, pepper and nutmeg. It should be moist but not too wet. Keep hot while you preheat the grill.

Spread the cooked spinach in the base of a small buttered gratin dish. Make four little hollows and nestle the eggs in them. Cover them (and some of the spinach) with Gruyère cheese and drape a good spoonful of *béchamel* over each egg, so that they are fully covered. Grate the Parmesan cheese over everything and put the dish under a medium grill for around 3 minutes, until the sauce is spotted dark golden brown and bubbling.

Eat straight away, seasoning the eggs with salt as you go.

Baked Eggs with Rice & Gruyère
(Oeufs à la Monteynard)

SERVES 2

Here's a comforting mountain dish if ever there was one. The recipe comes from the Isère and I first saw it in *French Country Cooking* by Elizabeth David. It's a gratin of rice and soft-boiled eggs (runny yolks please!) with Gruyère.

This is a good way to use up leftovers – a little diced roast beef nestled under the egg, moistened with some of its gravy, would fit the bill nicely, and chicken is excellent too – but the dish is also delicious plain.

2	EGGS
150G/ 5½OZ/ ¾ CUP	RISOTTO RICE
500ML/ 18FL OZ/ 2 CUPS	MILK
500ML/ 18FL OZ/ 2 CUPS	LIGHT CHICKEN STOCK OR USE WATER
	A HANDFUL OF LEFTOVER ROAST OR BOILED MEAT, CHOPPED
ABOUT 100ML/ 3½FL OZ/ SCANT ½ CUP	LEFTOVER GRAVY FROM THE ROAST, OR REDUCED BROTH FROM THE STEW
30G/1OZ /2 TBSP	UNSALTED BUTTER
100G/ 3½OZ/ GENEROUS 1 CUP	GRATED GRUYÈRE CHEESE
	SALT AND FRESHLY GROUND BLACK PEPPER
	CHOPPED CHIVES, TO SERVE (OPTIONAL)

Preheat the oven to 180°C fan/200°C/400°F/ gas mark 6.

Soft-boil the eggs in a small pan of simmering water for about 4–5 minutes, then cool in cold running water. Peel and set aside.

Wash the rice once in cold water. Bring the milk and stock to the boil in a large saucepan, drop in the rice and a good pinch of salt and simmer for around 15–20 minutes, or until the rice is cooked. Leave the rice quite soupy – add more milk or water if it has dried too much because it will firm up quickly once baked. Adjust the seasoning, then pour the hot rice into a gratin dish that will have the rice sit at a depth of about 2.5cm/1in. Allow to settle for a moment, then make four little hollows in the rice with the back of a spoon.

Fill the hollows with the meat and the gravy. Carefully halve the soft-boiled eggs and nestle them on top, yolk facing upwards. Dot the rice with slivers of butter and sprinkle the grated Gruyère cheese all over the dish – add a double layer of cheese to each egg half to protect the runny yolk.

Bake the gratin in the hot oven for a few minutes until the cheese is golden and bubbling but try not to cook for too long; see that the egg yolk stays soft. Sprinkle with chives if you have some, crack over plenty of black pepper, and dig in.

Trout in the Chambéry Style

Chambéry is home to the Dolin distillery, a company credited with the invention of the pale French version of the famous red vermouth from Turin. Its inventor, a Monsieur Joseph Chevasse, was no doubt inspired by the monks making their infusions in the nearby Grande Chartreuse monastery. His vermouth, from 1821, is a fortified wine made with Alpine roots, flowers and herbs. Excellent in a cocktail, of course, but cooking with vermouth is a joy; infused with complex, herbal flavour, it has a slight sweetness that can really make things pop. This is a lovely recipe for trout: the fish is doused in vermouth, then baked in the oven with soft herbs and cream.

3	GRAPE-SIZED KNOBS OF UNSALTED BUTTER
2	GOOD-SIZED TROUT FILLETS, PINBONED
½	SHALLOT, FINELY DICED
I	MIXED HANDFUL OF TARRAGON, CHERVIL AND SORREL, CHOPPED
100ML/ 3½FL OZ/ SCANT ½ CUP	CHAMBÉRY DRY VERMOUTH (DOLIN IS THE BRAND TO LOOK FOR)
50ML/ 2FL OZ/ SCANT ¼ CUP	DOUBLE CREAM
	SALT

Preheat the oven to 200°C fan/220°C/425°F/ gas mark 7.

Grease a baking dish well with one of the knobs of butter – choose a dish that will accommodate the fish snugly. Season the trout with salt on both sides. Mix the diced shallot with the chopped herbs and arrange in two piles on the dish. Put the trout on top and pour in the vermouth. Top the trout with the other knob of butter. Bake in the hot oven for 5 minutes, then pour in the cream. Continue to cook for another few minutes, until the fish is almost cooked. Remove from the oven, allow to rest for a few minutes to finish cooking gently and take the trout to the table in the dish. The skin can be removed before serving if preferred. This needs a salad of soft leaves and plenty of crusty bread.

Tartiflette

Along with *raclette* and fondue, *tartiflette* is one of Savoie's most famous dishes, a gratin of potatoes, onions, bacon and the local Reblochon cheese. Its origins are a little confused. The name undoubtedly derives from the local patois for potato, *tartiflâ*, and *tartiflette* was first mentioned in a 1705 book written by the chef François Massialot, *Le Cuisinier Royal et Bourgeois*: there a recipe more similar to the local *péla*, a simpler dish of potatoes, bacon and onions, named after the spade-like long-handled pan in which it was cooked.

The modern recipe was developed as a marketing strategy by cheese producers looking to sell more of their Reblochon and this is the version that the ski resorts have made famous. Bravo lads! There's no arguing that it's delicious. This version follows fairly closely the 'official' recipe of the Syndicat Interprofessionnel du Reblochon.

750G/ 1LB 10OZ	POTATOES — A RED VARIETY, BETWEEN WAXY AND FLOURY, IS BEST
150G/ 5½OZ	LARDONS, SMOKED FOR PREFERENCE
2	KNOBS OF UNSALTED BUTTER
1	ONION, FINELY SLICED
1	GLASS OF WHITE WINE
ABOUT 3 TBSP	CRÈME FRAÎCHE (OR 6 TBSP IF YOU HAVE NO DOUBLE CREAM)
ABOUT 3 TBSP	DOUBLE CREAM (OR 6 TBSP IF YOU HAVE NO CRÈME FRAÎCHE)
	OLIVE OIL
	A HALF-WHEEL (APPROX. 250G/9OZ) OF REBLOCHON CHEESE
	SALT

Preheat the oven to 180°C fan/200°C/400°F/ gas mark 6.

Peel then cut the potatoes into 1.5-cm/ ⅝-in pieces. Simmer them in a saucepan of lightly salted water until just cooked, then drain and allow to steam.

Meanwhile, fry the lardons in a roomy frying pan. When the fat is rendered, add a knob of butter and the onion slices with a little pinch of salt. Fry slowly until soft and golden brown. Add the white wine, simmer for a minute until reduced to 2 tablespoons, add the cream(s) and a good 2 tablespoons of water. Mix well, then pour this tasty mixture into a bowl and rinse and dry the pan.

When the potatoes have steamed dry they can be fried. Reheat the clean pan, add a little oil and the remaining knob of butter and sauté the potatoes over a medium-high heat. They should brown and crisp up nicely without being crunchy all the way though. Once browned, transfer the potatoes to a gratin dish big enough to fit all the potatoes without them spilling out the top. Pour over the onion/bacon mixture and mix a bit. Slice the cheese with the rind on and lay over the top of the gratin.

Bake in the oven for 15–20 minutes, until the cheese has browned and melted fully. Eat hot, with a green salad and wine to wash it down.

Matefaim

Thick fluff pancakes from the mountains of Savoie. *Matefaim* or *matafan*, means literally 'kill-hunger'. These are made in different ways, and can be either savoury or sweet, but always with what are winter staples in the mountains: flour, eggs, butter and sometimes potatoes. Bacon (or at least bacon fat) is a common addition. They are usually served for dinner with a green salad, but I must say the version here reminded me of potato farls, so feel free to eat them for breakfast with bacon and eggs.

The warm water helps to keep them fluffy and the whisked egg white helps the batter to soufflé slightly. The recipe is for individual pancakes, but it's also quite fun to make one enormous one and bake it for a bit in the oven.

100G/ 3½OZ	FLOURY POTATO(ES), UNPEELED
60G/ 2¼OZ/ GENEROUS ½ CUP	FLOUR
120ML/ 4FL OZ/ ½ CUP	WARM WATER
2	EGGS, SEPARATED
1 TBSP	MELTED UNSALTED BUTTER OR BACON FAT, PLUS EXTRA FOR FRYING
	SALT

Boil the potato(es) in a pan of salted water. Drain and allow to cool, then peel and mash; don't worry if there are a few little lumps. Mix the flour with the potato, then whisk in the warm water and melted butter, followed by the egg yolks and a pinch of salt.

Whisk the egg whites to stiff peaks and fold into the batter. Melt a knob of butter or some bacon fat in a hot frying pan and cook the *matefaims* like pancakes. If desired, keep warm in a low oven while you prepare the others. This can sometimes result in slightly crispy edges to the pancakes, which is no bad thing. What really helps to keep the pancakes fluffy is to pop them onto a cooling rack rather than a plate, because the trapped steam will soften and deflate them somewhat.

As a variation, sprinkle some chopped ham and grated mountain cheese into the batter before frying, which is especially nice with a simple green salad for lunch. Or serve the *matefaims* with bacon and fried eggs for breakfast or, for extra points, sandwich your breakfast items inside two pancakes and eat it like a sandwich. This last one is perhaps not advisable for health reasons if you don't live and work in the high mountains.

Italian Influence and the de' Medici Myth

In *The Oxford Companion to Food* Alan Davidson begins his chapter on 'Culinary Mythology' with one of the biggest myths of all in French food: that the young queen-to-be Catherine de' Medici and her retinue transformed French cookery from something primitive and medieval into something much more sophisticated in the Italian fashion.

Catherine was born in 1519 into the powerful de' Medici dynasty that ruled Florence. By the age of fourteen she was orphaned and her marriage to the then Prince Henri of France was arranged by her uncle, Pope Clement VII, who was keen to form alliances that would quell the expansionist ambitions of the French in Italy. It seems obvious that a teenaged orphan could not have exerted any influence on culinary habits at the French court, and the reality is that there was no noticeable change during the mid-sixteenth century. Modern-day researchers generally agree that French cooking of this period was little changed from that of the Middle Ages.

The story of Catherine de' Medici is clearly apocryphal; a way of understanding an undeniable Italian influence over the centuries that is difficult to prove or even to define. It is certain that ideas filtered over the Alps to France, and vice versa. Davidson writes: 'Whatever view one takes of the contribution of Catherine de' Medici to the development of cookery in France, it is indisputable that Italy was leading the way during the Renaissance. By the end of the 16th century, however, the genius displayed by Italian artists working in many fields, including the kitchen, showed signs of fatigue, even exhaustion. As Anna del Conte (1987) observes, it was around then that "the leadership of European gastronomy moved over the Alps to France".'

M. F. K. Fisher's imagining of the story makes no claims to be authentic. In one chapter in her book *Serve It Forth*, entitled 'Catherine's Lonesome Cooks', Fisher muses on how Catherine's skilled cooks found their new life in France: 'Paris seemed harsh and boorish to the lonesome Florentines … Catherine's cooks shuddered, and conferred together in low voices. It was not long before they acted. Their innovation burst like a bomb all over the noble tables of Paris … Roughened tongues were made smooth, and hot throats cooled; palates, long calloused by the indiscriminate spicings of the dark centuries, slowly grew keen and sensitive.'

The truth of the matter is that Italian innovation had already made its influence felt on French cuisine. In fact the publication and widespread diffusion of a book by Italian writer Platina, *De Honesta Voluptate et Valetudine* (On Honest Indulgence and

> *It is indisputable that Italy was leading the way during the Renaissance. By the end of the 16th century, however, the genius displayed by Italian artists working in many fields, including the kitchen, showed signs of fatigue, even exhaustion.*

Good Health), in 1474 had started the trend decades earlier. Platina's work is widely accepted as the first cookbook ever printed, and it was translated into French in 1505, under the title *Platine en François*. No single event or a sudden awakening brought Italian influence to bear on French cuisine, rather a subtle dissemination; a slow creep.

If we are to look for evidence of the changing nature of French cuisine, cookbooks are an excellent resource. Taillevent's *Le Viandier* (*c.* 1300), was the defining work of the Middle Ages, featuring rich and spicy dishes, typically roasted or boiled, but we must wait until 1651 for the publication of *Le Cuisinier François* by the chef François Pierre Sieur de La Varenne. His book was published at a time when France was the dominant power in Europe, and Paris one of Europe's most influential capitals. The famously gourmand Louis XIV, the 'Sun King', was on the throne and French cuisine entered a new era, one that would cement its reputation as one of the most refined in the world.

> *It is fun to imagine that a contingent of Italians crossing the Alps changed the course of French cuisine, but equally captivating to realize that the influences also ran the other way.*

La Varenne's work documented the changing fashions in the French kitchen, a move away from sugar and rich spices that had hallmarked medieval cuisine, with a new focus on regional ingredients, seasonal produce and 'a great deal of butter', tenets that still seem familiar to us centuries later. Vegetables, which had previously been considered an afterthought, sometimes took centre stage: spinach fritters, artichoke hearts with butter sauce, asparagus with cream and herbs, and vegetable soups by the dozen. La Varenne introduces the concepts of *bouillon*, *jus* and *liaisons* (emulsifiers), and outlines such techniques as *potages* and *ragoûts* which have been central to French cuisine for hundreds of years since. Complicated as some of the recipes might seem at first glance, this cooking has at its heart a simple approach, and champions the idea that the cook should let good ingredients speak for themselves.

Many of the recipes in *Le Cuisinier François* were adapted by Carême and Escoffier, two chefs who greatly influenced the direction of French cuisine during the nineteenth century. Varenne's 'Trout with short broth' is trout poached in court *bouillon* – what became Escoffier's *truite au bleu*. And a 'pottage of young pigeons' is remarkably similar to Escoffier's *pigeonneaux aux petits pois*: pigeons braised in a pot with bacon, fresh peas, button onions and stock, finished with butter – a dish that I would be more than happy to put on a menu today.

It is fun to imagine that a contingent of Italians crossing the Alps changed the course of French cuisine, but equally captivating to realize that the influences also ran the other way. In the late seventeenth and early eighteenth centuries, with Piedmont under France's control and its cuisine firing on all cylinders, the Italians were on the receiving end of a body of French wisdom. The two countries shared an Italianate Renaissance history, yet 200 years later the barometer had swung the other way, and French cooks were the toast of the courts of Europe. The cooks of the Neapolitan court in the eighteenth century were French; and in Sicily it became the fashion in the *palazzos* of the wealthiest families to serve ostentatious French cuisine. Cooks, either of French or French-trained Piedmontese origin, were given the title *monsù*, from the French *monsieur*. The *monsù* created their own French-inflected cuisine with the ingredients at hand, adapted to the tastes of the Italian court, resulting in a sort of fusion cuisine: the French *ragoût* became *ragù*; *gâteau* became the Neapolitan *gattó*; and the famous *sartù*, a timbale of rice filled with a rich *ragù*, chicken livers, peas, mozzarella, boiled eggs, cheese, ham and the rest, took its name from the French *surtout* for the mould it was baked in.

Pellegrino Artusi's *La scienza in cucina e l'arte de mangiar bene* (Science in the Kitchen and the Art of Eating Well), first published in 1891 not long after the unification of Italy, can perhaps be regarded as the Italian equivalent of Escoffier's *Guide Culinaire* (1903). Artusi's book was a statement of pride in Italian cookery, one that helped to define what was then a nascent national cuisine.

From the introduction by Luigi Ballerini in the English edition of Artusi's classic, we learn that it was published at a time 'of transition, listlessness, and decadence in Italian cuisine, which was on one hand regional, and on the other entirely French'. Victor Emmanuel II, first king of a united Italy and a lover of French food, took up residence in Florence as it became the country's temporary capital. As Artusi wrote his book it seemed to him that something had to be done to resist the dominance of the French, to champion Italy's own cuisine, and to present it in a way that would be understandable to his bourgeois readership.

The introduction continues: 'Artusi's pages, written in Florence during those years … showed not only that French and Italian culinary traditions ought to be viewed as parallel experiences, but that the common Renaissance denominator they share, thanks to Catherine de' Medici, patron saint of both Italian and French cuisine, was perhaps more "common" on the southern side of the Alps than in the land of the Sun King.' Ballerini goes on to make the claim that de' Medici introduced several celebrated dishes to France that later made their way back to Florence: '*crespelle*, a quintessential Tuscan dish, returned as *crêpes suzette*; *colletta*, which dates back to the times of Ancient Rome, came back as *béchamel*.' I find this claim a most intriguing one; that dishes that perhaps made their way over the Alps – not necessarily with Catherine de' Medici or her entourage, but more probably over several hundred years of cultural exchange – reappeared at their plausible origin, reimagined, and just maybe (whisper it, in Italian) improved upon.

I can understand Artusi's frustration at the supremacy of French terms for basic culinary techniques ('Prepare, as the French say, a *roux*, or as I would say, a paste …'), or indeed the supremacy of the French in general – of *salsa alla maître d'hôtel* he writes: 'What a pompous title for a trifling little thing! Yet here, as in other matters, the French have claimed the right to lay down the law. Their dictates have prevailed and we must conform. This is a sauce that goes well with steak …' How frustrating for Artusi that French food is so delicious!

What is interesting to me is that this great work on Italian cuisine at the turn of the twentieth century is peppered throughout with recipes that read as French. Artusi's recipe for pigeon with peas – *piccioni coi piselle* – is (almost) identical to Escoffier's *pigeonnaux aux petits pois*, and there are recipes for *vol-au-vents* with sweetbreads, *béchamel* and truffles, or *animelle all bottiglia*, for sweetbreads, floured, browned in butter, moistened with Madeira and enriched with meat stock and butter. The *sformato della Signora Adele* is a cheese soufflé by another name (Gruyère, no less), and two of the frittatas are *folded* like a French omelette. Steady on!

Of *balsamella* (*béchamel* sauce), Artusi writes: 'this is the same sauce as the French *béchamel*, except that theirs is more complicated.' A sly dig there, of course, but of *sauce ravigote* he writes that it is a recipe that 'deserves to become part of Italian cuisine because it goes well with poached fish, poached eggs, and so forth'. Indeed Artusi, always gracious, includes more than a handful of French recipes that he deems worthy of inclusion: kidneys Parisian style (skewered and grilled, with anchovy butter), two recipes for peas *alla Francese*, *macaroni alla Francese*, and the aforementioned *salsa alla maître d'hôtel*.

Funny as it is to see Artusi railing against the horrid French, he begrudgingly accepts that they might well be good at cooking. Artusi's recipes are a marvel and connect remarkably well with the household cook despite the inclusion of recipes of advanced technique. This is a book that has been in print since its publication more than 130 years ago, not least because it engages with the reader in a practical way that previous cookbooks simply did not. Artusi writes with humour and flair, and crucially his instructions are clear and uncondescending. This was a work that helped launch Italian cookery into the twentieth century and introduced a new repertoire to the home cook; a repertoire peppered with references to French food. Here we can see the birth of modern Italian food: a ship launched with a bottle of champagne as celebration.

The cuisines of Italy and France have been intertwined so often that they have never really run just in parallel as over time each country has accepted the influence of the other. Nowadays we see the two cuisines as distinct, but in reality they have never been far apart: two neighbouring countries with inseparable stories and undeniable sway on each other. French cuisine lives on in Italy just as Italian cuisine lives on in France, even though many on each side of the borderlands would be hesitant to admit it.

Tagliatelle with Walnuts & Lovage (Taillerins)

SERVES 2

This recipe is adapted from *Madeleine Kamman's Savoie: The Land, People, and Food of the French Alps*. Her version calls for the Swiss seasoning known as Maggi ('a modern use of old ideas'), but I think the flavours here are interesting enough without. In Kamman's recipe the tagliatelle – *taillerins* in Savoyard dialect – are infused with powdered celery seeds and Maggi powder, and tossed in a sauce of butter, garlic, walnuts, lovage and cream. Celery leaf can be substituted for lovage if you wish, but it is something that I often see in good greengrocers, so if you spot some, consider this recipe.

2	PORTIONS FRESH OR DRIED TAGLIATELLE
50G/ 1¾OZ/ 3 TBSP	UNSALTED BUTTER
2	GARLIC CLOVES, FINELY SLICED
50G/ 1¾OZ/ ½ CUP	WALNUTS, COARSELY CHOPPED
½	BUNCH LOVAGE, COARSELY CHOPPED
4 TBSP	DOUBLE CREAM
I TBSP	CRÈME FRAÎCHE
	SALT AND FRESHLY GROUND BLACK PEPPER
	GRATED GRUYÈRE , BEAUFORT OR FONTINA CHEESE, TO SERVE

Boil the pasta in a pan of salted water until *al dente*. Meanwhile, melt the butter in a saucepan and slowly fry the garlic until it sticks together but has no colour. Add the walnuts and continue to fry for a minute or two, then add the lovage. Stir, and swiftly follow with the cream and crème fraîche. Toss the drained cooked pasta in the sauce, moistening it with a little of the cooking water. Serve immediately, topped with grated cheese and a grinding of black pepper.

Macaroni au Pilaf

This recipe is a slight hybrid. It reminds me very much of the classic *macaroni au jus* that is served as an accompaniment to stews – little macaroni pasta moistened with some of the *jus* from the *daube* or gravy from the roasting tin, with a little butter stirred through: delicious.

Here the idea is the same but the cooking method is a little different. Cooking pasta like a risotto produces a wonderfully starchy result and the French love of cooking *au pilaf* imparts an excellent flavour.

30G/1OZ/ 2 TBSP	UNSALTED BUTTER
I	ONION, FINELY DICED
I	SPRIG OF THYME
4	SLICES OF DRIED CEP (PORCINI), SOAKED IN HOT WATER
250G/ 9OZ	SMALL MACARONI — FOR ME, THE STRAIGHT TUBULAR KIND WORKS BEST (TUBETTI OR DITALINI), BUT ALSO GOOD WITH ORZO OR LITTLE ELBOW MACARONI
I LITRE/ I ¾ PINTS/ 4 CUPS	HOT CHICKEN OR BEEF STOCK
IOOG/ 3½ OZ/ GENEROUS I CUP	COARSELY GRATED BEAUFORT, COMTÉ OR GRUYÈRE CHEESE
2 TBSP	FINELY GRATED PARMESAN CHEESE
	SALT AND A GOOD AMOUNT OF FRESHLY GROUND BLACK PEPPER

Melt the butter in a large, lidded saucepan and fry the onion and thyme with a good pinch of salt until soft. Add the soaked and drained porcini and the pasta and stir until well coated in the fat. Pour in a ladleful of the hot stock and stir as it absorbed then pour in another and repeat. Do this once more, then add the rest of the stock, taste for salt and cover with a tight lid. Cook over a low heat for 10 minutes, occasionally lifting the lid to stir the bottom so the pasta doesn't stick. The pasta should be just cooked and stay slightly soupy. Sprinkle in the grated cheeses, crack in some black pepper, stir and transfer to a serving dish.

Chestnut Gnocchi & Porcini Sauce

This recipe is ostensibly northern Italian but the flavours here are found wherever there are chestnut trees and wild mushrooms – Liguria, the High Alps and in Corsica where both the pasta recipes and the chestnut trees are remnants of five centuries of Genoese rule of the island (not to say that this recipe is traditionally Corsican!).

Here, the earthy sweetness of the chestnut flour is delicious in a rich sauce of fresh porcini and cream. In the absence of fresh porcini (admittedly not a regular find at my local supermarket), use other wild mushrooms, or chestnut mushrooms with a bit of soaked dried porcini fried in the mix.

Scrub the potatoes but don't peel them. Bring slowly to the boil in a pan of salted water and cook until tender. Drain and leave the potatoes to dry until cool enough to handle. Peel them, allow to dry for a few further minutes, then pass through a potato ricer or food mill.

500G/ 1LB 2OZ	OLD, FLOURY POTATOES (KING EDWARDS OR MARIS PIPER WORK WELL)
150G/ 5½OZ/ GENEROUS 1 CUP	CHESTNUT FLOUR
75G/ 2¾OZ/ ½ CUP	PLAIN FLOUR, PLUS EXTRA FOR DUSTING
1	EGG YOLK

FOR THE PORCINI SAUCE:

50G/ 1¾ OZ/ 3 TBSP	UNSALTED BUTTER
250G/ 9OZ	FRESH PORCINI OR OTHER WILD MUSHROOMS, CLEANED AND THINLY SLICED
1	GARLIC CLOVE, CRUSHED SLIGHTLY WITH THE FLAT OF A KNIFE
1	SPRIG OF THYME
100ML/ 3½FL OZ/ SCANT ½ CUP	DOUBLE CREAM
1 TBSP	GRATED PARMESAN CHEESE, PLUS EXTRA TO SERVE
	SALT AND FRESHLY GROUND BLACK PEPPER

Spread the mashed potato out onto a work surface. You want to allow as much steam to escape as possible so you have nice dry, fluffy mash to work with. When the potato has dried out but is still warm, sprinkle over the flours and work into the potato; I like to have a dough scraper in one hand to help. When the dough starts to come together, add the egg yolk and mix in well. The amount of flour that the potato will take depends on the potatoes; add as much flour as you think you need so that the dough no longer sticks to your hands and, if you poke a finger in, it comes out more or less clean.

Lightly flour the work surface and cover the dough with a tea towel while you slice off pieces and roll them into sausages about 2cm/¾in thick. Cut the sausages into 1-cm/½-in lengths. If you like, you can roll the gnocchi on a ridged board or over the tines of a fork to make a nice shape that will help the sauce stick as well.

To make the porcini sauce, melt the butter in a saucepan and fry the porcini, garlic clove and thyme until they are soft and lightly browned. Season with salt and pepper, remove the garlic and thyme, then add the cream. Bubble slowly for a minute, then add the grated Parmesan cheese. Keep warm while you cook the gnocchi.

Bring a large pan of salted water to the boil. Throw in the gnocchi, stir once, and wait a minute or so for them to float to the surface. Remove with a slotted spoon and toss gently in the porcini sauce. Use a little of the cooking water to loosen the sauce. Serve immediately, with more Parmesan and plenty of pepper on top.

Pizzoccheri alla Valtellinese

SERVES 4–6

Pizzoccheri is a recipe from the Valtellina valley in Lombardy, made with a thick buckwheat noodle. The similarity with the Savoyard *crozets* (see page 206) suggests a shared heritage that perhaps spread over the Alpine passes. Either way, extremely delicious and a proper rib-sticker on a cold day, given that the pasta is supplemented with potato, boiled cabbage, Fontina and lots of garlic butter before a quick trip into the oven: a buttery buckwheat noodle and cheesy potato bake. Yes please.

I've never seen *pizzoccheri* for sale back home, but don't be put off: the making process is easy, requires no pasta machine and considerably less skill than a *soba* master. I should however warn you that this recipe is not particularly healthy.

To make the pizzoccheri — Mix the flours well in a bowl and add the water. Bring together to form a dough, knead for 5 minutes or so until smooth(ish), then roll out on a lightly floured board to a thickness of 3mm/⅛in. Cut the dough into strips 10cm/4in wide. Stack these strips on top of each other, lightly dusting with flour between layers, then cut into noodles approximately 1cm/½in wide. Set aside on a floured board.

2	RED POTATOES, PEELED, CUT INTO 2CM/¾IN CUBES
I	SAVOY CABBAGE, COARSELY SHREDDED
125G/ 4½OZ/ GENEROUS ½ CUP	UNSALTED BUTTER
8	GARLIC CLOVES, HALVED
I2	SAGE LEAVES
200G/ 7OZ/ 2 CUPS	GRATED MOUNTAIN CHEESE, SUCH AS FONTINA
50G/ I½OZ/ ½ CUP	GRATED PARMESAN CHEESE

FOR THE *PIZZOCCHERI*:

200G/ 7OZ/ SCANT I½ CUPS	BUCKWHEAT FLOUR
50G/ I¾OZ/ SCANT ⅓ CUP	'OO' FLOUR, PLUS EXTRA FOR DUSTING
I20ML/ 4FL OZ/ ½ CUP	WATER

Preheat the oven to 200°C fan/220°C/425°F/ gas mark 7.

Bring a big pan of salted water to the boil. Add the potatoes, bring back to the boil and simmer for 5 minutes. Add the noodles and the cabbage to the pot. Cook until the potatoes and cabbage are soft and the noodles cooked through – test the noodles regularly: they should take about 8–10 minutes.

Meanwhile, melt the butter in a small pan and fry the garlic slowly until it softens and infuses the butter with its flavour. Add the sage leaves, then remove from the heat.

Sprinkle a layer of the grated cheeses in a buttered gratin dish that will fit everything in snugly. Using a slotted spoon, scoop out the noodles, potato and cabbage, taking some of the cooking water with them, and arrange in a layer in the dish. Note that the amount of cooking water that goes into the gratin dish is important – too little and the dish will dry out as it bakes in the oven. Sprinkle more cheese on top. Return the pan with the butter, garlic and sage over the heat, and when it starts to bubble again, pour the contents over the noodles. Sprinkle again with the rest of the cheese and put into the hot oven for 5 minutes. Eat while still steaming hot.

Gratin de Ravioles du Royans

After some convoluted research I am none the wiser as to the origin of these little ravioli from the Dauphiné; 'Royans' is possibly a corruption of 'Romans'. In the absence of any actual historical cookbooks, historians and etymologists seem to have come to the conclusion that the word *ravioles*, despite the pasta being an obvious cousin of the Italian equivalent, has its roots in a contortion of the word *rissole*, a rust-coloured fried ball of meat, and the Lenten practice of using the greens from a turnip (*la rave*) in place of meat. This is all too academic for me, but it does seem that the *raviole* might well have a history of its own.

Traditionally they are stuffed with parsley and soft cheese and served in hot broth – not dissimilar to the Bolognese *tortellini in brodo* – but here is a preparation much more Alpine in character: the little *ravioles* are first poached then baked with finely chopped spinach, cheese and cream. Here I give a recipe for the *ravioles* themselves – if you do go to the trouble I would certainly also try them simmered in a rich chicken stock with a grating of Parmesan. Good small shop-bought ravioli with a cheese filling are an acceptable shortcut for when you want to minimize the time that it takes to get it into your face.

FOR THE DOUGH:

200G/ 7OZ/ 1½ CUPS	'OO' FLOUR, PLUS EXTRA FOR DUSTING
2	EGGS

FOR THE FILLING:

200G/ 7OZ/ SCANT 1 CUP	COTTAGE CHEESE OR RICOTTA
100G/ 3½OZ/ GENEROUS 1 CUP	FINELY GRATED COMTÉ, EMMENTAL OR PARMESAN CHEESE
2 TBSP	FINELY CHOPPED PARSLEY
	SALT AND FRESHLY GROUND BLACK PEPPER

OR

1	PACKET SMALL SHOP-BOUGHT CHEESE RAVIOLI

First, make the dough. Pour the flour onto a work surface, make a well in the centre and crack in the eggs. Whisk the eggs with a fork, then slowly incorporate all the flour until a dough is formed. Knead the dough for 5–10 minutes until smooth and soft. Wrap in clingfilm and leave to rest for at least 30 minutes.

Meanwhile, combine all the ingredients for the filling and taste for seasoning.

Cut the rested dough into two pieces. Use a pasta machine to roll out both pieces: for *ravioiles* you want the pasta to be as thin as possible – you should be able to read a newspaper headline through it. Set aside the first strip of pasta on a lightly floured surface while you roll out the other – cover with a tea towel to prevent it drying out.

When you have two evenly sized strips of pasta, ensure that your work surface is floured, then dot little chickpea-sized bits of filling on one of the strips, leaving roughly 2cm/¾in between each lump of filling. Gently lay the second strip over the top. Press very gently on each lump, then use your fingertips to press the pasta around the mounds of filling to seal. Squish well to ensure there are no big air pockets. Using a fluted wheeled cutter, cut in between each parcel. Separate the ravioli and set aside on a floured surface while you make the gratin.

FOR THE GRATIN:

500G/ 1LB 2OZ/ 10–12 CUPS	SPINACH
½	GARLIC CLOVE
150ML/ 5FL OZ/ ¾ CUP	DOUBLE CREAM
100G/ 3½OZ/ GENEROUS 1 CUP	GRATED COMTÉ, GRUYÈRE OR EMMENTAL CHEESE

Preheat the oven to 180°C fan/200°C/ 400°F/ gas mark 6.

Wash the spinach, then bring a big pan of salted water to the boil. Dunk in the spinach for a few seconds, scoop out with a slotted spoon, cool until you can handle it, give it a quick squeeze, then use a big knife to chop it to a rough purée.

Bring the water back to the boil, cook your *ravioles* until they float, then drain. Rub the half garlic clove around a gratin dish that will fit the *ravioiles* in two or more layers, then butter it well. Arrange the chopped spinach over the base of the dish and top with the blanched *ravioles*. Pour over the cream and grind over some black pepper. Top with the grated cheese and bake in the hot oven for about 20 minutes, or until all is bubbling and the cheese is golden.

Gratin de Crozets

Crozets are tiny little buckwheat pasta squares from the Savoie and this gratin is typically served with the local pork and pepper *diots* – a word that I have learned is Savoyard dialect for 'sausages'. *Diots* come in a few different varieties – smoked or unsmoked, for one, and some flavoured with nutmeg. *Diots* are difficult to find outside the French Alps but the smoked Polish *kiełbasa śląska* are a good substitute for the smoked ones found in the French Alps – either boiled in water or slashed and roasted hot in the oven. But I digress! A *gratin de crozets* is excellent either with sausages or on its own, perhaps with a salad for balance. I ate mine with a sausage and a slice of simmered Savoy cabbage.

Making *crozets* is a bit of a labour of love – not something to be done as a speedy midweek supper – but I thoroughly enjoyed myself last time I made them. It is possible to buy the *crozets* online, which would save you a fair bit of time. If you buy them, try to get the one made with buckwheat, as the plain one is a bit, well, plain. The buckwheat adds an interesting high note to the typically Alpine flavours of bacon, onion, cheese and cream.

I've seen some recipes that prescribe boiling the *crozets* in chicken stock. Not strictly necessary, but I wouldn't turn my nose up at it. Also, don't tell anyone, but I've made this gratin with macaroni when I didn't have any funny Alpine buckwheat pasta squares, and it was great.

FOR THE CROZETS:

300G/ 10½OZ/ 2¼ CUPS	BUCKWHEAT FLOUR
75G/ 2¾OZ/ ½ CUP	'00' FLOUR, PLUS EXTRA FOR DUSTING
180ML/ 6FL OZ/ ¾ CUP	WATER

First, make the *crozets*. Mix the flours in a bowl and stir in the water. Knead until the dough is smooth. Cover with a damp tea towel and let it rest for an hour.

On a well-floured surface, use a rolling pin to roll out the pasta to a thickness of 1mm/¹⁄₃₂in – its shape matters not as you will be cutting it into tiny squares. Using a long knife or, much better, a pizza cutter, cut the dough into 3mm/⅛in wide strips. Again, it doesn't matter so much how long they are – cut them into lengths that you are comfortable with. Realign the strips, dust with more flour and cut them into 3mm/⅛in squares – your *crozets*.

Toss the *crozets* in a little flour to prevent them from sticking together. They can be cooked straight away or dried out on a large platter – I dried mine on a big plate at room temperature for four days before using, so don't feel like you need to cook them all in one go if you don't need to.

When you're ready to cook, preheat the oven to 180°C fan/200°C/400°F/gas mark 6.

FOR THE GRATIN:

	OIL
150G/ 5½OZ	PANCETTA OR LARDONS – SMOKED IF YOU FANCY
1	ONION, DICED
1	PACKET OF DRIED *CROZETS*, OR A QUANTITY OF FRESH *CROZETS*, SEE LEFT
½	GLASS OF WHITE WINE
150G/ 5½OZ ¾ CUP	CRÈME FRAICHE
	UNSALTED BUTTER, FOR GREASING
200G/ 7OZ/ SCANT 2 CUPS	GRATED ALPINE CHEESE – GRUYÈRE OR BEAUFORT (OR SUBSTITUTE THE HARD CHEESE FOR SOME REBLOCHON, *ET VOILÀ: CROZIFLETTE!*)
	SALT, FRESHLY GROUND BLACK PEPPER AND NUTMEG

For the gratin, heat a little oil in a large pan and fry the lardons until the fat has rendered. Add the diced onion and gently fry until soft. Season with salt, pepper and nutmeg.

Meanwhile, boil the *crozets* until soft in a pan of lightly salted water. This will take just a few minutes if freshly made, but a couple of minutes longer if dried (see the packet instructions if you have bought some). Make sure you stir well as you put the *crozets* into the water, or they can stick. When soft, drain the *crozets* and add to the bacon and onion. Add the white wine, stir well and bubble for a minute. Remove from the heat and stir in the crème fraîche. Adjust the seasoning, transfer to a buttered gratin dish and sprinkle over the cheese. Bake in the hot oven for around 15–20 minutes, or until bubbling and browned on top. Eat hot with sausages and cooked cabbage, or on its own with a green salad.

Gratin Dauphinois (à la Fernand Point) SERVES 2

Fernand Point was one of the France's great chefs and by all accounts a man of both formidable character and waistline, who would famously eat a whole chicken or two for breakfast and drink a magnum of champagne in the late morning. Point is considered by many to be the founder of modern French cuisine, and his restaurant La Pyramide in Vienne near Lyon was revered; Curnonsky described it as 'the summit of culinary art'.

Point was well known for his maxims, one of the most famous being 'Butter, give me butter, always butter!': he would not shy away from richness. His recipe for *gratin dauphinois* differs from the way most people make it in that he specifies there must be only one thin layer of potatoes; a most interesting idea, that maximizes the ratio of golden browned crust to creamy potato. I must disagree with Fernand on the inclusion of eggs, as I have never quite succeeded in adding eggs to a gratin without slightly scrambling them, and I prefer to use more cream than milk, but we both agree that '*no cheese should ever be used*' (the italic is Point's).

What you want is for the potatoes to be soft, velvety slices, but not turned to mash, and still holding their shape but collapsing in the mouth. The dish should be lightly browned, all gold and cream with one or two darker spots, but the most important part of the recipe is not to cook it too fast or for too long, or the butter will separate from the cream and pool on top. The ideal is that the starch in the potatoes helps to thicken the cream to a sauce that will slowly ooze out of the potatoes onto the rest of your plate.

300G/ 10½OZ	RED-SKINNED, YELLOW-FLESHED POTATOES
15G/½OZ/ 1 TBSP	COLD UNSALTED BUTTER, PLUS EXTRA FOR GREASING
1	GARLIC CLOVE
50ML/ 2FL OZ/ SCANT ¼ CUP	MILK
220ML/ 8FL OZ/ GENEROUS 1 CUP	DOUBLE CREAM
	A GRATING OF NUTMEG (OPTIONAL)
	SALT AND FRESHLY GROUND BLACK PEPPER

Preheat the oven to 160°C fan/180°C/350°F/ gas mark 4.

Peel and slice the potatoes thinly (2mm/ ⅛in thick), ideally using a mandoline. Grease the inside of an earthenware dish (approximately 28 × 16cm/11 × 6¼in) with the extra butter, then lay the sliced potatoes in an overlapping pattern in the dish, to form a layer not much thicker than 1cm/½in. Season with salt and pepper.

Crush the garlic with the flat of a knife and put it in a saucepan with the milk and cream. Bring to a simmer. Season with a little salt to taste, then pour through a sieve over the potatoes, discarding the garlic. Dot the dish with the remaining butter. Grate over a little bit of nutmeg if you like (I do).

Cover the dish with foil and bake in the hot oven for about 40 minutes (test with a skewer to check the potatoes are soft all the way through), then remove the foil and continue to cook for a further 10–15 minutes or so, until golden brown on top. Remove the dish from the oven and allow to rest for 10 minutes before serving.

Gratin Savoyard with Wild Mushrooms   SERVES 2–4

A deeply savoury gratin to eat with a steak or a pork chop and a salad. This gratin is different from other mountain gratins, like its neighbour the *dauphinois*, in that instead of milk or cream it uses stock – more along the lines of a *boulangère* – to cook the potatoes.

1 KG/ 2 LB 4 OZ	RED POTATOES (BETWEEN WAXY AND FLOURY), PEELED
75 G/ 2¾ OZ/ 4 TBSP	UNSALTED BUTTER, PLUS EXTRA FOR GREASING
250 G/ 9 OZ	MIXED WILD MUSHROOMS – CHANTERELLES, TROMPETTES DE LA MORT, GIROLLES
1 TBSP	DRIED CEPS (PORCINI), REHYDRATED IN HOT WATER
4	GARLIC CLOVES, FINELY CHOPPED
1	SPRIG OF THYME, LEAVES PICKED
150 G/ 5½ OZ/ 1½ CUPS	COARSELY GRATED GRUYÈRE OR COMTÉ CHEESE
500 ML/ 18 FL OZ/ GENEROUS 2 CUPS	HOT GOOD BEEF OR CHICKEN STOCK
	NUTMEG
	SALT

Next time you go to the butcher's, ask them for a few cut-up beef bones. Roast them in a hot oven, pour off any fat and drop the bones into cold water with a few vegetables and aromatics. Simmer for a few hours, skimming, and you have your good beef stock.

Preheat the oven to 180°C fan/200°C/400°F/ gas mark 6.

Slice the potatoes into thin even rounds. Put them in a bowl, season with salt and toss well. Grease a gratin dish liberally with butter. Heat 50g/1¾oz/3 tablespoons of butter in a frying pan and sauté the mushrooms (including the soaked porcini) briefly until they just begin to soften and absorb some butter, but not to cook fully. After 30 seconds or so, remove from the heat, add the garlic and thyme and toss well. Layer the potatoes with the mushrooms and cheese, finishing with a layer of potatoes. Pour over hot stock to almost cover the potatoes, then dot the surface of the potatoes with the rest of the cold butter. Grate over a little nutmeg and cover the dish tightly with foil.

Bake the gratin in the hot oven for 1 hour, or until the potatoes are soft when you poke in a skewer. Remove the foil and continue to cook the gratin until all is bubbling and a dark golden brown. Remove from the oven and allow to cool slightly before you eat it.

Polenta au Gratin

I love polenta and in general see no reason to mess around with it, although this polenta gratin struck me as a good example of savoyard innovation. Polenta, made with a light chicken stock, is further enriched with tomato sauce, fried bacon, Alpine cheese and butter before a quick turn in the oven. Excellent on a cold night, with some sausages, or just in a bowl (on the sofa, in front of the telly) with grated cheese on top. Keep the polenta nice and wet, otherwise it will be too dry when it is baked in the oven.

I LITRE/ I ¾ PINTS/ 4 CUPS	LIGHT CHICKEN STOCK
200G/ 7OZ/ I ⅓ CUPS	GOOD-QUALITY COARSE POLENTA (INSTANT POLENTA IS MUCH QUICKER BUT FAR LESS TASTY, SO I ALWAYS STICK WITH THE PROPER STUFF)
	SALT

FOR THE TOMATO SAUCE:

I5G/ ½OZ/ I TBSP	BUTTER, PLUS EXTRA FOR GREASING
I TBSP	OLIVE OIL
I	ONION, DICED
2	GARLIC CLOVES, CRUSHED A LITTLE IN THEIR SKINS
I	BAY LEAF
400G/ I4OZ	CANNED PEELED PLUM TOMATOES

TO FINISH:

200G/ 7OZ	SLAB OF SMOKED BACON, CUT INTO FAT CUBES
4	GARLIC CLOVES, SLICED
	A HANDFUL OF PARSLEY, ROUGHLY CHOPPED
I00G/ 3½OZ/ GENEROUS I CUP	GRATED BEAUFORT, COMTÉ OR GRUYÈRE CHEESE

First, set the polenta to cook. Bring the chicken stock to the boil and whisk in the polenta in a steady stream. When it boils, reduce the heat to very low. Replace the whisk with a wooden spoon and cook slowly, stirring regularly, for 45 minutes–1 hour, until the coarse grains are no longer gritty and the polenta starts to come away from the sides of the pot. Season lightly with salt.

Meanwhile, make the tomato sauce: heat the butter and oil in a small pan, gently fry the onion, garlic, bay leaf and a pinch of salt, then add the tomatoes and half their juice. Squish the tomatoes well with your spoon. Cook for the same amount of time as the polenta, or until the sauce has thickened slightly and tastes delicious. Fish out the garlic cloves. The sauce should not be too thick.

Preheat the oven to 180°C fan/200°C/400°F/gas mark 6.

Heat a drop of oil in a frying pan and fry the smoked bacon until crisp and golden, then add the garlic. Fry briefly, then add the parsley, then set aside.

Butter a gratin dish that will hold the polenta but leave at least 1cm/½in of space at the top. Make sure the polenta is still nicely loose and wet, as it will dry out as it bakes in the oven – add more hot water if you think it looks a bit dry. Pour half the polenta into the dish, and sprinkle over the mixture of the fried bacon, garlic and parsley. Pour in the rest of the polenta, spread with the tomato sauce and sprinkle over the grated cheese. Bake in the hot oven for 15 minutes or so, until bubbling and golden.

Valpelline Soup

This thick soup from the Val d'Aosta closely resembles a French *panade* – a dish layered with stale bread and cheese before being baked in hot stock in the oven.

This version, from the Italian side of the border, uses rye bread and Fontina.

50G/ 1¾OZ/ 3 TBSP	UNSALTED BUTTER, PLUS EXTRA FOR GREASING
2 TBSP	OLIVE OIL, PLUS EXTRA FOR DRIZZLING
100G/ 3½OZ	PANCETTA, CUT INTO 2CM/¾IN DICE (OPTIONAL)
I	ONION, DICED
I	CELERY STICK, DICED
2	GARLIC CLOVES, SLICED
I	SAVOY CABBAGE
1.5 LITRES/ 2½ PINTS/ 6 CUPS	GOOD (HOMEMADE) BEEF, OR CHICKEN OR VEG STOCK
6	DRIED PORCINI (IF USING CHICKEN OR VEG STOCK)
8	SLICES OF STALE RYE BREAD
200G/ 7OZ	FONTINA OR OTHER ALPINE MELTY CHEESE, THINLY SLICED
	SALT, FRESHLY GROUND BLACK PEPPER AND NUTMEG

The traditional recipe calls for beef stock, which is very good indeed, but chicken or even veg stock works well with a few dried porcini thrown in for 'beefiness'. The bacon is optional; it's just as delicious without.

Preheat the oven to 180°C fan/200°C/400°F/ gas mark 6.

Heat the butter and oil in a large stockpot and slowly fry the pancetta, if using, onion, celery and garlic with a pinch of salt, until very soft.

Meanwhile, trim the outer leaves of the cabbage and discard, along with the toughest bits of the stalk. Cut the cabbage into 2cm/¾in slices. Pour the stock into the pot, bring to the boil, season with salt and add the cabbage (if using chicken or veg stock, add the dried porcini at this stage). Boil for 5 minutes, until soft. Drain the cabbage and reserve the stock. Roughly chop through the cabbage to ensure there are no big stringy pieces.

Grease a deep earthenware dish with butter. Layer the cooked cabbage, the sliced rye bread (torn to fit in an even layer), thin slices of Fontina cheese, black pepper and a touch of nutmeg. Finish with a layer of cheese and pour over hot stock to cover. Drizzle with oil and bake in the hot oven for 30 minutes, until the stock is bubbling and the cheese molten and golden.

Chicken with Morels & Vin Jaune

SERVES 4

A classic dish from the Jura, where the chicken would traditionally have been the most expensive part of the meal – the morels foraged for free in spring and the *vin jaune* (yellow wine) an affordable local wine. Nowadays the opposite is true, unless you happen to have a patch of morels in your garden. *Vin jaune* is a rather special thing; a slightly oxidized wine made from the Savagnin grape, with a flavour not unlike dry sherry – well worth tracking down if you have a pretty penny to spare.

When this is served in the Jura the chicken comes swimming in a vat of cream sauce: *c'est correct*, as the French say. This will feel luxurious, although it is really a very simple dish: use the best ingredients you can get your hands on and it's sure to be a winner. A little trick to boost the *vin jaune* flavour in the sauce is to splash in a little extra wine at the end, along with some butter and perhaps a squeeze of lemon.

This is traditionally, and best, served with a simple rice pilaf. At the restaurant where I work we add a few crispy curry leaves to the top of the rice – most untraditional, of course, but something that pairs nicely with your glass of *vin jaune* on the side.

FOR THE STOCK:

500G/ 1LB 2OZ	CHICKEN WINGS
	CARCASS FROM THE JOINTED CHICKEN (SEE PAGE 214)
½	SHALLOT
½	CELERY STICK
1	BAY LEAF
1	SPRIG OF THYME
	A FEW BLACK PEPPERCORNS

Preheat the oven to 200°C fan/220°C/425°F/ gas mark 7.

First, make the stock. Put the chicken wings and the carcass in a large roasting tin. Put in the hot oven and roast until a light golden brown. Transfer the wings and carcass to a large stockpot (leave the chicken fat in the tin) with the remaining ingredients and cover with cold water. Bring to the boil, skim well, then reduce to a simmer for 1½ hours, skimming periodically. Strain through a sieve, then reduce the liquid by half – you want 1 litre/1¾ pints/4 cups. Set aside while you prepare the chicken.

Recipe continues overleaf

Chicken with Morels & Vin Jaune continued

Season the chicken pieces with salt. Heat a little oil in a large saucepan and brown the pieces on both sides, adding a knob of butter towards the end. When the pieces are golden all over, remove to a plate and pour off the excess fat in the pan. Melt the 30g/1oz/2 tablespoons of butter, then add the diced shallot and a pinch of salt. Cook slowly until the shallot is very soft.

Halve the morels if they are large but leave any small or medium ones whole. Add the mushrooms to the pan and fry gently until they have softened and absorbed some of the butter – season them lightly with salt. Add the *vin jaune* and simmer until reduced to a syrupy consistency.

Reintroduce the chicken pieces, skin side up, and add the chicken stock – you might not need it all – to almost cover the chicken but leave the golden skin sitting above the liquid. Half-cover with a lid and cook for 30 minutes at a simmer. The sauce should reduce until it tastes powerful and delicious but bear in mind that the aim is to have a lot of it, so don't reduce too far (add a little more stock if you think it needs it). Now, pour in the cream and swirl the pot. Simmer slowly for a further 15 minutes or so, until the chicken is cooked and the sauce has thickened slightly.

Remove the chicken to a serving dish that will also hold the sauce. Taste the sauce for salt and finish by whisking in a good splash of *vin jaune*, the cold cubed butter and maybe a little squeeze of lemon juice. Pour the sauce over the chicken and serve, with a rice pilaf on the side.

1.5KG/ 3LB 5OZ	CHICKEN, JOINTED (YOU CAN ASK A BUTCHER TO DO THIS FOR YOU)
	OIL AND A KNOB OF UNSALTED BUTTER, FOR FRYING
30G/1OZ/ 2 TBSP	UNSALTED BUTTER, PLUS 15G/½OZ/1 TBSP (COLD, CUBED) TO FINISH THE SAUCE
½	SHALLOT, FINELY DICED
	AT LEAST 20 MORELS — FRESH WHEN IN SEASON, OR DRIED ONES SOAKED IN COLD WATER UNTIL SOFT
	A SMALL GLASS OF *VIN JAUNE*, PLUS AN EXTRA SPLASH AT THE END TO FINISH THE SAUCE
1 LITRE/ 1 ¾ PINTS/ 4 CUPS	GOOD CHICKEN STOCK (PREFERABLY HOMEMADE, SEE PAGE 112)
150ML/ 5FL OZ/ ¾ CUP	DOUBLE CREAM
	LEMON JUICE (OPTIONAL)
	SALT

Carbonada Valdostana

The name *carbonada* is remarkably similar to the Flemish *carbonnade*, a hearty stew of beef, onions and beer. This version from the Val d'Aosta has more in common with the famous *Bouef Bourguignon* in that they are both simmered in red wine.

The names of both stews suggest either that the preferred cooking method was long and slow over a charcoal (*carbon*) brazier or that they ended up very dark, almost charcoal, in colour.

Carbonada is undoubtedly a very old mountain recipe. The stew was traditionally made with salted, dried meat and spiced with cinnamon, cloves and nutmeg, perhaps to disguise a certain rancidity. Nowadays even those living in the most remote Alpine valleys have access to fresh beef, but I would encourage you to mimic the old practices and salt the meat overnight, not to disguise the flavour but to deepen it. This is best served with wet polenta that contains lots of cheese and butter.

500G/ 1LB 2OZ	BEEF CHUCK OR OTHER STEWING BEEF, CUT INTO 5CM/2IN CHUNKS
	FLOUR, FOR DUSTING
50G/ 1¾ OZ/ 3½ TBSP	UNSALTED BUTTER
	OIL
I	GOOD-SIZED RED ONION, DICED
I	CINNAMON STICK
4	CLOVES
	A SPRIG OF SAGE OR ROSEMARY
	NUTMEG, TO TASTE
½	BOTTLE OF RED WINE
	SALT AND FRESHLY GROUND BLACK PEPPER

Salt the beef as you would normally, toss the chunks thoroughly in the salt and refrigerate overnight.

The following day, pour off the excess liquid that comes out of the beef. Dredge the meat lightly in flour. Heat half the butter and a little oil in a large, lidded ovenproof casserole dish, and fry the meat, browning on all sides. Remove to a plate and add the onion with the rest of the butter – don't add any salt. Fry the onion slowly, scraping up any bits from the base of the dish. Cook until soft and sweet, about 20–30 minutes. Chuck in the cinnamon, cloves and your herb sprig. Stir into the onions, let them fry in the fat for a minute or two, then grate in a little nutmeg and stir again.

Reintroduce the beef, stir again, then cover with the red wine. Bring to the boil, then reduce to a slow simmer, covered by a lid. Cook for 3–4 hours, or until the beef is spoon-tender. Remove the meat and reduce the liquid if you would like it thicker. Adjust the seasoning; it will happily take pepper but it probably won't need salt. A little more nutmeg is sometimes desirable at the end, but don't overdo it. Serve with buttery wet polenta.

Farçon

Farçon, also known as *farcement*, is a hefty potato cake, and a traditional Sunday lunch in Savoie. The *farçon* would be put in the oven to slow-cook for hours while the family trooped off to mass. On their return, there would be a triumphant de-moulding and slicing of the steaming potato cake, served with roast or stewed meats, or a selection of sausages, and perhaps a salad.

Each village and valley in Savoie will have its own recipe for *farçon* but almost all preparations contain potato, bacon and some sort of fruit. Some include cheese, but I must say it's a relief to find an authentic Savoyard recipe without it. Raisins, soaked in a little brandy or *marc*, are a common addition, as

is grated apple, plus a little spice: pepper, cinnamon or nutmeg. The use of spices and fruit in a savoury dish like this is a relic of the Middle Ages, perhaps earlier. I tend to stick with a classic combination of potato, bacon and prune, with a touch of nutmeg, but feel free to add or alter according to what you like.

Don't be put off by the heft of the thing!

The next morning, fry leftover slices in butter for breakfast – with fried eggs, maybe another banger or two and some brown sauce, although maybe don't tell the Savoyards about this last bit. It is almost better than the day before.

1.5KG/ 3LB 5OZ	FLOURY POTATOES, PEELED
15G/ ½OZ/ 1 TBSP	UNSALTED BUTTER
1	YELLOW ONION, THINLY SLICED INTO HALF-MOONS
150G/ 5½OZ	SMOKED BACON LARDONS OR (EVEN BETTER) COOKED SMOKED SAUSAGE, CUT INTO 2CM/¾IN DICE – EITHER ONE FROM THE ALPS OR SOMETHING JUICY AND POLISH
24	RASHERS STREAKY BACON (THE NUMBER OF RASHERS WILL DEPEND ON THE SIZE OF YOUR TIN)
ABOUT 2 TBSP	FLOUR
2	LARGE EGGS
ABOUT 6 TBSP	CRÈME FRAÎCHE
12	PITTED PRUNES (AGEN PRUNES FOR PREFERENCE)
	SALT, FRESHLY GROUND BLACK PEPPER AND NUTMEG
27-CM/ 10-¾-IN	A FLUTED BUNDT TIN, BUT IF YOU HAVE A RINGED CHARLOTTE MOULD (OR A VERITABLE *MOULE AU FARÇON*) THAT WOULD BE MORE AUTHENTIC!

Preheat the oven to 180°C fan/200°C/400°F/ gas mark 6.

Grate the potatoes either by hand or using a grating attachment on a food processor. Put the grated mass in a colander and season with 3 teaspoons of salt. Leave for a few minutes, then wrap in a clean tea towel, twist together and squeeze well to expel all the water. Tip the potatoes into a large bowl.

Heat the butter in a small frying pan and gently cook the onion until soft. If using bacon lardons, add them to the pan and fry them with the onions (if using cooked sausage, no need to fry it). Season with black pepper and nutmeg. Set aside to cool slightly while you line the bundt tin with the slices of bacon. Try to leave an overhang over the sides that can be wrapped over the filling. The rashers can be squished and scraped with the flat of the knife if you need them to be longer and thinner. However, if it's difficult to leave an overhang, just reserve a few slices of bacon to put on top once the filling is in the mould.

Recipe continues overleaf

Farçon continued

Add the flour, eggs, crème fraîche, lardons or diced sausage, the cooked onions and the prunes to the potatoes. Mix well. Pack the filling into the lined tin: when transferring the mixture, leave any excess liquid at the bottom in the mixing bowl.

Fold over the overhanging strips of bacon (or line the top with your extra rashers), press down and tap the tin on the work top to level out. Don't worry if there's a little gap on the top that the bacon doesn't cover. Wrap the tin in foil and place it in a deep-sided baking tray. Make a bain marie by pouring boiling water into the tray – enough to come about a third of the way up the sides of the bundt tin. Carefully transfer the tray to the *hot oven* and bake for 3 hours.

After 3 hours, carefully remove the tray from the oven and increase the temperature to 200°C fan/220°C/425°F/gas mark 7. Remove the foil from the tin and return it to the oven, this time without the bain marie, and cook for a further 30 minutes to crisp and colour the bacon.

Take the *farçon* out of the oven and allow to cool for 15 minutes. At this stage the smell filling your kitchen will be ridiculous. Use a thin knife to make sure that the bacon rashers are not stuck to the tin, then place a serving platter on top and quickly invert the tin onto the platter. Serve the *farçon* steaming hot with sausages, boiled meat (or boiled sausages, for that matter) or just a salad. Remember to save some for breakfast the next day!

The Grand Feasting Pot of the Governor General of Lesdiguières (La Grande Marmite de Lesdiguières)

SERVES 6–8

This historic dish takes its name from a certain François de Bonne, Duke and Governor General of Lesdiguières, in the seventeenth century. The duke attended a wedding at which a gargantuan *marmite* (a grand feasting pot, if you will) was served to all fifty guests present, and the recipe, named after him, was duly recorded.

My recipe will not quite feed fifty, although the original does sound fun (take two whole veal heads, forty pig's feet, fifteen kilos of beef, eight large chickens, ten bottles of red wine, a litre of cognac etc). It is a quite splendid *pot-au-feu* variation for a special occasion. Although unmistakably French in accent, with its varied spicing and judicious use of cognac, the dish reminds me of a *bollito misto*, the Piedmontese speciality of slowly boiled meats. A *pot-au-feu* at its simplest might be a piece of beef, some vegetables, salt and mustard, but a true *gran bollito misto* might well contain up to fourteen (!) different meats and seven (!) different sauces.

Somewhere in the middle, then, lies this special recipe. It is adapted from that found in *The Auberge of the Flowering Hearth*, a book about a remarkable inn in the Dauphiné where the proprietress served her *marmite* with a side of saffron rice (shades of a traditional *risotto Milanese*) and some pickled cherries. I suggest you do the same – there are recipes overleaf but note that the cherries need a week to pickle.

1 KG/ 2LB 4OZ	BEEF BRISKET, ROLLED AND TIED
1 KG/ 2LB 4OZ	VEAL SHIN, ON THE BONE, CUT INTO 2 500-G/1LB 2-OZ PIECES
1	PIG'S TROTTER, OR A FAT PIECE OF ROLLED AND TIED PIG'S SKIN
	FINE SALT
1	BOTTLE OF RED WINE
½	BOTTLE OF WHITE WINE
2	WHOLE ONIONS, EACH STUCK WITH A CLOVE
6–9	CARROTS, PEELED OR WASHED WELL
1	HEAD OF GARLIC
3	RIPE TOMATOES, PEELED (SEE PAGE 143) AND QUARTERED, OR ½ CAN (200G/7OZ) QUALITY PEELED PLUM TOMATOES, RINSED OF THEIR JUICE
4	BAY LEAVES
	PARSLEY STALKS
	A FEW PIECES OF DRIED CEP (PORCINI)
	NUTMEG
1.2KG –1.5KG/ 2LB 10OZ –3LB 5OZ	CHICKEN
	A HANDFUL OF CHESTNUT MUSHROOMS, HALVED IF LARGE
	A GOOD SPLASH OF COGNAC OR ARMAGNAC
	SALT AND FRESHLY GROUND BLACK PEPPER

Recipe continues overleaf

The Grand Feasting Pot of Governor General of Lesdiguières (La Grande Marmite de Lesdiguières) continued

First, dry-salt all the meats by seasoning well on all sides with fine salt and leave in the refrigerator, preferably overnight. The next day, put the beef brisket, veal shin and pig's trotter in your biggest, grandest cooking pot (if you don't have one quite big enough, you can plan to remove the brisket or veal when it is cooked so you can fit in the chicken). Cover with cold water and add a big pinch of salt (this will stop your dry brine from leaching out of the meats as they blanch). Bring slowly to the boil and then discard the water.

Re-cover the meat with the wines, topping up with fresh cold water until the meats are almost covered. Turn on the heat to full. As scum appears, reduce the heat and skim well until the worst of it is gone, then add the whole onions, 1 of the carrots, the garlic and tomatoes. Tie the bay leaves, parsley stalks and dried porcini into a bouquet garni and pop it in the pot. Add a few grates of nutmeg, but go easy – this can be corrected later. Adjust the heat so that the liquid is at a slow simmer – blip-blip-bubble-blip. Continue to skim the broth from time to time.

Cook until the beef brisket and veal are almost soft. At this stage, remove the onions, carrot and garlic, and add the chicken, the mushrooms and the cognac. Cook at a slow simmer for a further 45 minutes or so. You are aiming for the beef and veal to be completely soft without starting to fall apart in the broth. As a rough guide, the brisket and veal should take about 2.5–3 hours while the chicken should be nicely poached after 45 minutes: do poke and prod your meats to get a feel of how they are coming along. Ensure that the broth never tips over into a boil, as that would dry out the meats. If you feel that one of the meats is cooked before the others are ready, take it out and cover with foil – it can be warmed through again later.

Meanwhile, make the horseradish cream and prepare the saffron rice.

Once all your meats are cooked, discard the pig's trotter, vegetables and bouquet garni – they have done their job. Arrange the meats on a large celebratory platter; keep warm. Cook the remaining carrots in the broth, then transfer them to the platter with the meats. Strain the broth and adjust the seasoning – it might well need some more salt.

Moisten the meats with the broth and present whole to your guests. Hurrah! Then, to serve, cut the chicken into eight pieces (drumsticks and thighs on the bone, breasts off), pull pieces of veal off the bone, and slice the brisket. Each person should have a plate with some of each meat all moistened with hot broth and sprinkled with flaky salt.

Serve with the saffron rice below and pickles of some kind. Cornichons or pickled red cabbage are an excellent accompaniment if you don't have any pickled cherries ready. Horseradish cream, I think, would be the only other thing I would want with this.

Horseradish Cream

Finely grate and then hand chop the horseradish. Combine with the other ingredients. Don't overmix.

5-CM/2-IN PIECE OF FRESH HORSERADISH, PEELED	
2 TSP	SUGAR
2 TSP	CRÈME FRAÎCHE
	LEMON JUICE, TO TASTE
	SALT, TO TASTE

Saffron Rice

Working carefully so as not to break the grains, wash the rice three times in cold water until the water runs almost clear. Soak the rice in fresh cold water for 30 minutes. If using bone marrow, soak it separately in cold water. Warm the vermouth slightly in a pan and add the saffron – remove from the heat and allow to steep.

Meanwhile, heat the butter in a large saucepan, add the onion slices and slowly fry with a good pinch of salt, until very soft but not coloured. Add the bone marrow to the onions. Drain the rice and add to the pan, along with a nice pinch of salt. Stir delicately with a wooden spoon to coat the grains in butter without damaging them.

Pour over boiling water to cover the rice by 1cm/½in and pour in the saffron vermouth. Bring to the boil, cover with a tight-fitting lid and cook on full whack for 3 minutes. Turn down the heat to the lowest possible, cook for a further 6 minutes, then turn off the heat.

Keep the lid on for at least 10 minutes more, then fluff the rice gently with a fork. If using, the marrow can now be scooped out of the bone and mixed back into the rice. The rice will keep hot in the covered pan for a while so that you can assemble the rest of the meal.

400G/ 14OZ/ GENEROUS 4 CUPS	BASMATI RICE
5-CM/2-IN	SECTION OF BONE MARROW (OPTIONAL), SOAKED IN COLD WATER FOR AN HOUR
2 TBSP	DRY VERMOUTH OR WATER
	A GOOD PINCH OF SAFFRON STRANDS
75G/ 2¾OZ/ 4 TBSP	UNSALTED BUTTER
2	WHITE OR YELLOW ONIONS, THINLY SLICED INTO HALF-MOONS
	SALT

Pickled Cherries

Pack the cherries into one or two sterilized glass jars. Bring the vinegar, water, sugar and spices to the boil in a small pan and pour the lot over the cherries. Seal tightly with the lids and leave to pickle for a week or so. Delicious with boiled meats or *charcuterie*.

300G/ 10½OZ/ ABOUT 2 CUPS	PITTED SOUR CHERRIES
100ML/ 3½FL OZ/ SCANT ½ CUP	WHITE WINE VINEGAR
100ML/ 3½FL OZ/ SCANT ½ CUP	WATER
100G/ 3½OZ/ ½ CUP	BROWN SUGAR
1	CINNAMON STICK
4	CLOVES
6	PEPPERCORNS

Panade

Panade, literally 'big bread thing', is a kind of layered bread and onion soup-gratin hybrid. It can be wet, soft and yielding, or firmer and wobbly, like a savoury bread and butter pudding. Bake it firmer as a side dish, or wetter if it's to be eaten on its own as a main course: either way it is very good.

At its simplest it is a quintessential mountain peasant dish: stale bread, onions and a few herbs baked with some stock or water, but made with good homemade stock,

enriched with greens and a little cheese, and given a lot of care, this is completely delicious. Any greens are good in this – Savoy cabbage, cavolo nero or chard – and it is a good vehicle for good mountain cheese like Fontina or Gruyère.

Be sure to use a good-quality sourdough bread with a firm crumb, and to scoop strategically from the dish so that each person has a nice ratio of custardy wobble to crisp edge.

100G/ 3½OZ	PANCETTA OR SMOKED BACON, DICED (OPTIONAL, BUT VERY GOOD)
50ML/ 2FL OZ/ SCANT ¼ CUP	OLIVE OIL
100G/ 3½OZ/ ½ CUP	UNSALTED BUTTER, PLUS EXTRA FOR GREASING
4	YELLOW ONIONS, THINLY SLICED INTO HALF-MOONS
6	CLOVES GARLIC, THINLY SLICED
	A SPRIG OF SAGE, PICKED
2	BAY LEAVES
1 KG/ 2LB 4OZ	SWISS CHARD OR A LARGE SAVOY CABBAGE
I	STALE SOURDOUGH LOAF (APPROX. 600G/1LB 5½OZ), TOUGH CRUSTS REMOVED, CUT INTO ROUGH 2.5-CM/1-IN OR 5-CM/2-IN PIECES
100G/ 3½OZ/ I CUP	PARMESAN CHEESE, GRATED
I LITRE/ 2 PINTS	LIGHT CHICKEN OR VEGETABLE STOCK (YOU MAY NOT NEED IT ALL)
100G/ 3½OZ/ GENEROUS I CUP	GRUYÈRE, FONTINA, OR OTHER GOOD MELTING MOUNTAIN CHEESE
	SALT, FRESHLY GROUND BLACK PEPPER AND NUTMEG

Preheat the oven to 170°C fan/190°C/375°F/ gas mark 5.

Fry the bacon, if using, in a drizzle of olive oil in a deep pot. When golden brown and frazzled, remove and reserve. Add half of the butter, a little more olive oil, and the sliced onions to the pot. Season with salt, stir well, and cook slowly, for at least 30 minutes, until the onions are very soft and sweet but with little colour. Halfway through, add the sliced garlic, sage leaves and bay. Cover with a lid if it looks like the onions are drying out.

Meanwhile, blanch the chard. Trim the bottom of the stalks, separate the ribs from the leaves, and cut the ribs into 2-cm/¾-in pieces. Cook the stalks in boiling salted water for about 2 minutes, until soft through, then remove with a slotted spoon. Add the chard leaves whole and boil for 10 seconds. Drain both leaves and stalks and set aside to cool.

To assemble the *panade*, grease a deep-sided baking dish with butter. Start with a layer of cooked onions, then follow with a layer of bread cubes, a drizzle of olive oil and a layer of cooked chard. Season the chard layer with a touch of nutmeg, grated Parmesan and black pepper.

Recipe continues overleaf

Panade continued

Continue in this fashion until everything is used up. Try to finish with a layer of bread, but don't be too precious about how the ingredients are arranged – a little roughness and variety is a good thing and will make for a more interesting eat – and it's good to be able to see a little of each ingredient when the panade is finished.

Heat the stock and carefully pour into one of the sides of the panade. The stock should come up to the top of the other ingredients, moistening the top layer but not drowning it. Drizzle with olive oil, dot with the remaining butter, loosely cover with foil and bake in the *hot oven*.

After 1 hour, take a peek – the *panade* should be lovely and soft, the bread slightly swollen from the stock, with the centre pale and the edges darker. If it still looks too wet and soupy, remove the foil and continue to bake slowly. At this stage it can be kept warm, well covered with foil in a low oven.

When you are almost ready to serve, increase the oven's heat to 200°C fan/220°C/425°F/gas mark 7. Remove the foil, grate over the Gruyere, and cook for 15 minutes. The *panade* should be custardy soft underneath a crisp browned top. Serve at once, scooping straight from the baking dish.

Civet of Hare with Green Chartreuse

SERVES 4

A recipe from the mountains, where hares are hunted in autumn and into the dark winter, the meat infused with the flavour of the myriad wild herbs and flowers that are used in Chartreuse. This stew is deep, dark and richly flavoured with red wine, cream and the hare's own blood and liver. (If you have neither the blood nor the liver, fear not: the stew will still be delicious, even though it cannot be a true *civet*.)

Start this recipe the day before you plan to eat it, as the hare will need marinating overnight. This would also work with wild rabbit.

FOR THE MARINADE:

I	BOTTLE OF FULL-BODIED RED WINE
2	ONIONS, QUARTERED
2	CARROTS, SLICED INTO CHUNKS
2	CELERY STICKS, CUT INTO PIECES
4	GARLIC CLOVES, LIGHTLY CRUSHED
	PARSLEY STALKS
2	BAY LEAVES
I	SPRIG OF THYME OR WINTER SAVORY
I TSP	BLACK PEPPERCORNS
I TSP	JUNIPER BERRIES

If you have the hare's blood, lucky you. Whisk the fresh blood with the red wine and red wine vinegar. Refrigerate until needed, along with the hare's liver – trimmed of any sinew. You can substitute the hare's liver with chicken liver.

If you are friends with your butcher, ask them to joint the hare into eight pieces. Otherwise, cut up the hare thus: cut off the head. Remove the front legs. Remove the hind legs and cut into two; thigh and drumstick. Cut away the rib section nearest the head from the saddle. Cut the meaty saddle into two pieces through the bone. Sit the hare in the marinade ingredients overnight.

The next day, strain the marinade from the hare and reserve the liquid. Pat the pieces of meat dry and season with salt and black pepper.

Preheat the oven to 150°C fan/170°C/340°F/gas mark 3½.

Heat the goose fat in a large, lidded ovenproof casserole dish and sauté the bacon until golden brown. Remove with a slotted spoon, then brown the seasoned hare until it has taken some colour. Add the shallots and garlic and sauté in the fat until they too turn golden. Add the soaked porcini, reintroduce the bacon and sprinkle with the *quatre épices*. Stir, then add the cognac and the Chartreuse, which will most likely set alight. Fun!

Pour over the strained red wine from the marinade and the soaking water from the porcini. Top up the liquid with enough stock to cover the hare and bring to the boil. Reduce to a low simmer, lay a cartouche of parchment paper over the hare and cover with a lid. Put the casserole into the *hot oven* and cook for 2½–3 hours, until the meat is very tender.

Remove the hare and keep warm. Skim off any excess fat from the surface of the braising liquid (I often dab the top of the stew with kitchen paper which usually does the job nicely), then stir in 100ml/3½fl oz/scant ½ cup of the cream. If you have neither the hare's blood nor liver, simmer the sauce for 10 minutes or so, then finish with a little cold butter and a glug of Chartreuse. If using blood and liver, follow the next step.

Simmer gently while you prepare a liaison. Put the liver, blood and remaining cream in a blender. Blitz well, to make a delicious smoothie. Whisk a ladleful of the hot braising juices into this mixture to temper slightly. Take the casserole off the heat, then quickly whisk the smoothie into the braising liquid. Bring back to a low simmer, stirring all the while, but do not boil, or the sauce will curdle. Cook for a few minutes until the sauce has thickened and tastes full. Whisk in a few cubes of cold butter and sprinkle over a glug of Chartreuse.

Adjust the seasoning and pour the sauce over the warm hare. Serve with boiled potatoes (peeled, in big pieces, hot, with cold butter melting onto them), mashed potato or some buttered noodles.

2 TBSP	RED WINE AND 1 TBSP RED WINE VINEGAR (IF YOU HAVE THE HARE'S BLOOD)
1	CHICKEN LIVER (UNLESS YOU HAVE THE HARE'S LIVER) (OPTIONAL)
1	HARE, PREFERABLY WITH ITS LIVER AND BLOOD, JOINTED INTO 8 PIECES – YOU CAN ASK YOUR BUTCHER TO DO THIS
2 TBSP	GOOSE OR DUCK FAT
100G/ 3½OZ	SMOKED BACON OR PANCETTA, CUT INTO 2-CM/¾-IN CUBES
100G/ 3½OZ	ROUND SHALLOTS OR PEARL ONIONS
6	GARLIC CLOVES
5G/⅛OZ	DRIED CEPS (PORCINI), SOAKED IN BOILED WATER (RESERVE THE SOAKING WATER FOR LATER)
	A PINCH OF *QUATRE ÉPICES* OR MIXED SPICE
50ML/ 2FL OZ/ SCANT ¼ CUP	COGNAC OR ARMAGNAC
100ML/ 3½FL OZ/ SCANT ½ CUP	GREEN CHARTREUSE, PLUS A SMALL GLUG TO FINISH (PLUS EXTRA IF YOU DON'T HAVE HARE'S BLOOD OR LIVER)
250ML/ 9FL OZ/ GENEROUS 1 CUP	CHICKEN OR GAME STOCK
150ML/ 5FL OZ/ ¾ CUP	DOUBLE CREAM
	A FEW SMALL CUBES OF COLD BUTTER, CUBED (PLUS EXTRA IF YOU DON'T HAVE HARE'S BLOOD OR LIVER)
	SALT AND FRESHLY GROUND BLACK PEPPER

Veal Cordon Bleu

Shamelessly retro and an excellent bit of Franco-Swiss cookery. A *Cordon Bleu* is the blue ribbon worn by a special order of French knights and, when applied to cookery, is a sash awarded only to cooks of the highest order. The dish is relatively new and thought to originate in Brig, Switzerland, although variants of the breaded 'cutlet' are much older.

There are two schools of thought: flat or rolled? The answer is obviously rolled. A flat *cordon bleu* is nothing but a ham and cheese schnitzel. Cooked ham is essential: no prosciutto here, *grazie mille*; the traditional cheese is I suppose something mild like Emmental. I see that and raise you some Reblochon. A little julienne of fresh black truffle will also do quite nicely.

2	VEAL ESCALOPES (APPROX. 150G/5½OZ EACH)
2	SLICES OF COOKED HAM (NOTHING TOO THINLY SLICED)
	A DUSTING OF GRATED PARMESAN CHEESE
125G/ 4½OZ	REBLOCHON CHEESE, THINLY SLICED
	A HANDFUL OF FLOUR
1	EGG, BEATEN WITH A SPLASH OF MILK
	FINE BREADCRUMBS
	BLACK TRUFFLE, JULIENNED (OPTIONAL, BUT GO ON)
	UNSALTED BUTTER PLUS A LITTLE OIL, FOR FRYING
	SALT

Preheat the oven to 160°C fan/180°C/350°F/ gas mark 4.

Bash out the veal escalopes between sheets of baking paper to a thickness of 2mm/ ⅛in. Season very lightly with salt. Arrange the sliced ham down the length of the escalopes and top with a dusting of grated Parmesan and thin slices of Reblochon cheese. Here is the moment to add your black truffle if you have it. Roll up the escalopes from the short side.

Lightly flour the rolls, tap off the excess, dip into the beaten egg and milk, then into the breadcrumbs. Press lightly on all sides to coat evenly.

Set the rolls aside while you heat the butter (with the addition of a little oil to stop it burning) in a frying pan over a medium heat. Fry the rolls on all sides until golden brown, then transfer to a baking sheet or dish and bake in the oven for 10–15 minutes, until hot through.

Slice in half and serve with salad.

Chapter Five

Alsace

Alsace

Alsace has continued to be passed between French and German hands ever since it officially became part of France in 1648. The name 'Alsace' is intriguing: it could be derived from the Old High German *Ali-Saz*, meaning 'foreign domain', or – equally likely – the Germanic *Ell-sass*, meaning the seat of the river Ill. Today it is part of France, but culturally this region stands apart. The author Waverley Root describes the Alsatian people as 'French-Germans', a term that they might not take kindly to, but is hard to argue with. The Alsatian language is a dialect of German, and Germanic influence can be seen everywhere from traditional dress to architecture to food.

At first glance the food of Alsace is obviously Germanic – all sausages, sauerkraut, smoked bacon, little dumplings, sweet mustard, horseradish and beer. Delicious! Alsace is indeed sausage country, the traditions learned from its neighbour, and I make no apology here for the inclusion of several recipes involving smoked pork sausages: *Knack*, *Cervelas* or the imposing *Maennerstolz* (see page 249). The most famous local product is surely *choucroute*, the sour pickled cabbage known as *Sauerkraut* in Germany which is common throughout central and Eastern Europe.

But Alsatian food is far more than pork and cabbage: there are onion tarts oozing with cream, or *tarte flambée*, a thin pizza-like tart topped with onions, crème fraîche and little lardons of smoked bacon. The famous *coq au Riesling* uses the most delicious local white wine, and there are stews of game served with buttered little noodles called *spaetzle* (see page 262). Roast goose is a speciality, as is *foie gras* made from the bird's fattened liver; a product perhaps of the Jewish community that came to settle in Alsace, a community that possibly has influenced the local cuisine more than one might presume.

> *Germanic influence can be seen everywhere from traditional dress to architecture to food.*

At the Saturday farmers' market in Strasbourg there were more clues to the character of Alsatian cooking. The old Fish Market Square is where once river fishermen sold their wild salmon and the Dutch bargemen brought their salted herrings for pickling. Nowadays there are lots of river trout, whole, piled up and glistening on the slab, for poaching with a butter sauce (although no live trout were spotted for making *truite au bleu*: plans foiled!). Otherwise there are sides of wood-smoked trout to be sliced thinly and piled onto brown bread with butter, and trout terrines flavoured with morels and herbs.

Come summer, there are *myrtilles* – small wild blueberries – by the punnet, and deep red cherries by the kilo, fresh flowering mint and chives and fat sweet white onions piled high. On the cheese stalls are stacks of *munster fermier*, or big *tommes d'Alsace*, and next to them is the *charcutier* selling slabs of smoked bacon, links of sausages and a delectable *pâté en croûte au foie gras* – an Alsatian invention.

Alsace may be a tiny region of France but it has a sophisticated cuisine that borrows from and improves on that of its neighbour. On this subject Root writes: 'The cooking of Alsace would seem, indeed, to be to a considerable extent artificial – a borrowing, rather than a school imposed by the nature of the land. The cuisine of Germany has been moved bodily across the Rhine. There it has undergone naturalization, for the better. The Alsatians have added a French subtlety to the often rather unimaginative heaviness of German food.'

It is true that the cooking in Alsace does have a certain *je ne sais quoi*, even if it is hard to put your finger on: a *salade Strasbourgeoise* is not exactly a *wurstsalat*, and I would much rather a *choucroute garnie* (see page 239) than a *schlachteplatte*. This is most interesting: the idea that a cuisine could be borrowed, learned, but then improved upon, with the addition of some sort of Gallic flair.

Onion Tart

Elizabeth David, writing of Alsace in *French Provincial Cooking*, describes a meal that commenced with an onion tart 'flat as a plate but still somehow oozing with cream'. The ideal Alsatian onion tart should indeed ooze; the filling is a wondrous suspension of melting onion and cream that sets to the gentlest of wobbles. Take care slicing the tart; the pastry is short and the filling delicate – both for the better. It should be served warm, not piping hot from the oven with a little green salad: a glass of Riesling will do very nicely alongside.

FOR THE PASTRY:

250G/ 9OZ/ GENEROUS 2 CUPS	PLAIN FLOUR
I TSP	FINE SALT
I	EGG YOLK
115G/ 4OZ/ ½ CUP	SOFTENED BUTTER, DICED
3 TBSP	WATER

FOR THE FILLING:

100G/ 3½OZ/ ½ CUP	UNSALTED BUTTER
6	LARGE YELLOW ONIONS, SLICED INTO HALF-MOONS
2	EGG YOLKS
I	WHOLE EGG
100ML/ 3½FL OZ/ SCANT I CUP	MILK
200ML/ 7FL OZ/ SCANT I CUP	DOUBLE CREAM
	GRATED PARMESAN CHEESE
	SALT, FRESHLY GROUND PEPPER AND NUTMEG
28-CM/ 11-IN	LOOSE-BASED FLUTED TART TIN

To make the pastry, mix the flour and salt in a bowl. Mix in the egg yolk, followed by the butter. Bring together, then add the water. Work briefly to form a smooth dough without overworking. Flatten gently into a circular shape, wrap in clingfilm and chill for at least an hour.

Meanwhile, melt the butter in a large frying pan, add the onions, season with salt and cook, covered by a lid, for a good hour or so, until the slices have collapsed completely. Stir once in a while to prevent sticking – there should be very little colour on them. Remove the onions to a bowl.

Preheat the oven to 170°C fan/190°C/ 375°F/gas mark 5.

Roll out the chilled pastry to a thickness of 2mm/¼in. Drape the pastry over the tart tin and gently ease it into the edges. Trim the excess but leave a 1-cm/½-in overhang on all sides. Line the pastry with baking paper and fill with baking beans, dried chickpeas or whatever you have that fits the purpose. Blind-bake the tart for 15 minutes, then remove the beans and paper and return to the oven for a further 5 minutes. The pastry should be crisp and golden brown. Remove from the oven and increase the temperature to 180°C fan/200°C/400°F/gas mark 6.

Whisk the eggs, milk and cream together, season with pepper and nutmeg, and mix well through the cooked onions. Taste for salt. Carefully pour the onion mixture into the tart shell. It must come right up to the top, or you risk an uneven onion:pastry ratio. Grate with Parmesan.

Return the filled tart to the oven and bake for 35–40 minutes. When the filling is cooked there should still be the slightest of wobbles. Remove from the oven and leave until the tart is just warm. Slice carefully with a large knife.

Split Pea & Ham Soup

Classic Northern European fare this; split pea soup is very popular in Alsace. Green split peas are also nice here – slightly sweeter. This is a good way to use up the tasty stock left over from boiling a ham. I like the sweetness that the rye croutons and caraway lend it, and sizzling the seeds in the butter reminds me of making a tempering to pour over a dhal.

100G/ 3½OZ/ ½ CUP	YELLOW SPLIT PEAS, WASHED WELL AND SOAKED OVERNIGHT
½	ONION
I	CARROT, PEELED
I	STICK CELERY
½	SMALL LEEK
2	GARLIC CLOVES
50G/ I¾OZ/ 3 TBSP	UNSALTED BUTTER, PLUS 2 TBSP EXTRA FOR FRYING
I LITRE/ I¾ PINTS/ 4 CUPS	HAM OR CHICKEN STOCK OR WATER
	A SMALL CHUNK OF LEFTOVER HAM
I	SLICE OF RYE BREAD, CUT INTO I-CM/ ½IN DICE
I TSP	CARAWAY SEEDS
	SALT AND FRESHLY GROUND BLACK PEPPER
	CRÈME FRAÎCHE, TO SERVE

Drain and rinse the soaked split peas. Transfer them to a pot with fresh cold water and bring to the boil. Skim well the scum that rises, then reduce to a fast simmer. Continue to skim periodically.

Meanwhile, finely dice all the vegetables and sweat slowly in the butter. Season at the start with salt (only a little, the ham stock is salty) and pepper, and cook for around 15 minutes, until everything is soft. Drain the simmering split peas, add them to the vegetables, then pour in the ham stock (if your ham stock tastes salty, replace half of the stock with water).

Bring to the boil, then reduce to a simmer. Cook for about 1 hour, until the split peas are completely soft. If the split peas absorb a little too much stock, top it up, or use water. When cooked, whizz half of the soup in a blender for a slightly smoother texture (this step is optional). Tear up the ham into thick pieces and add to the soup; simmer for a few minutes while you make the croutons.

Fry the cubes of rye bread until crisp in the 2 tablespoons of butter. When the croutons are crisp, add the caraway seeds and sizzle them in the hot fat for a moment or two. Put the soup into bowls, introduce a dollop of crème fraîche, and spoon the croutons, caraway and a bit of the browned butter over the soup. Eat.

Clams with Peas, Bacon, Spices & Riesling SERVES 2

Not an authentic recipe, of course: there are no clams in the rivers of Alsace, but here's a reminder that Alsatian white wine pairs very well with both sweet shellfish and salty smoked bacon. The spices are an interesting addition but use them with a light touch or your tasty broth will be overwhelmed.

250G/ 9OZ	PALOURDE CLAMS
	OIL
I TBSP	DICED SMOKED BACON
½	GARLIC CLOVE, FINELY SLICED LENGTHWAYS
I	HANDFUL FRESHLY PODDED PEAS
I	SPRIG OF THYME
I	GLASS OF RIESLING
I5G/ ½OZ/ I TBSP	UNSALTED BUTTER
I TBSP	CHOPPED PARSLEY
	A SMALL PINCH OF CARAWAY SEEDS, CRUSHED TO A POWDER
	A SMALL GRATING OF NUTMEG
	LEMON JUICE
	FRESHLY GROUND BLACK PEPPER

To clean the clams — Give the shells a good rinse then set them in cold water for 30 minutes, then rinse again.

Heat a little oil in a large, lidded frying pan and slowly fry the bacon so that the fat renders and it starts to colour. Add the garlic, peas and thyme and swirl everything around in the hot fat. Cook slowly until the garlic sticks to itself, then add the clams and the wine. Cover with a lid and cook over a medium heat for a minute or two, until the shells open. Scoop out the open clams into two bowls.

Simmer and reduce the liquid in the pan until it tastes full and delicious, then add the butter, parsley, caraway, nutmeg and pepper and swirl the pan around again. Taste for seasoning – it probably won't need any salt depending on the clams. Finish with a squeeze of lemon juice, then pour the sauce and all its contents over the clams. Eat with some crusty bread and drink some more Riesling.

Poached Trout with Girolles & Butter Sauce

SERVES 4

This is a classic bit of fish cookery but don't let that put you off! It's a lovely late-summer plate of food – trout poached in an aromatic *court bouillon* (stock) and lightly sautéed girolles tied together with a butter sauce.

Chives are important here, breaking up the gold and cream motif and adding a bit of freshness. A just-warm puff pastry crescent (a *fleuron* if we're being all fancy) really does set things off nicely.

4	FILLETED PORTIONS OF TROUT OR SALMON, OR I LARGE WHOLE RAINBOW TROUT
15G/½OZ/ I TBSP	UNSALTED BUTTER
250G/9OZ	FRESH GIROLLES, CLEANED
	SALT AND FRESHLY GROUND BLACK PEPPER
I TBSP	FINELY CHOPPED CHIVES, TO FINISH

FOR THE *COURT BOUILLON*:

I	SHALLOT, HALVED
½	FENNEL BULB, HALVED
I	CELERY STICK
	A FEW PARSLEY STALKS
I TSP	BLACK PEPPERCORNS
I TSP	FENNEL SEEDS
I	BAY LEAF
I	SPRIG OF THYME

FOR THE BUTTER SAUCE:

100ML/ 3½FL OZ/ SCANT ½ CUP	WHITE WINE
50ML/ 2FL OZ/ SCANT ¼ CUP	WHITE WINE VINEGAR
½	SHALLOT, SLICED
4	PEPPERCORNS
I	BAY LEAF
I TBSP	DOUBLE CREAM
200G/ 7OZ/ I CUP	UNSALTED BUTTER, VERY COLD, DICED
	LEMON JUICE

Preheat the oven to 180°C fan/200°C/400°F/gas mark 6.

First, make the *court bouillon* and the reduction for the butter sauce, as they need time to simmer. Put all the ingredients for the *court bouillon* in a wide saucepan and fill with cold water. Bring to the boil and simmer gently for 20 minutes, then remove the gubbins. Season with salt.

Meanwhile, make the reduction for the butter sauce. Put the wine, vinegar, shallot, peppercorns and bay leaf in a small pan, bring to the boil, and simmer until reduced to 2 tablespoons. The idea is to evaporate almost all of the liquid and then replace it with butter. Strain through a sieve into another small pan, squeezing to extract all the liquid. Discard the solids and set aside the reduction.

To make the *fleurons*, use a 10-cm/4-in fluted cookie cutter to cut out a circle of puff pastry, then cut an overlapping circle to form a crescent. Repeat until you have made eight little crescents. Score the surface with a paring knife to form a decorative pattern. Brush the tops with the beaten egg – be careful not to allow the egg to drip down the sides as this will inhibit the pastry from rising. Bake in the hot oven for 10 minutes or so until fully risen, flaky and golden. Remove and allow to cool. Turn the temperature down low to use later to warm things through.

Lower the trout into the simmering court *bouillon*. Simmer gently for only a minute, then turn off the heat and cover the pan. The trout should be cooked in 5–10 minutes, depending on the size and thickness of your fillets; it should be just warm in the centre of the fillet.

While the fish poaches, finish the sauce. Gently reheat the reduction. Whisk in the double cream, followed by a couple of cubes of the butter. When this has almost all disappeared add another couple of cubes. Repeat until the butter is used up – ensure you never boil or simmer the sauce or it will split. Season well with salt and a squeeze of lemon juice. Keep warm.

FOR THE *FLEURONS*:

1	SHEET OF PRE-ROLLED PUFF PASTRY
1	BEATEN EGG, FOR GLAZING

To cook the girolles, melt the butter in a frying pan, add the girolles and season with salt. Fry until soft then keep warm in the oven (pop the *fleurons* back in to warm through as well) until the fish is cooked.

Skin the trout and place on plates. Nestle a pile of girolles next to the trout, then pour over a copious amount of butter sauce. Garnish with a *fleuron* or two and sprinkle the chives over the fish. Black pepper is optional but very good.

Pictured overleaf

Salade Strasbourgeoise

A Strasbourg salad is sort of unashamed in that the salad part is mostly minimal and it consists mostly of sausage and cheese, which is obviously brilliant. There are a few ways to go about this, and a little careful thought, I think, can make all the difference. This kind of thing is known in other parts as *Wurstsalat* (sausage salad in German) and sometimes comes bound in a thin mayonnaise, other times seasoned with pumpkin oil and pickle juice, or made with a vinaigrette using sweet mustard. I favour vinaigrette, which seems more appropriate, and for this to be a Strasbourg salad it should made with Dijon rather than a sweet German mustard, because we are on the western side of the border.

There should be no potato. Potato salad is delicious and you can find a recipe for one on page 251, but this eats better without. The cheese should really be Emmental, although I bet this would be great with a young Gruyère. Either way, buy a piece in a block so that you can cut it the way you want. There should also be young lettuce – something snappy rather than floppy – and some excellent ripe tomatoes. Cornichons

and a bit of raw onion add a little zip. Boiled egg gilds the lily.

Most importantly, the sausage. This is made with *Cervelas*, a slightly smoked, chubby, pale boiling sausage, which is common to Alsace, Switzerland and parts of Germany. The word *cervelas* refers to the brain that was once the stuffing for this type of sausage, as well as for the related Saveloy, which is easier to source. Am I suggesting you buy some Saveloys from the chip shop in order to make this salad? Yes, obviously. Alternatively, buy some raw and boil yourself, or get some decent Frankfurters, or check out a Polish deli where there will definitely be something very good. The sausages should be mild, only lightly smoked and emulsified within.

There are varying schools of thought as to how to cut the salad. A fine julienne? Thin, flat, long strips? Cubes? Sausages sliced lengthways into quarters? I do like the look of the sausage and cheese cut the same way – into chunky strips that will tumble down into the salad. Do it any way you want. I found making this great fun.

Recipe continues overleaf

Salade Strasbourgeoise continued

2	*CERVELAS* SAUSAGES, OR SAVELOYS, FRANKFURTERS, OR SOMETHING GREAT FROM THE POLISH DELI, COOKED AND CHILLED
100G/ 3½OZ/ GENEROUS 1 CUP	EMMENTAL OR YOUNG GRUYÈRE CHEESE
2	RIPE TOMATOES
2	HEADS BABY GEM LETTUCE, LEAVES SEPARATED, WASHED AND DRIED
1	SMALL SWEET WHITE ONION, SLICED THINLY
2	HARD-BOILED EGGS, QUARTERED
	A SMALL HANDFUL OF CORNICHONS
	CHOPPED CHIVES, TO GARNISH

FOR THE VINAIGRETTE:

	A SCRAP OF GARLIC
2 TSP	DIJON MUSTARD
½ TSP	HONEY
1 TBSP	WHITE WINE OR CIDER VINEGAR
3 TBSP	OLIVE OIL
1 TBSP	WATER

Slice the sausage into strips about 5cm/2in long and 4mm/¼in thick. Cut the cheese into pieces the same size and shape. Cut the tomatoes into thin wedges. Arrange the tomatoes, sausage and cheese on top of the lettuce. Sprinkle over a few slices of the onion, and tuck in quarters of hard-boiled egg. Chop the cornichons and sprinkle over the top.

Mix together the ingredients for the mustard vinaigrette and spoon over enough to moisten the whole salad but not drown it. Finish with a sprinkle of chopped chives.

Smoked Sausage with Potato Salad

Winstub means literally 'wine bar', but in Alsace this was originally a type of restaurant opened by a winemaker to sell surplus stock by the pitcher on their own premises. The food served is hearty local fare – onion tarts, foie gras, snails in garlic butter, pig's head terrine, *choucroute garni*, *coq au Riesling avec spaetzle*. Chez Yvonne, on an innocuous corner spot near the cathedral in Strasbourg, is famous for having been a regular meeting place between the newly elected Jacques Chirac and the German Chancellor Helmut Kohl. On the menu: choucroute, beer and discussions about the reforging of a great Franco-German friendship and the construction of a new Europe. Beer and sausage: common ground.

For the main event I order a smoked sausage called 'Man's Pride', because how could I not? *Maennerstolz* is a pork and beef sausage, a local speciality of Strasbourg. I'd say it was 10 inches long and a good inch thick, semi-emulsified, with cubes of fat running through, and a good snap. It came with enough potato salad for three people.

The potato salad is not the mayonnaise-based style that we know and love, but instead moistened with stock and a vinaigrette, sliced raw red onion and a sprinkle of chives.

There's a little pot of mustard on the table, slightly sweet. The other pot is filled with some quite hardcore grated horseradish. I piled it all on.

FOR THE POTATO SALAD:

4	WAXY POTATOES, SUCH AS PINK FIR
I	RED ONION, VERY THINLY SLICED
	A FEW CORNICHONS, CHOPPED INTO 5-MM/¼-IN LENGTHS, PLUS A LITTLE OF THEIR PICKLING JUICE
I TBSP	SWEET MUSTARD
50ML/ 2FL OZ/ SCANT ¼ CUP	OLIVE OIL
2 TBSP	CRÈME FRAICHE
50ML/ 2FL OZ/ SCANT ¼ CUP	LIGHT CHICKEN STOCK
	SALT AND FRESHLY GROUND BLACK PEPPER

TO SERVE:

2 TBSP	FINELY CHOPPED PARSLEY AND CHIVES
I	COOKED SMOKED SAUSAGE (MY LOCAL SHOP SELLS PORK AND BEEF POLISH *KIEŁBASA ŚLASKA* THAT ARE VERY DELICIOUS), EITHER BOILED OR SLIGHTLY SCORED AND ROASTED IN A HOT OVEN
	SWEET MUSTARD
	HORSERADISH CREAM (SEE PAGE 222)

Boil the potatoes in a pan of lightly salted water until soft. Drain and cool until you can handle them (but try to keep warm as they will absorb the dressing better), peel and slice across the diameter into slices no smaller than 1cm/½in thick.

Toss the still-warm potatoes in a bowl with the sliced onion and cornichons. Add the sweet mustard, the olive oil, crème fraiche, and moisten with a little chicken stock to your preference – more stock will make the salad looser. Drizzle in a little of the pickle juice from the cornichons jar, to taste. Season well with salt and black pepper.

Mix well and serve warm or at room temperature, sprinkled with the parsley and chives, alongside the hot sausage and the condiments.

Choucroute

Choucroute, aka *sauerkraut*, is a European relic of a time before refrigeration, when slicing, salting and fermenting cabbages would see a family through winter when nothing was growing. Alsace's most famous dish, *choucroute garnie* (garnished *choucroute*), is a celebration of pork and fermented cabbage like no other. I tried quite few in Strasbourg and regret to report that the *chou* itself was dry – this is to be avoided. Keep it moist, luscious and lightly glistening with duck fat.

I realize that making your own *choucroute* from scratch makes this at least a two-week rather than a two-hour process, but there is very little work involved, and most of this incubation period is spent watching and waiting; observing your salted cabbage's slow journey into something more special.

Wash the cabbages and discard any discoloured or floppy outer leaves. Cut in half, remove the core, and weigh the cabbages. Slice as thinly as possible by hand with a big sharp knife. Alternatively, use a mandoline, but resist the urge to slice extremely thinly: 2mm/⅛in is perfectly fine. Put the slices in a large bowl and add correct amount of salt. Toss the cabbage with the salt and sprinkle on the caraway seeds, peppercorns and juniper berries, if using. Leave for 30 minutes.

Use your hands to massage and squish the cabbage forcefully: the goal is to work the salt into the cabbage and to draw the water from it. You can leave the cabbage for a period to let the salt do its work, then return to pummel it some more.

Once the cabbage has released a good amount of water and has started to soften, it can be tightly packed into sterilized glass jars with its water. Squish the cabbage down firmly until it is completely covered by its own water. Weight the cabbage down with something heavy so it remains underneath the water – use a clean smooth stone, or fill a ziplock sandwich bag with water to use as a weight.

2	WHITE CABBAGES
I TSP	CARAWAY SEEDS
I TSP	BLACK PEPPERCORNS
4	JUNIPER BERRIES (OPTIONAL)
	FINE SALT – 3% SALT TO CABBAGE WEIGHT (FOR EVERY I KG/2LB 4OZ OF CABBAGE ALLOW 30G/I OZ SALT)

Leave the cabbage at room temperature for 2–3 weeks: fermentation time will depend on the ambient temperature. If any cabbage becomes exposed to the air it must be squished down again. Alternatively you can make a 3% brine and use this to top up the water inside the jar. Any cabbage that has been exposed to air might have picked up some unwanted moulds. This cabbage can be discarded without harming the good stuff underneath it. The *choucroute* is ready when it has softened but retains a delicious crunch. The flavour will be acidic, fresh and full of umami. This will keep for a few weeks more in the fridge.

Choucroute Garnie

It helps to brine the fresh meats before cooking – this will keep them juicy and pink. For the pork collar or belly, brining for two days in a 10% brine (for every 1kg/2lb 4oz of meat allow 100g/3½oz salt) should do it, or just salt the meat overnight. It is usually quite easy to buy a pre-brined ham hock from a butcher, which should save you some trouble as hocks are a little bulky.

The whole piece of bacon can be bought at a good Eastern European deli. You are after the one that is smoked but still quite soft. Cut into thick slices so they don't fall apart as they soften. I would definitely go to the trouble to find some proper Alsatian-style *Knack*, the slightly fatter equivalent of a Frankfurter, but either one is acceptable. Maybe both!

THE MEATS:

1	UNSMOKED HAM HOCK, BRINED, WASHED
500G/ 1LB 2OZ	BONELESS PIECE OF PORK COLLAR (PORK NECK) OR PORK BELLY, BRINED, WASHED
2	THICK (2CM/½IN) SLICES OF SMOKED ALSATIAN (OR POLISH) BACON
	A MIXTURE OF SMOKED SAUSAGES – *MONTÉLIARD, MORTEAU,* POLISH SMOKED *KIEŁBASA ŚLĄSKA, KNACK* (STRASBOURG) OR FRANKFURTER SAUSAGES – TRY TO AIM FOR AT LEAST TWO TYPES

Start cooking the ham hock first in a large, lidded saucepan: bring the ham up to the boil in cold water, discard the water then repeat with fresh cold water. Bring to the boil, reduce to a simmer, skim well, and cook at a simmer for about two hours with the pan half-covered, or until the ham begins to soften but is not yet falling off the bone – you want it to be two-thirds cooked.

Meanwhile, heat the duck fat in a large stockpot and slowly fry the onion slices with the bay leaves and a pinch of salt. Cook until the onion is good and soft but with little colour. Tie the spices and crushed garlic in a muslin bundle and pop it in. Taste a bit of your *choucroute* – it will need washing to mellow its sourness. With homemade *choucroute* I usually only wash once, but the commercially made stuff can be sourer and will need two washes under cold running water. Once washed, squeeze well, then add to the soft onions in the pot. Give everything a good stir together to coat the cabbage in the fat.

Recipe continues overleaf

Choucroute Garnie continued

Pour in the Riesling, bring to a bubble, then add enough stock to almost cover the cabbage. Add a little of the (skimmed) ham cooking liquor too. Bring to the boil then reduce to a slow simmer. Nestle in your brined pork collar. Cover with a lid but leave a little 1-cm/½-in gap for some steam to escape and flavour your kitchen. Cook the pork collar for 1½ hours, or until almost soft, then add in your partially cooked ham hock and thick slices of smoked bacon. Add a little more stock if the *choucroute* is threatening to dry out – keep the whole assembly moist at all stages.

When the meats are soft, quivering and just threatening to fall apart, turn the heat off and cover with a lid. Taste the cabbage for seasoning – it might need a little salt, but probably not. Meanwhile, boil the potatoes in a pan of lightly salted water, and boil the sausages according to the packet instructions. Keep warm.

Pour a splash of kirsch into the *choucroute* pot and return briefly to the heat. When all is hot, it is time to eat. Serve the choucroute on a large platter, garnished like this: pile steaming cabbage in the centre, with the boiled meats and sausages in, on and around it, surrounded by the potatoes. The cabbage should be nice and moist but leave any excess liquid in the pot rather than pouring it all onto the platter. Serve with the mustards, horseradish and pickles on the side, and make merry.

THE *CHOUCROUTE*:

2 TBSP	DUCK OR GOOSE FAT
2	YELLOW ONIONS, FINELY SLICED INTO HALF-MOONS
2	BAY LEAVES
6	PEPPERCORNS
1 TSP	CARAWAY SEEDS
4	JUNIPER BERRIES
2	CLOVES
4	GARLIC CLOVES, UNPEELED, CRUSHED LIGHTLY WITH YOUR HAND OR THE FLAT OF A KNIFE
2	BIG DOUBLE HANDFULS OF *CHOUCROUTE*; HOMEMADE IS BEST, SEE PAGE 254
¼	BOTTLE OF DRY RIESLING
500ML/ 18FL OZ/ 2 CUPS	LIGHT CHICKEN OR HAM STOCK OR WATER
	A GOOD GLUG OF KIRSCH (CHERRY BRANDY)

THINGS TO EAT WITH IT:

POTATOES, PEELED
MUSTARDS – DIJON, SWEET, WHOLEGRAIN …THE MORE THE MERRIER
CREAMED HORSERADISH (THAT'S THE GERMANIC INFLUENCE FOR YOU)
CORNICHONS
PICCALILLI (OBVIOUSLY UNHEARD OF IN ALSACE, BUT MORE FOOL THEM)

Pasta

I've developed a liking for the French way with pasta. I'm sure it's all a joke to the Italians, who – let's face it – do it a lot better. When I lived in Paris and spent hours with my friends in the local bistro drinking coffee after coffee, we would look on with amusement as the lunchtime dishes rolled out, where a mound of sorry-looking, overcooked tagliatelle (nouilles or 'noodles', as the French put it) was served as an accompaniment to coq au vin or the braised meat du jour. How we chuckled! For we knew that Italians always serve pasta with the sauce, not alongside.

Years later, bored of boiled potatoes for some reason, and remembering the fondness the French have for pâtes (pasta), I ventured to serve a pile of fresh tagliatelle with my coq au vin. A revelation! Carefully cooked, lightly buttered and dusted with Parmesan, the sauce gradually winds its way into the pile of pasta as you eat it: a real joy. Plus, there's a certain nostalgic element to a pile of buttered cheesy pasta.

The Alsatian *spaetzle*, an import from southwest Germany, have a similar appeal: dressed with fried onions and cheese they are delicious on their own, and the little squiggles of this eggy pasta are excellent plainly buttered and served alongside a rich stew – a gravy mopper of the highest order. Plain *spaetzle* are commonly served alongside a coq au Riesling, civets of game, or pork knuckles braised in Pinot Noir, but I quite enjoy treating them as one would any other pasta: tossing them with fresh spring mushrooms and cream, topping them with a veal, pork and radicchio *ragoût* or blitzing nettles into the dough and serving the green noodles with poached trout, crème fraîche and lots of black pepper (see page 264).

> *Despite the similarities between neighbouring regions, it's more likely that the origin of pasta as we know it dates back to the Greeks and the Arabs.*

There are a few other French pasta dishes that are indisputably delicious: nouilles fraîches with butter and Parmesan, for instance, and macaroni *au jus* to serve alongside a roast or a *daube* – boiled macaroni, either straight or elbow, heavily buttered, moistened with some of the cooking juices from the meat, layered with grated Parmesan and served alongside. There's the famous green gnocchi of Nice – merda de can (see page 136) – and the city's former mayor Jacques Médecin proffers a few noteworthy pasta recipes in his book Cuisine Niçoise: a green lasagna baked with a pork, beef and chicken liver *ragù*; cannelloni with beef and Swiss chard; raviolis *à la daube*, and the fabulously French Les macaronis Jetée-Promenade – a baked pasta with chicken breast, ham, mushrooms, *béchamel* sauce and fresh black truffle ('serve with hot veal juices' is Médecin's advice).

Above all, Nice is famous for its pâtes au pistou. Pistou is similar to pesto Genovese but without the intense perfume of its Italian cousin; maybe the basil is different. The chef at the renowned La Merenda in Nice, Dominique Le Stanc, tosses each portion carefully in a warmed earthenware bowl, and his pasta is perfect – green with spinach and basil, fresh, toothsome, cut slightly flat but textured like that made alla chitarra.

It is in exploring the Alpine regions of southeast France that the history of pasta gets really interesting. Jean-Noël Escudier, an authority on Provençal cuisine, writes of gnocchi in his book The Wonderful Food of Provence: 'Contrary to what is generally supposed, the origin of this dish is not Italian but Provençal-Niçois. Even the name "gnocchi" is derived from the Niçois dialect … We think of ravioli as an Italian dish. And so, indeed, it is. But actually, its long-forgotten origin was the ancient "ralhôla" (railloles in French), which was made – and still is – in the hilly Provence of the East and in Nice.' The plot thickens.

Chef and author Madeleine Kamman's work Savoie: The Land, People, and Food of the French Alps documents the old culinary traditions of Savoie, and echoes Escudier's observations. She writes: 'It would be wrong to believe that the Savoie learned its pasta making from Italy. Pasta was there historically among the Ceutron, Graiocèle and Médulle populations that, centuries before the opening of the Alpine passes, made tiny squares of dough, which they called crozets.' Crozets are perhaps the most famous of mountain pastas and are still regularly encountered in the Savoie. A mixture of flours would have been typical: buckwheat and rye for flavour, wheat for substance. The flavour marries well with cabbage and cheese, just like the northern Italian pizzoccheri, a thick, largely buckwheat, noodle quickly boiled then baked with Fontina cheese, boiled cabbage and lashings of melted butter flavoured with sage and garlic (see page 202).

Taillerins are Savoie's equivalent of tagliatelle. The seasoning would be simple – butter fried until nut brown, and sweet onions or shallots stewed until melting, the pasta dusted with cheese before serving. Bacon and cream, quintessential mountain ingredients, are also popular. Kamman offers a delicious recipe for taillerins flavoured with lovage, an idea that I have approximated on page 198.

I was also very interested to learn about the Savoyard fides, a fine spaghettini that would be dried and cooked in a similar way to the Spanish fideuà (think paella but using pasta instead of rice): the dried pasta first toasted in oil then moistened with stock. The origin of fidés is difficult to pinpoint, as it's likely that dried pasta such as this would have been traded throughout the Mediterranean and would have been a valuable staple of the Savoyard mountain folk. Ligurian seafaring traders were known as the Fidellari after their dried spaghetti-like fidelli, which was easily exported on long sea voyages.

Despite the similarities between neighbouring regions, it's more likely that the origin of pasta as we know it dates back to the Greeks and the Arabs. The first recorded instance of something resembling pasta, made from milled wheat mixed with water and cooked on a hot stone, dates back to the first millennium BC, most likely from the Greeks. Arab pasta-making is documented from the thirteenth century, when the original fidawsh was cooked much in the style of a fideuà today. Kamman's recipe for a pilaf of fides is made with chicken broth, peas and saffron, a custom she suggests was introduced by the Arabs along with their pasta. We may naturally assume that the origin of French pasta dishes is in Italy, but the roots of these traditions may well extend far wider.

Spaetzle

Alsace's famous noodle is an import from southern Germany and *spätzle* (here with an umlaut) is also made in Austria. This is a basic recipe for *spaetzle*, one for serving alongside a rich stew cooked in red wine, for example, or on its own, loaded with cheese, naturally, and plenty of onions, which you should cook slowly in butter until they melt.

Once cooked these keep very well – perfect for making ahead and then reheating in a sauce or in lightly browned butter. A *spaetzle*-maker is cheap and readily available from popular online retailers – worth the investment!

2	EGGS
100G/ 3½OZ/ SCANT ⅔ CUP	BREAD FLOUR
100G/ 3½OZ/ ⅔ CUP	FINE SEMOLINA
70ML/ 2½FL OZ/ ⅓ CUP	MILK
I TSP	VEGETABLE OIL
	PINCH OF SALT
	GRATED NUTMEG, TO TASTE
	UNSALTED BUTTER, FOR FRYING

Whisk all the ingredients together well. Once the batter is made, let it rest for at least 30 minutes at room temperature.

The idea is that your batter will drop through your *spaetzle*-maker (or a colander) into simmering water. The batter should be just thin enough that it will drop through the holes without too much encouragement – too thick is a pain to work with, but too thin will result in soft *spaetzle* without any of their characteristic chew.

Set your *spaetzle*-maker or colander above a pan of lightly salted simmering water. Ladle in some of the batter and it will drop through the holes into the water. If using a colander, a bench scraper will encourage the batter down through the holes, but don't be too forceful. You can stir the *spaetzle* gently in the pot as the batter is dropping through, which will ensure that they don't stick while still in the water.

Set the *spaetzle*-maker on a small tray (so as not to create a large mess!) and scoop out the *spaetzle* as soon as they float – this will take very little time at all. Lay the cooked *spaetzle* on a shallow tray and lightly oil and gently toss to prevent sticking. Repeat until all the *spaetzle* are made.

At this stage the *spaetzle* can be stored in the fridge until ready to eat. They keep well overnight if cooled and stored properly.

When ready to eat, heat a large pan, throw in the *spaetzle* and toss well with lots of butter, frying them until golden. This is a great accompaniment to a rich game stew. Also very good tossed with slowly cooked onions as in the introduction above; choose a cheese that melts well without stringing too much (Comté is delicious, for example, or a Tomme de Savoie), then grate it in and toss briefly before serving.

Spaetzle au Gratin with Munster & Bacon

SERVES 4

Leftover *spaetzle* is an excellent thing to have around, and in the restaurant where I work everyone is very pleased to see something like this on the table for staff food: underneath a thick golden brown crust hide the little noodles, bobbing around in a bath of molten cheese with bits of smoked bacon.

I ate this in a hurry as I had half an hour before my train left Colmar for the airport. The temperature outside was 32 degrees celsius, and the portion was gargantuan. As I was in a rush I ate it too fast, burned my mouth on it, sweated buckets and didn't manage more than half. The waitress laughed at me, but here I am with a recipe to show for it.

It's not a particularly subtle one: Munster is a pungent Alsatian cheese and if you want to make the dish more mellow, try using Gruyère instead. In autumn, this would be lovely made with some dried ceps and fresh wild mushrooms.

I TBSP	OLIVE OIL
200G/ 7OZ	SMOKED BACON, CUT INTO LARDONS
2	YELLOW ONIONS, FINELY SLICED INTO HALF-MOONS
6	GARLIC CLOVES, SLICED LENGTHWAYS
I	SPRIG OF THYME, LEAVES PICKED
30G/1OZ/ 2 TBSP	BUTTER, PLUS EXTRA FOR GREASING
2 TBSP	PLAIN FLOUR
500ML/ 18FL OZ/ 2 CUPS	MILK
250G/ 9OZ	MUNSTER CHEESE
	COOKED *SPAETZLE* (SEE OPPOSITE)
	A FEW RASHERS OF SMOKED STREAKY BACON
	SALT AND FRESHLY GROUND BLACK PEPPER

Preheat the oven to 200°C fan/220°C/425°F/ gas mark 7.

Heat the olive oil in a large, ovenproof casserole dish and fry the bacon until crisp and the fat rendered. Add the onions, garlic and thyme, with a pinch of salt and some pepper. Cook slowly until all is very soft and quite sweet. Add the butter and, when melted, chuck in the flour and stir around for a bit. Add the milk gradually until you have a sauce with the consistency of a loose *béchamel*. Melt in a quarter of the Munster cheese, then add the *spaetzle* and pour into a buttered gratin dish that will hold them all.

Slice the remaining Munster and layer on the *spaetzle*. Top with the bacon rashers. Bake the gratin in the oven for 15–20 minutes until the cheese has melted and formed a crust with the crisp bacon, and all within is bubbling molten delicious goo. Serve extremely hot with lots of wine, and maybe a salad (for health).

Nettle Spaetzle with Poached Trout & Crème Fraîche

In the north of Italy near the Austrian border they make a delicious spinach *spätzle*, often served with fried *speck* (cured ham). Here, nettles are used to the same verdant effect. Nettles pair very well with fish and cream, to create a perhaps untraditional idea with a slightly more Alsatian flavour. There's something interesting about using *spaetzle* with seasonal sauces, and there's plenty more to explore for those who aren't sticklers for tradition. Plus, apart from anything else, 'nettle *spaetzle*' is fun to say.

During the spring, and wearing thick gloves, pick the young nettle tips from the top of the plants. Strip them off the stalk and blanch for a second or two in boiling salted water before use – this takes out their sting. Reserve a tablespoon or so of cooked, chopped nettles to stir into the *spaetzle* at the end.

300G/ 10½OZ	FILLETED TROUT OR SOCKEYE SALMON, PIN-BONED
50G/ 1¾OZ/ 3 TBSP	UNSALTED BUTTER
2	SMALL SHALLOTS, SLICED INTO HALF-MOONS
	A PINCH OF CARAWAY SEEDS
	A SPRIG OF THYME, LEAVES PICKED
I TBSP	CRÈME FRAÎCHE
	LEMON ZEST AND JUICE
	SALT AND FRESHLY GROUND BLACK PEPPER
I TBSP	FINELY CHOPPED CHIVES, TO GARNISH

To cook the nettles, blanch them in lightly salted boiling water for a few seconds, then drain, cool and squeeze well of water. Blitz to a smooth paste with the eggs (reserve a tablespoon full of cooked nettles to add in at the end).

Whisk the *spaetzle* ingredients together. Note that, depending on how well you squeezed out the nettles, you may not need all of the milk – add gradually until you have a smooth but very thick gloopy batter that drops slowly off a spoon.

Allow the batter to rest for 30 minutes before passing through a *spaetzle*-maker or colander into a pan of lightly salted simmering water (see page 262 for full instructions). Set aside the *spaetzle* once cooked.

While the batter rests, make a court *bouillon* for poaching the trout. Put all the vegetables in a wide saucepan, cover well with cold water, bring to the boil, skim, and simmer for 20 minutes. Remove the vegetables using a spotted spoon, season with salt, and slip in the trout.

Recipe continues overleaf

Nettle Spaetzle with Poached Trout & Crème Fraîche continued

Bring back to a simmer then turn off the heat and leave the fish in the liquid for a few minutes until it is cooked – slip a thin skewer into the flesh and if it passes through easily the fish is done. Take care not to overcook the fish as you will be reheating it with the *spaetzle*. Lift out the fish and allow to cool. Reserve a few tablespoons of the poaching liquid.

Skin the trout and flake it gently into large pieces.

To finish, heat the butter in a large frying pan and slowly fry the shallots with the caraway seeds, thyme leaves and a pinch of salt. They should be soft, sweet and golden. Add the *spaetzle*. Stir to coat the *spaetzle* with butter and ensure they are not stuck together. Add a couple of tablespoons of the poaching liquor, followed by the cooked, flaked trout and the reserved cooked nettles. Stir and toss gently, then add the crème fraîche and toss again. Take care not to break the trout up too much.

Taste for salt. If the sauce looks thin, add a little more cream, or if it looks thick, add another spoon of liquor. Season sparingly with lemon juice and a little scrape of lemon zest. When all is hot and tasty spoon the *spaetzle* onto waiting plates. Sprinkle over the chives and grind over plenty of black pepper.

FOR THE NETTLE *SPAETZLE*:

6 TBSP (APPROX. 150G/ 5½OZ)	COOKED NETTLES, PLUS 1 TBSP COOKED, CHOPPED NETTLES TO FINISH
2	EGGS
100G/ 3½OZ/ SCANT ⅔ CUP	BREAD FLOUR
100G/ 3½OZ/ ⅔ CUP	FINE SEMOLINA
1 TSP	VEGETABLE OIL
	PINCH OF SALT
	GRATED NUTMEG, TO TASTE
ABOUT 70ML/ 2½FL OZ/ ⅓ CUP	MILK

FOR THE *COURT BOUILLON*:

1	CELERY STICK
	A THICK SLICE OF FENNEL BULB
½	SHALLOT
	A FEW PARSLEY STALKS
1 TSP	BLACK PEPPERCORNS
1	BAY LEAF
1	SPRIG OF THYME

Baeckeoffe

I once had a spectacularly bad *baeckeoffe* in Strasbourg, a masterclass in how not to choose a restaurant or a dish for dinner; a self-inflicted meal. It was a very hot day, I had ordered a hot-pot, the portion was big enough for four, and it was garbage. Anyway, I thought, at least now I can cook it myself. *Baeckeoffe* means 'baker's oven', a reference to a way of life before each household had its own oven when a hot-pot would have been made up at home and taken to the local baker in the morning where it could cook slowly as the oven cooled, the earthenware lid sealed with a dough to keep all the juices in.

This is as traditional as the food gets in Alsace – a mixture of lamb, pork and beef, marinated in juniper and Riesling, stewed with alliums and topped with a layer of sliced potatoes like they do in Lancashire. The reason I ended up at the terrible restaurant in Strasbourg was because they advertised the inclusion of pig's trotters as well as the cubed meats: good idea, poorly executed. If you want to include them, you'll need to cook the trotters the day before, which will give you both some sticky delicious meat to chop into the mix and a flavourful stock to use.

This is proper winter stuff – don't order it on a hot summer's day at a tourist trap in Strasbourg. Make this when you want something that tastes satisfyingly plain and you are happy to serve piping hot.

FOR THE TROTTERS AND STOCK:

2	PIG'S TROTTERS, HAIRS REMOVED
4	CHICKEN WINGS
I	LEEK, HALVED
I	ONION, UNPEELED AND HALVED
I	CARROT
I	SPRIG OF THYME
I0	BLACK PEPPERCORNS
	A FEW PARSLEY STALKS
I	SMALL GLASS OF RIESLING

(IF THIS LOOKS TOO MUCH OF A FAFF, USE ABOUT 500ML/18FL OZ/ 2 CUPS OF NICE CHICKEN STOCK INSTEAD, OR EVEN WATER)

Boil the pig's trotters in a pan of water for 5 minutes, then discard the water and rinse. Put them in a clean stockpot with the other ingredients, then cover with water. Bring to the boil, then turn down to a simmer and cook for 3 hours, or until the pig's feet are totally giving. Remove the trotters and allow to cool. Strain the stock. Pick all the meat, fat and skin from the trotters and roughly chop. Keep the trotters and the stock in the refrigerator until the following day.

Recipe continues overleaf

Baeckeoffe continued

FOR THE *BAECKEOFFE*:	
300G/ 10½OZ	BEEF SHIN, CUT INTO 4-CM/1½-IN PIECES
300G/ 10½OZ	LAMB SHOULDER, CUT INTO 4-CM/1½-IN PIECES
300G/ 10½OZ	PORK SHOULDER, CUT INTO 4-CM/1½-IN PIECES
6	JUNIPER BERRIES, CRUSHED
2	BAY LEAVES
1	SPRIG OF THYME
1	BOTTLE OF RIESLING
4 TBSP	DUCK FAT, PLUS EXTRA FOR GREASING
2	ONIONS, SLICED THINLY INTO HALF-MOONS
2	LEEKS, SLICED INTO ROUNDS
1	CARROT, SLICED INTO ROUNDS
8	FAT GARLIC CLOVES
4	MEDIUM RED POTATOES, PEELED AND SLICED THINLY
	A FEW RASHERS OF SMOKED STREAKY BACON
	FLOUR AND WATER, TO MAKE A PASTE TO SEAL THE POT
	CHOPPED PARSLEY, TO SERVE
	SALT AND FRESHLY GROUND BLACK PEPPER

Place the prepared meats in a non-metallic bowl, add the juniper, bay and thyme leaves and pour over the Riesling. Cover and leave in the fridge overnight to marinate.

The following day, when you are ready to cook, preheat the oven to 150°C fan/170°C/375°F/gas mark 5.

Melt the duck fat in a large saucepan and sweat the onions with a good pinch of salt. Cook them slowly until they are soft, then add the leeks, carrot and garlic. Stew until everything has softened, then add the marinated meats (reserve the marinade) and the prepared trotters, if using, to the pan. Cook, stirring, for a few minutes, then add the marinade and top up with stock or water to cover. Bring to the boil and taste for seasoning. Remove from the heat.

Take a shallow earthenware dish with a lid (at a push you can use two layers of foil), and grease it with duck fat, then make a layer of sliced potatoes, slightly overlapping. Season with salt and pepper. Spoon over your stew and cover with a second layer of potatoes. Season again with salt and pepper. There should be enough liquid so that it sits just underneath the top layer of potatoes. Cover the potatoes with a layer of bacon rashers.

Put the lid on the dish. Make a dough out of the flour and water (roughly two parts flour to water) and press around the rim of the lid to seal it. Transfer to the oven and bake for 3 hours. Chip away at the dough sealing the lid and remove the lid – be careful of the hot steam. Spoon onto plates and sprinkle with chopped parsley.

Rabbit with Mustard & Bacon SERVES 4

This one is an absolute classic: mustard and bacon are a great match for rabbit. Based on Robert Carrier's recipe for rabbit with two mustards: he uses French and English; I like Dijon for depth of flavour, and grain mustard for nubbly texture. Some recipes tell you to smear the mustard on the rabbit before it cooks, but I like this better when the mustard is added just before serving, as it keeps the taste somehow fresher. Serve this with something green – blanched spinach or green beans – to offset the rich, savoury sauce.

If using a whole rabbit, cut into six pieces: remove the hind and front legs, then cut away the head and ribcage and discard (keep any offal for a tasty snack). Cut the loin into two pieces. Season the pieces of rabbit with salt and pepper, and dust with the flour.

I	RABBIT, OR 4 RABBIT LEGS
2 TBSP	FLOUR, FOR DUSTING
60G/ 2¼OZ/ 4 TBSP	UNSALTED BUTTER, PLUS 30G/1OZ/ 2 TBSP, COLD, CUBED TO FINISH THE SAUCE
2 TBSP	OLIVE OIL
2	SHALLOTS, SLICED INTO HALF-MOONS
I	HEAD OF GARLIC, BROKEN INTO CLOVES
I	NICE BIG SPRIG OF THYME
½	BOTTLE OF WHITE WINE
250ML/ 9FL OZ/ GENEROUS I CUP	LIGHT CHICKEN STOCK OR JUST USE WATER
4	RASHERS OF SMOKED STREAKY BACON
200ML/ 7FL OZ/ SCANT I CUP	DOUBLE CREAM
2 TBSP	DIJON MUSTARD
2 TBSP	GRAIN MUSTARD
	SALT AND FRESHLY GROUND BLACK PEPPER
	BLANCHED SPINACH OR GREEN BEANS, TO SERVE

Preheat the oven to 160°C fan/180°C/350°F/ gas mark 4.

Brown the rabbit in butter and olive oil in a roomy pot. When a lovely golden-brown crust has formed, remove the rabbit and set aside. Add the shallots, garlic and thyme to the pot and soften the shallots for 5–10 minutes, adding more butter if it looks a little dry. Put the rabbit back in and pour over the white wine. Bring to the boil, then add the stock or water, so that the rabbit is mostly covered by the liquid but the top bit is above the surface.

Cover with a lid and put the put into the oven. Cook for 1 hour, or until the rabbit is soft and will come off the bone if given a nudge. When cooked, remove the rabbit, put the pieces on a baking tray, and keep warm. Put the slices of bacon into the oven to crisp them up, then remove and keep warm with the rabbit.

To finish the sauce, strain the juices from the braise and return to the pot. Bring to a simmer. You might feel like the juices need to reduce slightly if they are underwhelming. When you are happy that the sauce tastes full, pour in the cream. Bring again to a simmer and cook for 5 minutes, then whisk in both mustards and the 2 tbsp of (cubed, cold) butter. Taste again for seasoning – the sauce should have a full mustardy flavour. Put a portion of rabbit (either a hind leg or a piece each of loin and front leg) on each plate, dress with the spinach or green beans, pour over the sauce, and put a piece of crisp bacon on top.

Roast Wild Duck with White Grapes, Riesling, Chicory & Cinnamon

SERVES 2

Game birds are delicious cooked with grapes and wine. Best not to faff around making a separate sauce for your duck – instead cook it in the pot with all the other bits and let the juices from the bird seep out into the bubbling liquid.

In autumn I often pot-roast grouse or partridges with red muscat grapes and Pinot Noir: savoury and sweet, and delicious with the gamey meat. Mallard is less pongy than grouse, but no less rich, and here's a recipe with a slightly different colour palette. Riesling for acidity, grapes for sweetness, chicory for bitterness, cinnamon for mystery and butter because it's French. The worst things that can happen with this recipe is that the duck overcooks and the sauce dries out, so keep the duck pink and the sauce juicy.

Preheat the oven to 220°C fan/240°C/475°F/gas mark 9.

Season the duck all over with salt, and sprinkle some inside the cavity. Set a deep-sided, heavy-based ovenproof casserole dish over a medium heat, heat the duck fat and olive oil, and slowly brown the bird until some of the fat has rendered and the skin is golden brown all over. This will take a good 10–15 minutes to do properly: don't rush it or the fat won't render and the duck may burn.

Tip out the excess fat. Roast the duck, breast side up, in the hot oven for 5 minutes, remove the excess fat again, then add the grapes, chicory, bay leaf, cinnamon stick and Riesling. Roast for a further 15 minutes, until the thickest part of the breast has a slight bounce to it when you squeeze it – like a ripe peach. If the liquid in the dish threatens to dry out while the bird is roasting, add a splash of water. Transfer the dish to the hob.

Remove the duck and rest in a warm place. Use a slotted spoon, squish half the grapes into the sauce and simmer for a few minutes until the sauce is a nice balance of salty, bitter and sweet. Add more water periodically if it looks a little dry – you should be left with around 100ml/3½fl oz/scant ½ cup. Finish the sauce by whisking in the cold butter. Taste for seasoning – if it is slightly too sweet add a little splash of good white wine vinegar.

After the duck has rested for 10 minutes, pour any juices into the sauce, then scoop out the bits from the sauce and arrange on a plate; keep the sauce hot on the hob. Carve the duck – take off the legs and arrange on the plate with the other bits, then take off the breasts and slice them up. Arrange the carved duck on the plate and pour over the sauce.

I might eat this with a salad – something made with sweet rather than bitter leaves – and dressed lightly with a vinaigrette.

1	MALLARD DUCK, ABOUT 600G/1LB 5OZ, OVEN READY (HEAD AND NECK REMOVED, GUTTED)
1 TBSP	DUCK FAT OR OLIVE OIL
2	SMALL BUNCHES (APPROX. 250G/9OZ) OF WHITE GRAPES – MUSCAT FOR PREFERENCE
2	SMALL HEADS OF WHITE CHICORY, SHREDDED COARSELY ACROSS THE DIAMETER
1	BAY LEAF
1	CINNAMON STICK
200ML/7FL OZ/SCANT 1 CUP	DRY RIESLING
2 TBSP	COLD UNSALTED BUTTER, CUBED
1 TSP	GOOD QUALITY WHITE WINE VINEGAR (OPTIONAL)
	SALT

Fried Duck Livers with Raisins Soaked in Gewürztraminer & Kirsch

SERVES 2
as a starter, or a satisfying lunch with a salad on the side

Foie gras is a delicacy in France, quite possibly originating in the Jewish tradition – those who settled in the region, opting not to farm pork, instead raised geese and fattened their livers. I do not quite share the adoration of *foie gras* that some have (although it is delicious, in moderation), but fried duck livers are wonderful whether they are *gras* or not.

As with true *foie gras*, a little booze, spice and sugar help to cut through the richness. Soak some raisins in the local sweet wine with a good glug of cherry brandy – if you have the foresight to do it overnight the dried fruits will swell until they are plump. Work quickly if you want to keep your livers pink inside. If you can't find duck livers, chicken livers are also very good done like this.

Soak the raisins in the kirsch and Gewürztraminer overnight.

The following day, heat half the butter in a small pan and slowly fry the shallot until very soft and sweet. Set aside.

2 TBSP	RAISINS, IDEALLY HALF LIGHT, HALF DARK
4 TSP	KIRSCH (OR OTHER FRUIT BRANDY – *VIEILLE PRUNE* SPRINGS TO MIND)
4 TSP	SWEET GEWÜRZTRAMINER (OR OTHER SWEET WINE)
2 TBSP	UNSALTED BUTTER
I	SHALLOT, HALVED AND SLICED INTO HALF-MOONS
2	CLOVES
8	DUCK OR CHICKEN LIVERS, TRIMMED OF SINEW, BUT OTHERWISE LEFT WHOLE
I TBSP	NEUTRAL OIL (GROUNDNUT OR SUNFLOWER)
50ML/ 2FL OZ/ SCANT ¼ CUP	LIGHT DUCK OR CHICKEN STOCK
4 TSP	DOUBLE CREAM
	SALT, FRESHLY GROUND BLACK PEPPER AND NUTMEG
	BUTTERED TOAST, TO SERVE

Crush the cloves to a powder using a pestle and mortar, then add the same quantity of grated nutmeg and of black pepper. Give it a few smashes and mix together. Set aside ready for use; you should have ½ tsp of spice mix.

Season the livers with salt. Heat a heavy non-stick pan over a medium-high heat, add the oil, wait until it just starts to smoke, then add the livers and colour to an even golden brown. Make sure that the pan is not overcrowded – work in two batches if necessary – and don't move the livers around too much until they have formed a golden crust, which should only take a minute. Add the remaining 1 tbsp butter and flip the livers. Sprinkle the ground spices over the frying livers, give the pan a shake, and reduce the heat. The spices burn easily, so be careful. Once the spices have started to fry in the butter and smell fantastic, but while the livers are still pink inside, add the softened shallots, then the raisins and their marinade.

Simmer quickly, reduce the liquid to a syrup, then add the stock. Continue to simmer until the stock has thickened slightly. Add the cream, simmer briefly, correct the seasoning, and serve on top of buttered toast. The livers should ideally still be a bit pink.

Quatre-epices Ham with Baked Potatoes & Choucroute

A celebratory meal for, say, New Year's Day but this would make for a very satisfying Sunday lunch on any cold winter's day. Roast glazed ham, sticky, salty and sweet, spiced with fragrant *quatre-épices*, sliced steaming hot over a mound of *choucroute* moistened with the ham's cooking liquor. Yum. Make a sauce from the liquor and some good Riesling, and serve with heavily buttered baked potatoes, cornichons and mustard.

2.5KG/ 5LB 8OZ	BONELESS UNSMOKED (BRINED) GAMMON, SKIN ON, ROLLED AND TIED
¼	BOTTLE OF DRY RIESLING
500ML/ 18FL OZ/ 2 CUPS	HAM STOCK (SEE BELOW)
I	COOKED *CHOUCROUTE* (SEE PAGE 256)

FOR BOILING THE HAM/THE STOCK:

I	ONION, HALVED
I	CARROT
I	CELERY STICK
I TSP	BLACK PEPPERCORNS
I TSP	FENNEL SEEDS
4	BAY LEAVES
I	SPRIG OF THYME
	A FEW PARSLEY STALKS
7-CM/3-IN	PIECE OF ORANGE PEEL

FOR THE GLAZE:

2 TBSP	DIJON MUSTARD
I	GLASS OF RIESLING
6 TBSP	HONEY
2 TBSP	DEMERARA SUGAR

Put the gammon in a large stockpot and cover with cold water. Bring to the boil, then discard the water, wash out the pot and cover the joint with fresh cold water. Add the stock vegetables and flavourings, bring to the boil then reduce to a simmer. Cook for 2 hours, skimming well, and topping up the water if need be.

Preheat the oven to 170°C fan/190°C/ 375°F/gas mark 5. You'll use the oven to roast the ham after it's been boiled, but also bear in mind you'll want to bake some jacket potatoes to be ready at the same time as the roast ham. I won't give you a recipe for jacket potatoes!

Meanwhile, cook the choucroute following the recipe on page 256. As it cooks, moisten the *choucroute* with (skimmed) ham stock from the pot that is bubbling alongside.

Carefully lift out the ham and allow to cool on a big plate. Strain the stock and discard the vegetables and flavourings but reserve the tasty stock to make the sauce. When the ham has cooled enough to handle, remove the string, then cut off the skin, leaving a good, thick and even layer of fat. Lightly score the fat in a cross-hatch pattern making cuts 1.5cm/⁵⁄₈in apart.

Put the ham into a roasting tin. Pour in the Riesling and the measured ham stock – this will prevent the glaze from burning on the roasting tin and form the basis of a tasty sauce.

Make the glaze by whisking together the mustard, Riesling, honey and sugar in a small pan and bring to a simmer. Bubble for a few minutes until thickened slightly, then set aside to cool. Meanwhile, mix together the four spices to make the *quatre-épices*. Sprinkle the mix over the ham then brush with some of the glaze.

Roast the ham in the hot oven for 15 minutes or so, until the fat has started to colour, then brush again with more glaze. Return to the oven and roast for a further 30 minutes, brushing every now and then with the glaze. If the liquid in the roasting tin threatens to dry out, add a splash more stock. The ham is ready when the glaze is a gorgeous golden brown. The liquid in the bottom of the tin should taste salty/sweet, but if it has thickened too much, add a splash or two of water.

Remove the ham and rest for a while. Skim off excess fat from the liquid left in the roasting tin. Taste this sauce for seasoning. If you feel it could do with thickening, put it in a pan and reduce it until you are happy that it tastes full but not too salty.

Present your ham on a mound of steaming hot *choucroute*. Pour over a little of the sauce – keep the rest to have on the side – and serve with jacket potatoes, preferably slathered in butter and stuffed with grated cheese. Have some cornichons and mustard at the ready.

Note — You might need more liquid than stated depending on the size of your tin: put in enough that you are confident it won't dry out and catch – the sauce can always be concentrated later.

FOR THE *QUATRE ÉPICES*:

I TBSP	GROUND GINGER
I TBSP	GROUND WHITE PEPPER
I TBSP	GROUND CLOVES
I TBSP	GROUND NUTMEG

TO SERVE:

JACKET POTATOES
SALTED BUTTER
BOG-STANDARD CHEDDAR CHEESE (SACRILEGE!), GRATED ON THE CHUNKY SIDE OF THE GRATER
CORNICHONS
DIJON MUSTARD

Pictured overleaf

Index

Glossary

alla chitarra	square-cut pasta
anchoïade	a provençal dip made using anchovies, capers and garlic
au jus	served with the natural juices (jus) released during cooking
aziminu	Corsican version of bouillabaisse (fish soup)
bagna cauda	literally 'hot bath', a sauce of anchovies and garlic served as a dip for vegetables
bollito misto	a north Italian dish of mixed boiled meats similar to a French pot-au-feu
brik filo	pastry packets
bottarga (poutargue or boutargue in Provence)	the salted, cured roe sac of fish, particularly grey mullet
bourride (burrida in Italy)	another version of the classic provençal fish stew
brandade	a dish made with salt cod, often mixed with bread or potatoes to form a spread
brasucade	a Languedoc speciality for cooking mussels over a wood fire
caccuicco	Italian fish stew originating from Livorno on the coast of Tuscany
caldero	Spanish version of fish stew
confit	meat cooked slowly in its own fat
chouckchouka (chakchouka)	shakshuka
cotriade	a fish and potato soup from coastal Brittany
daube	a stew of meat, often beef, slowly braised in wine and flavoured with orange zest
figatellu	Corsican sausage
garbure	garbure
gésiers	chicken gizzards
Kiełbasa Ślaska	Polish sausage
lahmacun	flatbread topped with minced meat, vegetables and herbs
lablabi	Tunisian chickpea soup
magret	duck breast
mahjouba	Algerian pancake or flatbread
merguez	spicy sausage from the Maghreb
m'semen	flatbread
ojja	name used in Tunisia for shakshuka or chakchouka
panade	layered bread casserole
pan bagnat	a sandwich using the classic salade niçoise ingredients
pâtes	the French word for pasta, not to be confused with pâtés
pot-au-feu	classic rustic stew served as separate courses, with the broth first
Pieds-Noirs	term used for those of French descent born in Algeria during the time of colonial rule
pistou	garlicky sauce similar to pesto but without pine nuts
pizzoccheri	type of flat ribbon pasta
raclette	an alpine cheese that has lent its name to a shared dish of melted cheese served with cured meats, vegetables and baguette
rouille	an egg-based sauce typically served as a garnish for bouillabaisse
Schlachteplatte	a platter of sausage and belly pork, typically served with sauerkraut
tartiflette	a baked dish from the Haute-Savoie of cream, potatoes and onion
tian	a baked vegetable dish from Provence
traiteur	delicatessen
ttoro	a version of fish soup from the Basque Country
verjus	verjus
zarzuela	Spanish fish soup

UK/US Terms

aubergines / eggplant
baking paper / parchment paper
baking tin / pan
broad beans / fava beans
chicory/endive
colander / strainer

coriander / cilantro
crème fraîche - use sour cream
French (green) beans
frying pan/skillet
gelatine / gelatin
grill/broiler
kitchen paper / kitchen towel

mouli-légumes / food mill)
passata (strained tomatoes)
peppers / bell peppers
pine kernels / nuts
runner beans/ string beans
spring onions / scallions
stoned = pitted for US

Bibliography

Colman Andrews *Catalan Cuisine: Europe's Last Great Culinary Secret* (paperback edn Grub Street, 1997)

Pellegrino Artusi *La scienza in cucina e l'arte de mangiar bene* (1891; English edn Science in the Kitchen and the Art of Eating Well trans. Murtha Baca, Univ of Toronto Press, 2003)

Jean-Baptiste Reboul *La Cuisinière Provençale* (1897; reprinted Tacussel, 2001)

Robert Carrier *A Taste of Morocco* (Ebury Press, 1987)

Maurice Curnonsky *Recettes des Provinces de France* (Les Productions de Paris, 1959)

Elizabeth David *A Book of Mediterranean Food* (1st edn John Lehmann, 1950; reissued many times since)
— *Elizabeth David's French Country Cooking* (1951; reprinted Penguin, 2001)
— *French Provincial Cooking* (1960; reprinted Penguin, 1998)

Alan Davidson *The Oxford Companion to Food* (1999; reprinted Oxford, 2006, 2014, ed. Tom Jaine)

Irving Davis *A Catalan Cookery Book: A Collection of Impossible Recipes* (paperback edn Marion Boyars/Prospect, 2002)

Roy Andries De Groot *The Auberge of the Flowering Hearth* (1973; reprinted Ecco, 1991)

Georges Auguste Escoffier *Le Guide Culinaire* (1903; English edn trans. H.L. Cracknell & R.J. Kaufmann, Wiley International, 2011)

Jean-Noël Escudier and Peta J. Fuller *The Wonderful Food of Provence* (1968; reprinted HarperCollins, 1988)

Maïté Escurignan *Manuel de Cuisine Basque* (Harriet, 1993, reprinted 1997)

M.F.K. Fisher *Serve it Forth* (Harper Bros, 1937)

Jean-Claude Izzo *Garlic, Mint & Sweet Basil: Essays on Marseilles, Mediterranean Cuisine and Noir Fiction* (Europa Editions, 2013)

Madeleine Kamman *Madeleine Kamman's Savoie: The Land, People, and Food of the French Alps* (Atheneum, 1989)

Raymond Oliver (trans. Claude Durrell) *The French at Table* (Michael Joseph, 1967)

Richard Olney *Lulu's Provençal Table: The Exuberant Food and Wine from the Domaine Tempier Vineyard* (Ten Speed Press, 2002)

Platina [Bartolomeo Sacchi] *De Honesta Voluptate et Valetudine* (c. 1474)

Fernand Point *Ma Gastronomie* (1969; English edn Overlook/Rookery, 2008)

Jean-Baptiste *Reboul La Cuisinière Provençale* (Tacussel, 2001)

Waverley Root *The Food of France* (Knopf, 1958; reissued by Vintage, 1992)

Taillevent [Guillaume Tirel] *Le Viandier* (c. 1300)

François Pierre Sieur de La Varenne *Le Cuisinier François* (1651)

Paula Wolfert *The Cooking of South-West France: Recipes from France's Magnificent Rustic Cuisine* (2nd edn Wiley, 2005)

Paula Wolfert *The Food of Morocco* (Bloomsbury, 2012)

Clifford A. Wright *A Mediterranean Feast* (William Morrow, 1999)

Acknowledgements

Firstly, a massive thank you to my agent Emily, for helping to turn my rambling thoughts for this book into a coherent idea, and for letting us turn up en masse to make a mess in the kitchen (thanks also to Pete and Jerry the cat).

Further thanks to:

The team at Pavilion Books, particularly Steph Milner and Laura Russell, and all my editors past – Helen, Cara, Sophie and Ellen – for making the process such an absolute pleasure.

Jane Birch for proofreading and Stephanie Evans for copyediting.

Charlotte Bland, for her beautiful photography.

Hanna Miller, for doing all the actual cooking.

Jo and Pip, for helping to make the book look so gorgeous.

Tom Hughes and Joe Ghinai, for their (mostly doom-free) companionship.

Guillaume Aubert and family, for welcoming me into their home.

Alex Mackay, for introducing me to Jean-Claude Izzo.

My brother Tom, for being a brilliant sounding board.

Lloyd Morse, for listening to my mad ideas.

Sarah Johnson, for gifting me my copy of *The Auberge of the Flowering Hearth*.

Jonathan Meades, for his musings on Marseille, and to John Mitchinson, for the introduction.

The team at Noble Rot Soho, for listening to me bang on about finishing my book and for holding the fort in my absence.

Pavilion
An imprint of HarperCollins*Publishers* Ltd
1 London Bridge Street
London SE1 9GF

www.harpercollins.co.uk

HarperCollins*Publishers*
Macken House
39/40 Mayor Street Upper
Dublin 1
D01 C9W8
Ireland

10 9 8 7 6 5 4 3 2

First published in Great Britain by Pavilion
An imprint of HarperCollinsPublishers 2023

ISBN 978-1-91-166378-2

This book is produced from independently certified
FSC™ paper to ensure responsible forest management.

For more information visit:
www.harpercollins.co.uk/green

Publishing Director: Stephanie Milner
Editors: Ellen Sandford O'Neill and Stephanie Evans
Design Director: Laura Russell
Design Assistant: Lily Wilson
Senior Production Controller: Grace O'Byrne

Creative Direction and Design: Bell Blood Studio
Photographer: Charlotte Bland
Food Stylists: Alex Jackson and Hanna Miller
Prop Stylist: Charlie Phillips
Artworks: © Gus & Stella 2023
Proof-reader: Jane Birch
Indexer: Hilary Bird

Reproduction by Rival Colour Ltd
Printed in Malaysia